Mystical Stories from the

MAHABHARATA

Twenty Timeless Lessons in Wisdom and Virtue

Mystical Stories from the

MAHABHARATA

Twenty Timeless Lessons in Wisdom and Virtue

Amal Bhakta

TORCHLIGHT
PUBLISHING

First printing 2000

Cover and interior design by Kurma Rupa Dasa
Illustrations by Bhavasindhu Dasa (Ben McClintic)
Printed in India by Indira Printers, New Delhi - 110020
Published simultaneously in the United States of America and Canada
by Torchlight Publishing, Inc.

Library of Congress Cataloging-in-Publication Data

Amal Bhakta, 1932-
    Mystical stories from the Mahabharata : twenty timeless lessons in
    wisdom and virtue / Amal Bhakta
        p. cm.
ISBN: 1-887089-19-5 (cloth)
1. Mahabharata

BL1138.25 .B34 2000
294.5'92304521—dc21   99-053807

**Attention Colleges, Universities, Corporations, Associations, and
Professional Organizations**: *Mystical Stories from the Mahabharata* is available at
special discounts for bulk purchases for fund-raising or educational use. Special
books, booklets, or excerpts can be created to suit your specific needs.

For more information, contact the Publisher:

TORCHLIGHT
PUBLISHING

Torchlight Publishing, Inc.
PO Box 52
Badger, CA 93603
Telephone: (559)337-2200
Fax: (559)337-2354
Email: Torchlight@spiralcomm.net
Web: www.Torchlight.com

DEDICATION

This book is respectfully dedicated to my spiritual
master, His Divine Grace A. C. Bhaktivedanta Swami
Prabhupada. By his grace I was privileged to hear many
of these enlightening stories, to derive countless spiritual
benefits from them, and to be encouraged to share them
with as many devotees of the truth as possible. His own
remarkable books remain a constant source of
inspiration to me, not only for acquiring wisdom and
virtue, but also for developing in self-realization.

ACKNOWLEDGMENTS

I would like to thank Lord Sri Krishna for His inconceivable love and mercy; my mother, Sally Raleigh, for her constant support and encouragement; Alister P. Taylor, the publisher, for his many creative suggestions; His Holiness Hridayananda dasa Goswami for his guidance and help; Bhavasindhu Dasa (Ben McClintic) for his well-crafted story illustrations; Pushkara Dasa (Matthew Goldman) for his excellent painting for the front cover; Kurma Rupa Dasa for his splendid book design; Michael A. Cremo for his kind suggestions and inspiration; Caru Dasa and Vaibhavi Dasi for broadcasting some of the stories on their radio station; Raga Makeda Cannon and Sujan Dasi for their thoughtful and creative editing; Dravida Dasa and Arcita Dasa for their guidance and encouragement; Jalundar Dasa for assisting in the glossary preparation; Terry Cole Whittaker for her assistance in choosing the cover illustration; all the devotees of the Los Angeles ISKCON temple who inspire and help me daily by their devotional service; and anyone else whom I may have regretfully omitted who helped me to better appreciate and enjoy these remarkable stories.

CONTENTS

LINE ILLUSTRATIONS

CHAPTER ONE: As Yama dragged the soul southwards, Savitri followed him. (pg. *xviii*)

CHAPTER TWO: Ganga took her baby to the river, threw it in, and as it drowned, said, "This is for your benefit." (pg. 12)

Taking her child with her, Ganga vanished and went to a heavenly planet. (pg. 16)

CHAPTER THREE: As Amba's body was consumed, she cried out, "This is for Bhishma's death!" (pg. 24)

She discovered that her 'husband' was a young lady like herself. (pg. 38)

CHAPTER FOUR: "When your flesh weighs as much as the pigeon, you can give it to me. That will satisfy me." (pg. 48)

CHAPTER FIVE: When he was only six, he was so strong he would grab lions and tie them to trees in the retreat. (pg. 54)

CHAPTER SIX: "By taking the milk foam, you're preventing the calves from enjoying a full meal." (pg. 62)

CHAPTER SEVEN: Sharyati immediately gave his young daughter to the aged, high-souled Chyavana. (pg. 74)

CHAPTER EIGHT: "Yes, please go to King Nala and tell him I would like to marry him." (pg. 80)

The serpent sprang and coiled itself around her body, making it impossible for her to escape. (pg. 94)

"The two branches of the tree have fifty million leaves and 2,095 fruits. I would like you to check this." (pg. 107)

CHAPTER NINE: The prostitute led Rishyashringa to the boat that was disguised as an ashram. (pg. 118)

CHAPTER TEN: As the sage Durvasa was talking, a heavenly messenger on a chariot appeared in front of Mudgala. (pg. 126)

INTRODUCTION

The *Mahabharata* is a great epic poem of India that was written by Krishna Dwaipayana Vyasa, compiler of the Vedic scriptures, about 5,000 years ago. One of the longest poems in the world, it has eighteen *parvas* or books and about 220,000 lines. It is not only a moralistic and philosophical story but also a historical one. Though filled with intrigue, excitement and adventure, it nonetheless stands as a glorious primer for learning how to achieve spiritual enlightenment.

Not only does the *Mahabharata* contain a main story—in which virtue fights against, and ultimately triumphs over, evil—but it also has many peripheral stories. These teach us, through the exemplary deliberations, decisions, and actions of the chief characters, how to acquire noble characteristics, virtue and culture, peace and wisdom, and inner, transcendental happiness.

This particular presentation consists mainly of some of the peripheral stories, although it also contains a few instructive incidents from the main plotline. These twenty tales are about famous ancient heroes and heroines—kings, queens, sages and saints—who, when confronted by disturbing and harrowing situations, acted in ways that are outstandingly exemplary and inspirational. Thus the stories have the uncanny ability to challenge and motivate us to live up to, in our daily living, the highest principles of virtue. This can impart a sublime and tranquil quality to our otherwise stressful and confused lives. And in today's world of intense speed and pressure, we should find this quite welcome.

The poet Krishna Dwaipayana Vyasa recited the *Mahabharata* to his student Vaishampayana, who later narrated it at a sacrificial ceremony to King Janamejaya for the king's spiritual enlightenment. The main subject of the story was the colossal war between the Kauravas and the Pandavas. They were descendants, through King Bharata, of King Puru, a glorious ancestor of one branch of the lunar dynasty. The basis of the monumental conflict was rulership of the kingdom, the capital of which was Hastinapura, located fifty-seven miles north-east of today's New Delhi.

Perhaps a brief summary here of the *Mahabharata* will help us to better understand why the peripheral stories were introduced into the epic and what value they served.

* * *

SUMMARY

Krishna Dwaipayana Vyasa not only wrote the *Mahabharata* but was the source from whom the main characters of it originated. He was born from the union of Parashara, a great sage, and Satyavati, a beautiful maiden. But just after birth, he miraculously became a full-grown youth. Then, with his father, he left his mother and resided in the forest to perform spiritual austerities. However, by Parashara's mystic power, Satyavati's virginity was completely restored.

The reigning monarch of Hastinapura at that time was King Shantanu. He had been married to Goddess Ganga, who had borne him a son named Devavrata. This son later became famously known as Bhishma. But when the king violated an unusual agreement he had made with Ganga, she abandoned him and, with her son, left for the heavenly world. About sixteen years later, Ganga returned Bhishma, now fully educated, to his father and again departed. Then King Shantanu, after meeting Satyavati, and with his son's help, married her.

The king's wife gave birth to two sons—Chitrangada and Vichitravirya. The former became the next king, but was soon killed in battle. The latter succeeded him on the throne but shortly afterwards died, leaving two childless widows, Ambika and Ambalika. Fearful that the dynastic line might become extinct, Satyavati summoned her saintly son Vyasa and begged him to impregnate the widows on behalf of his deceased half-brother. Even though her request was totally inharmonious with his ascetic lifestyle, out of respect for and obedience to her, and because her petition at that time was scripturally lawful, he assented.

Vyasa had been living the harsh life of a recluse in the forest, and this had made his countenance unsightly. Ambika, during sexual intercourse with him, became so horrified by his looks that she shut her eyes. Consequently, she gave birth to a blind son named Dhritarashtra. Ambalika, during sex, became similarly revolted and turned frightfully pale. Thus she delivered a very pale-complexioned son named Pandu.

Satyavati, anxious about the children, desired that her daughters-in-law produce offspring that had no defects. She thus urged Ambika to try again to become pregnant. But Ambika, still repulsed by Vyasa's appearance, asked a gorgeous maidservant to substitute for her. Acting very respectfully towards the sage, the maidservant gave birth to a flawless boy named Vidura.

The children were raised by their uncle Bhishma, who acted as regent until they grew up. When the sons were of age, the older Dhritarashtra, because of his blindness, was considered incapable of ruling. Consequently, Pandu assumed the throne. Defeating many enemies, amassing large amounts of wealth and property, and maintaining the stability of the country, Pandu proved himself to be an exceptional king.

Sometime later, on a hunting expedition, Pandu fatally shot a deer while it was involved sexually. For this offense, the deer, who was empowered, cursed Pandu to die during the next time he would be involved sexually. To avoid an untimely death, Pandu took a vow of abstenance and, with his two wives, Kunti and Madri, retired to the Himalaya Mountains.

During this time, Dhritarashtra, with Bhishma's assistance, acted as the interim king.

Since Pandu could no longer produce progeny, he became worried as to who would succeed him on the throne. There appeared to be no solution until he learned that his wife Kunti possessed a mystical power. When she had been a teen at her foster-father's palace, she had served a visiting yogi, Durvasa, very devotedly. In gratitude, he blessed her by giving her a mantra which, if uttered, could invoke the physical presence of any god for the purpose of producing a child.

After Pandu urged her to use this power on his behalf, she gave birth to three sons— Yudhishthira, Bhima and Arjuna—fathered by the gods of righteousness, wind and rain respectively. And later, after she conveyed the mantra to her co-wife, Madri gave birth to twin sons, Nakula and Sahadeva, sired by the twin physician gods, the Ashwini Kumaras. These divine children came to be known as the Pandavas [Pandu's sons]. They developed into virtuous, strong, courageous, generous and chivalrous youths.

The heroic Pandu kept his vow of abstinence for many years. But one balmy spring day, he lost his self control and, forcing himself on his resisting wife Madri, died in her arms. A funeral pyre was then prepared. Madri, quite saintly and fully devoted to her husband, voluntarily lay on it beside Pandu. After the fire was lit and the flames enveloped them, she happily joined him in the afterlife.

Some years earlier at Hastinapura, just after Kunti had delivered her first child in the forest, Dhritarashtra's wife, Gandhari, also gave birth. Owing to a mystical blessing from Vyasa, she produced one hundred sons and one daughter. Since their renowned ancestor was King Kuru, they became known as the Kauravas. The oldest of the males was named Duryodhana, and he grew up to be a cunning, envious, malicious prince.

After Pandu died, Kunti brought her five children to the palace at Hastinapura. There, Dhritarashtra took charge of them, treating them respectfully and educating them with his own sons. Despite the youths receiving equal attention, the Pandavas excelled the Kauravas in all the military arts. This incensed Dhritarashtra's sons, who then regarded their cousins as arch rivals. Later on, when Dhritarashtra nominated Yudhishthira to be the next king—as was legally required—Duryodhana's hatred of the Pandavas became even more intense.

For Duryodhana believed that he himself—not Yudhishthira—should be the ruler. He thus embarked on a course of deadly schemes to implement this. To begin, he convinced his father—who desired that Duryodhana become the next king—to persuade the Pandavas to spend about a year at the beautiful city of Varanavata. After Dhritarashtra succeeded, Duryodhana had a flammable house built there for the Pandavas to occupy. His plan was to have the house burned down with them and their mother in it and thereby make their deaths look like an accident.

Nonetheless, while the Pandavas stayed there, their uncle Vidura apprised them of the plot, sent a miner to secretly dig an escape passage for them, and also informed them of the exact night Duryodhana's spy, Purochana, would burn down the house. On that fateful night, the Pandavas held a party for their friends. However, six uninvited low-class guests—a woman and her five sons—also attended. After becoming extremely drunk, they staggered into one of the rooms and fell deeply asleep—without the hosts knowing this. When the party ended and the Pandavas thought that all the guests had departed, Bhima set fire to the house. The Pandavas and their mother then fled through the underground tunnel.

When the Kauravas learned of the fire and the six charred bodies, they happily believed the Pandavas had perished. Duryodhana was now confident that he would surely be the next ruler, for there was no one now to oppose him. Meanwhile, the Pandavas, having no allies and few weapons, could not risk returning to Hastinapura—lest Duryodhana again try to kill them by some other crafty means. They therefore decided to hide in the forest for a while, disguising themselves as Brahmans and living on donations.

The Pandavas then learned that King Drupada of the Panchala dynasty would soon be holding an archery contest. To the winner, he would offer for marriage his gorgeous and accomplished daughter Draupadi. The Pandavas therefore journeyed to Kampilya and, still disguised as Brahmans, resided at a potter's cottage. After they went to the contest arena, Arjuna skillfully won Draupadi as his wife. On arriving home, Arjuna, referring to Draupadi, told his mother that he had just received a nice donation. Not yet seeing her, Kunti replied that he should share it with his brothers. Although polyandry was not the prevailing custom then, Arjuna agreed to share her as a wife with them. This he did to uphold the truth of his mother's words and thereby assure spiritual merit for her, himself and his brothers.

Now allied with the powerful Panchala dynasty, the Pandavas discarded their disguises. King Dhritarashtra, surprised to learn that the Pandavas were still alive, invited them back to Hastinapura. Wanting to avert a confrontation, he gave the Pandavas a vast tract of jungle territory, bordered by the holy Yamuna River, to rule. They, in turn, developed it into a most magnificent and opulent city called Indraprastha (close to today's Delhi, where the name still exists). And Duryodhana continued to rule Hastinapura.

Yudhishthira reigned with justice and wisdom. After some time, by the military might of his brothers, he established his supremacy over all the existing kings. This led to his performing the Rajasuya sacrifice in which he was proclaimed and acknowledged by all leaders as the emperor of the world. This, of course, inflamed the envy and hatred of Duryodhana and his brothers even more. So, with the help of their uncle Shakuni, they hatched another devious plot to deprive the Pandavas of their honestly earned wealth, power and land.

This time Duryodhana induced his father to invite Yudhishthira to Hastinapura for a "friendly" dice game. Though Yudhishthira was opposed to gambling, it was his duty as a warrior to accept the challenge. When he, along his brothers and wife, arrived there, he discovered that Shakuni, Duryodhana's uncle, would be playing on behalf of his nephew. In gambling, Shakuni was invincible, for he had mystic power over dice and could thus influence the outcome of each game.

Consequently, Yudhishthira lost all his possessions—including his brothers, himself and his dear wife.

Duryodhana's brother Dushasana then attempted to dishonor Draupadi by dragging her before the male assembly and trying to disrobe her. However, after Draupadi helplessly prayed to Lord Krishna, He protected her honor by making her sari unlimitedly long. Frustrated and exhausted by his fruitless efforts, Dushasana finally desisted. Draupadi then won Dhritarashtra's sympathies and prevailed on him to order Duryodhana to return all the possessions he had won from Yudhishthira.

However, shortly afterwards, as the Pandavas were proceeding towards their capital, Dhritarashtra, under Duryodhana's evil influence, summoned Yudhishthira back to the gambling hall to play one more game. The stake now was that the loser would have to spend twelve years in the forest and the thirteenth year unrecognized in some kingdom. Yudhishthira was again defeated; therefore he, his brothers and his wife went into exile. During this period they met several exalted sages who narrated to them some of the mystical stories contained in this book. These stories served to encourage, strengthen, uplift, and enlighten the Pandavas during their dark days of deprivation.

When the thirteenth year arrived, the Pandavas disguised themselves and entered the service of King Virata. At the end of the thirteenth year, the Pandavas revealed their true identities and were determined to recover their kingdom from Duryodhana. But when their cousin refused to return it, the Pandavas and the Kauravas prepared for war.

Seeking Lord Krishna as an ally, both Arjuna and Duryodhana reached Him at about the same time. But Krishna decided that He Himself would not fight. Nonetheless, He was willing to offer Himself to one party and His army to the other. Since Arjuna was given first choice, he selected his friend and cousin Krishna, who, soon after, agreed to Arjuna's request that He drive his chariot during the battle. Since Duryodhana considered Krishna's army more valuable than Krishna Himself, he was quite happy with this arrangement.

At Kurukshetra, a plain north of Delhi, the rival armies lined up and faced each other on the battlefield. It was then that Arjuna lost his courage to fight against his teachers, relatives and friends. But Krishna, to help him understand his moral duty and life's true purpose, spoke His famous divine song, the *Bhagavad-gita*. Consequently, Arjuna regained his confidence and proceeded to fight.

Thereafter, many bloody battles were fought and virtually all the warriors were killed—except for the Pandavas and a few others. Yudhishthira, along with his brothers, then went to Hastinapura and, after reconciling with Dhritarashtra, was coronated king.

But Yudhishthira was greatly depressed and troubled by the loss of so many relatives and friends. However, after some time, he was able to rule with justice, kindness, and firmness, and he and his brothers lived in peace and prosperity. Dhritarashtra could not forget or forgive the loss of his sons and mourned especially for Duryodhana. But at last he, his wife, and the Pandavas' mother retired to a hermitage in the woods. After two years, they perished in a fire.

When it was time to retire, Yudhishthira abdicated his throne to his grandson and departed with his wife and brothers for the Himalaya Mountains.

* * *

It is hoped that the following twenty timeless stories will encourage and inspire the reader to cultivate the numerous positive qualities expressed by the main characters—patience, forbearance, compassion, sacrifice, austerity, enthusiasm, faith, devotion, and selflessness. Without a doubt, such attainments can enrich our lives immensely and help us achieve true fulfillment through Divine enlightenment.

For persons unfamiliar with Vedic names and terms, an extensive glossary has been provided at the end of this book. The author has opted for a liberal rather than a literal re-telling of these tales—to make them more interesting, understandable, and reader friendly. It is hoped that such license will help fulfill the overall purpose of this book, namely, to increase the wisdom and virtue of everyone who reads it.

Amal Bhakta

As Yama dragged the soul southwards, Savitri followed him.

CHAPTER ONE

SAVITRI SAVES HER HUSBAND

Something very tragic happens to Savitri's husband. However, by her stead-fast perseverance, she completely reverses the situation. Likewise, in our pursuit of wisdom and virtue, although we may encounter many obstacles or difficulties, we must manifest similar perseverance to succeed.

Ashwapati, the king of Madras, was very pious and religious. He always served the Brahmins, was highly spiritual, and was firm in fulfilling his pledges. He restrained his senses, performed sacrifices, and worked for the welfare of all beings. The best of donors, he was competent and adored by both the residents of the city and the country. However, this forgiving and truthful king, though married, had no child, and as he grew older, this distressed him.

Therefore, in order to have children, the king decided to practice austerities and thereby atone for whatever sins he had committed in the past that resulted in his present childlessness. With a firm vow he ate sparingly, observed celibacy, and curbed his senses. Moreover, he daily offered ten thousand oblations into the sacrificial fire, chanted mantras honoring Goddess Savitri, and ate moderately at the sixth hour. After the king observed this vow for eighteen years, during one of the sacrifices Goddess Savitri finally arose from the fire and said, "Ashwapati, I have been pleased with your celibacy, purity, self-control, observance of vows, and all your efforts and reverence. Therefore, without violating the code of righteousness, how would you like me to bless you?"

"Goddess, please bless me with many sons who may be worthy of my family line. For the Brahmins have advised me that there is tremendous merit in having children."

"Since I had already known your desire, I spoke to Lord Brahma about it. By his favor, you will soon have a daughter of great power."

"A daughter?" thought the king, somewhat disappointed.

1

"Though I know you want a son, Lord Brahma asked me to tell you not to answer me now. You will understand later."

"All right."

Goddess Savitri disappeared and the king entered his city.

Soon after, his eldest and virtuous queen, the princess of Malava, became pregnant and gave birth to a daughter. In honor of Goddess Savitri, the baby was named after her. When the child grew up and reached puberty, she had a golden complexion, gorgeous face, slender waist and ample hips. She looked like the goddess of fortune, and when people saw her they thought, "Indeed, we have received a goddess!"

Her spiritual splendor, force and beauty were so overwhelming that possible suitors, feeling unequal to and inadequate for her, refused to ask her to marry them.

One day when the moon changed its phase, Savitri observed the usual sacrifice: She ate no food, bathed her head, went before the family Deity and had Brahmins perform a ceremony and offer oblations into the fire. Taking the flowers that had been offered to the Lord, she proceeded to her father, who happened to be with his counselors. There, she bowed to his feet, presented him with the flowers and, with joined palms, stood beside him.

As the king looked at her, he saw she was of marriageable age. But since no man had sought her hand, this made him unhappy. "My daughter," he said, "it is now time for you to get married. But no man has asked to marry you. Therefore, it would be best for you yourself to look for a husband. His qualities, of course, should be equal to yours. Choose a man you feel strongly attracted towards. When you find him, let me know. If, after thorough consideration, I think he's suitable, I'll surely give you to him. The Brahmins say that the father who does not get his daughter married will be disgraced. But remember: When you look for a husband, act in such a way that the gods will not disapprove."

After the king instructed his attendants to accompany Savitri, she offered him her respects and compliantly left the palace. Along with the king's elderly counselors, she mounted a vehicle and had the driver take her to a lovely sanctuary where royal sages lived. There, she worshiped the elders' feet and wandered about the forest distributing gifts to the Brahmins.

Sometime later Savitri returned to the palace. She went to her father's court and saw he was conversing with the great sage Narada. When she approached them respectfully, Narada asked the king, "Where did your daughter go? And where is she coming from? She is now marriageable, so why don't you obtain a husband for her?"

"That was the reason I sent her away—to find a spouse." The king turned to Savitri. "Now tell me about the man you've chosen."

Savitri replied, "There was a righteous king among the Shalwa people named Dyumatsena. But after some time, he went blind. Then, one of his former enemies, taking advantage of the king's weakness, took away his kingdom. After that, the king, along with his wife and only child, left to live in the forest, take vows, and practice asceticism. His son is now a young man and worthy of becoming my husband. I've taken him into my heart as my lord."

Narada turned to the king. "That's too bad. Savitri has made a wrong choice."

"Wrong?"

"Yes. The youth she's referring to is called Satyavan. And he does have exceptional qualities. Both his father and mother are truthful. That's why the Brahmins named him Satyavan."

"And is he energetic, intelligent, forgiving, and courageous?"

"His energy is like the sun's, his wisdom like Brhaspati's, his courage like that of the king of the gods, and his forgiveness like the earth's."

"But is he generous in gift-giving and devoted to the Brahmins? And is he handsome, unselfish, and stunning to look at?"

"In gift-giving he's like King Rantideva, who fed innumerable beggars. In truthfulness and devotion to the Brahmins, he resembles King Shivi, who offered his body as a sacrifice to protect a pigeon from a hawk. In unselfishness he's like King Yayati, in handsomeness like the moon, and in physique like the stunning Ashwins. He restrains his senses and is humble, courageous and truthful. With controlled passion, he's dedicated to his friends, devoid of hatred, unassuming, and forbearing. Indeed, great sages say that his behavior is always proper and his honor firmly established."

"Those are his *good* qualities. But what about his flaws? Does he have any?"

"He has only one flaw and it overpowers all his virtues."

Ashwapati wondered what it was.

"It's this: In one year from today—Satyavan will die!"

The king turned to Savitri. "Well, my daughter, you heard what the sage said. It will be best for you to choose a different man."

But Savitri replied, "Death can come only once! A daughter can be given away only once! And a person can say only once, 'I give this away.' Only once can any of these events occur. Similarly, whether Satyavan's life is short or long, virtuous or evil, I'll only choose my husband once. And I've done so."

Narada said, "King, your daughter's mind is firm. It's not possible to dissuade her from this virtuous course. As no one else has Satyavan's virtues, I approve of this marriage."

"I will do as you say," the king replied, "for you are my teacher."

"May Savitri's marriage be peaceful and may you all be blessed. Farewell," said Narada as he departed for the heavenly planets.

The king proceeded to arrange for the wedding. He summoned all the aged Brahmins with their assistants. Then, on a favorable day, he, Savitri, and the priests started out for Dyumatsena's hermitage. When they arrived there, they approached the wise but blind royal sage, who was sitting on a kusha grass mat under a sal tree.

After properly offering his respects, King Ashwapati identified himself. Dyumatsena, in turn, presented the king with arghya [water, milk, kusha grass, rice, durva grass, sandalwood, and flowers], as well as a seat and a cow. "What's the purpose of your visit?" he asked.

"Dyumatsena, this is my lovely daughter, Savitri. I'd like you to accept her from me as your daughter-in-law."

"But we've been dispossessed of our kingdom. That's why we are living here. Our lives consist of practicing asceticism to acquire virtue. How will your noble daughter bear the burden of doing the same?"

"My daughter and I know that happiness and distress come and go. Therefore, your words are inappropriate. I've come here with my mind made up. And out of friendship I've offered my obeisance to you. So I entreat you not to destroy my hope. We are equal in rank—kings—and are fit for an alliance. Therefore, please accept my daughter as your daughter-in-law and as the wife of your son."

Dyumatsena recollected, "In the past I desired to have an alliance with you. But I hesitated. Then my kingdom was taken away from me. Thus, let my former desire be fulfilled now. Indeed, you are a welcome visitor!"

The kings called all the Brahmins living in the surrounding retreats and, with proper rituals, had the marriage performed. Ashwapati gave Savitri away with suitable robes and ornaments and then departed happily for his palace. Satyavan and Savitri were also very happy, for he had obtained a wife who possessed every attainment, and she had acquired a husband whom she truly loved.

When Savitri's father left, she discarded all her ornaments and dressed as a hermit—in tree bark and red-colored cloth. By her services and good qualities, her gentleness and austerity, and by her congenial attendance on all, Savitri satisfied everyone. She pleased her mother-in-law by waiting on her person and by clothing her with robes and adornments. She pleased her father-in-law by honoring him as though he were a god and by restraining her speech. And she satisfied her husband by her sweet words, her skill in all kinds of chores, her balance of emotion, and her affectionate expressions in private.

Nonetheless, as time elapsed, Saint Narada's prophesy echoed through her mind day and night and made her lament. When only four days remained before Satyavan was to die, Savitri began a three day fast. Her father-in-law, hearing about this, became sad and said, "My Daughter, you are observing a difficult vow. Perhaps you should not—"

"Don't be sad, Father. I'm determined to fulfill it. And I will."

"All right, if you insist." And he stopped trying to discourage her.

Looking gaunt, Savitri spent the eve of Satyavan's predicted death in dire agony. As the sun rose, she brooded, "Today is the day!" Then she completed her morning rituals and made sacrificial offerings to the fire.

Having genuflected to the Brahmins, her father-in-law, and her mother-in-law, Savitri stood before them with joined palms and controlled senses. The Brahmins blessed her to never become a widow, and Savitri welcomed this with the thought, "May this come true!" Nevertheless, she could not help expecting Saint Narada's prophesy to soon materialize. Since she had completed her fasting vow, her parents-in-law urged her to eat.

"I've resolved to eat when the sun sets today."

At that moment Satyavan placed his ax on his shoulder and proceeded towards the woods. Noticing this, Savitri followed him and said, "I'd like to go with you today."

"Go with me?" He was surprised.

"Yes, because I can't tolerate your absence."

"But—you never go to the woods with me. The paths are hard to cross. And you're very weak now."

"But I don't feel weak. And I definitely would like to go. So please—let me."

"Well, all right. But first ask my parents' permission. I don't want to be responsible for any difficulties you may encounter."

Savitri went to them and asked. Then she added, "I can't stand to be away from him. Please let me go. It's almost a year since I last left the ashram. And I so much want to see the blossoming forest."

Her father-in-law replied, "I don't recall you ever saying anything with a hidden motive. So yes, you may go. But please don't divert Satyavan from his work there."

Savitri left the hermitage with her husband. Outwardly she was smiling, but inwardly she was agonizing. As they proceeded, they took in the beauty of the forest—its rivers, trees, flowers and birds. Continually glancing at Satyavan, Savitri considered him as already dead. It was only a matter of moments now.

Satyavan filled up his sack with fruits. Then, as he began to chop branches, he started perspiring. Soon his head began to hurt. Feeling very weary, he said, "Savitri, due to this heavy work, my head, limbs, and heart are aching. I can scarcely stand up. I think I'll go to sleep for awhile." He then sat down on the ground.

Savitri sat beside him and placed his head on her lap. As she felt the moment of death coming, she saw a strange-looking being coming towards her. He was dressed in red and wearing a crown. His dark-complected body was large and radiant, his eyes fiery red. Holding a noose in his hand and gazing at Satyavan, he looked dreadful.

Satyavan's wife placed his head on the ground gently. Then she stood up, her heart trembling. "You look superhuman," she said painfully, "so I assume you're a god. Who are you? And why have you come here?"

The visitor replied, "You are always devoted to your husband. And you've acquired the merit of performing austerity. That's why I am talking to you."

Savitri stared at him.

"I'm Yama, the lord of death. Your husband's days on earth are over. I've come to take his soul away."

"But usually only your servants come. Why have you personally come?"

"Because this prince has excellent qualities, achievements and bodily beauty. He's above being carried away by my servants."

Lord Yama tied his noose around Satyavan's soul. Then he yanked the soul out of the body, so that it was completely under his control. Satyavan's body, now lacking breath, luster and motion, looked repulsive. As Yama dragged the soul southwards, Savitri followed him. Seeing this, he turned to her and said, "Stop! Go home and perform your husband's funeral ceremony. You have no more obligations to him. Don't follow me any farther."

"I'll follow my husband wherever you're carrying him and wherever he goes. This is the eternal tradition. As a result of my austerities, my respect for my superiors, my love for my husband, my fulfilling of vows, and also your kindness, nothing is stopping me."

She continued: "The wise say that he who takes seven steps with another person makes a friendship with him. Now that we're friends, please hear what I have to say:

"Even if a person passes through the four spiritual orders of life—student, householder, retiree and renunciant—but has no control over his soul, he acquires no merit. What is known as spiritual merit is made up of true knowledge. The wise say that acquiring spiritual merit rather than merely passing through these four orders is the best of all things. If one practices the duties of even one of these orders, according to the instructions of the wise, he achieves spiritual merit. Therefore, it is not necessary for one to desire to enter the first or the fourth order."

"Savitri, I am pleased by your knowledgeable and distinctive speech, founded on reason. Therefore, ask me for any blessing—except your husband's life."

"All right. My father-in-law leads a life of seclusion in our ashram because lost his eyesight and kingdom. By your grace, may he regain his vision and become powerful."

"Granted. You look tired from walking. Don't tire yourself any longer. Just stop following me and return home."

Respectfully, she contradicted him. "How can I feel weary in my husband's company? His fate is surely mine also. Wherever you carry him, I will also go. Lord Yama, even one conversation with saintly persons is very desirable; friendship with them is even more so. And a relationship with them is always productive. Therefore, one should always live with saintly souls."

"Your words are very rich, Savitri. They satisfy the heart and increase the wisdom of even the wise. Therefore, ask me for another blessing—except your husband's life."

"Sometime ago my father-in-law, who is very learned and brilliant, lost his kingdom. I would like him to recover it now and never give up his duties."

"Granted. Now please stop following me and return home."

"You control all beings and carry them away, not by your fancy but by justice. That's why you're called Yama—the lord of justice or death. Kindly listen to this: The constant responsibility of the virtuous is to never harm anyone in thought, word or deed, but to love them and to give them what they deserve. To me, everything in this world is like my husband now—dead. People are empty of both devotion and grace. But the virtuous are merciful even to enemies who ask for protection."

Yama replied, "As water is to a thirsty person, so are your words to me. Therefore, ask me for a third blessing—except Satyavan's life."

"My father, Ashwapati, has no sons. But to continue our family line, I'd like him to father one hundred sons."

"Granted. Now that I've satisfied your wish, please stop following me. You've walked far enough."

"Walking beside my husband, I haven't noticed how far I've walked. In fact, I would like to walk farther. Please hear what I say now: You are the mighty son of the sun god, Vivaswata. Giving equal justice to all, you are called the lord of justice. One is not as confident even about oneself as he is with the virtuous. Thus, everyone especially desires friendship with the virtuous. It is virtue alone that inspires confidence in all beings. That is why people depend especially on the virtuous."

"Savitri, I've not heard anyone but you speak such words. They greatly delight me. Therefore, ask for another blessing—except Satyavan's life. Then return to your hermitage."

"I would like to give birth to a hundred sons. They should be powerful, skillful, and able to perpetuate our family line."

"Granted. Now please stop following me. You already have come too far."

"The virtuous always practice goodness. And when they associate with each other, this is always productive. Neither person jeopardizes the other. By the truth of the virtuous, the sun moves in the sky. By their austerities, the earth is maintained, and the past and future depend on them. The virtuous are always cheerful in the company of the virtuous. The virtuous help others without expecting any reward. Therefore, serving the virtuous is never a waste. It never hurts one's interest and dignity. Because of such service, the virtuous often become the protectors of everyone."

Lord Yama replied, "The more you speak such significant words— full of sweet phrases, invested with virtue and pleasing to the mind— the more I feel respect for you. Therefore, ask me for a great blessing."

"The last blessing you granted me can't be fulfilled unless I unite with my husband sexually. Therefore, please revive him. Without a husband, I'm like a dead person: I don't want happiness, heaven, or prosperity, and I don't wish to live. You've blessed me to have a hundred sons. Yet you've taken away my husband. Please bring him back. Only then will your words prove true!"

Realizing he had no other choice, Yama said, "So be it!" Then he untied the noose around Satyavan's soul. "Savitri, I've freed your husband

and he has no illness anymore. He will achieve prosperity and, along with you, live for four hundred years. When he performs sacrifices, he'll attain great renown. Moreover, he'll have a hundred sons with you. And all their sons and grandsons will become celebrated monarchs. Your father will also have a hundred sons with your mother Malavi. These sons will look like gods. They'll be known as Malavas. Along with their sons and daughters, they'll be very famous."

Lord Yama then departed for his own planet.

Savitri returned to Satyavan's body, sat down on the ground and placed his head on her lap. Satyavan suddenly regained consciousness and repeatedly and lovingly gazed at Savitri. "How unfortunate," he said. "I've been asleep for a long time. Why didn't you wake me? And—where is that dark-complexioned person, the one who was pulling me away?"

"That was Lord Yama. He has departed. You're now reinvigorated. If you can, stand up."

Satyavan sat up, refreshed, and glanced at the darkening woods. "Savitri, I remember that while I was chopping wood my head began to pain me. Then I couldn't stand up any longer. So I rested on your lap. And as you embraced me, I fell into a strange slumber. Though all around me it was dark, I saw a highly luminous being. Was I dreaming or—was it real?"

"I'll tell you everything tomorrow. I hope you're feeling well now. If so, we can return to your parents' place."

But as she gazed about, her mind began to change. "It's getting dark. Listen to the wild animals roaring and barking. They're prowling about now. It's very frightening. I think we should spend the night here rather than traipsing through the woods. We can return home tomorrow when the sun comes up. Besides, you may not be fully recovered from your illness."

"No, the pain in my head is gone. And my legs feel all right. I prefer to return tonight."

"But why?"

"Well, I've never stayed away from the hermitage for longer than expected. When I leave it during the day, my parents worry about me. Sometimes my father goes out with our neighbors to search for me—to be sure I'm all right. Even before twilight comes, my mother makes me stay in the ashram."

"I see."

"Thus, I must return tonight, otherwise my parents will be worried and distressed. They're old, my father is blind, and I'm their crutch. In fact, they once told me they'd stay alive only as long as I stay alive. Right now, my parents must be suffering because of my absence. This makes me miserable, for I live only for their pleasure. I should never have slept so long. Never!"

As Satyavan began to weep, Savitri wiped his tears and prayed, "If I've ever practiced asceticism, distributed wealth in charity and performed sacrifices, may this night be fortunate for my parents-in-law and husband. I've never, even in jest, told a lie. By reason of this truth, may my parents-in-law keep their lives."

"We should start for the hermitage immediately."

She stood up, tied her hair back and lifted Satyavan in her arms. When he got to his feet, he rubbed his legs and glanced at his fruit sack.

Savitri said, "You can pick fruits tomorrow. But now, to make things easy for you, I'll carry your ax."

She hung the sack on the branch of a tree, lifted the ax and escorted him. Placing his left arm over her left shoulder, Savitri held his waist with her right arm and began walking with him along the path.

"I feel well now," Satyavan said, "and my strength has returned."

They then proceeded towards the hermitage.

Meanwhile, at the ashram, Dyumatsena miraculously recovered his eyesight and could see everything clearly. But he was extremely distressed by Satyavan's absence, so he and his wife, Shaivya, anxiously searched all over for him. But they could not find him.

After a while, the Brahmins living in that sanctuary approached and consoled them. Then they escorted them back to their own ashram and comforted them with stories about ancient kings. Nonetheless, the parents continued to sorrow over the absence of Satyavan and Savitri. But the sages reassured the couple that, based on various signs, their son and daughter-in-law were definitely alive. With this news, the parents were somewhat solaced.

Satyavan and Savitri soon arrived at the ashram and entered it joyfully. After the Brahmins lit a fire and everyone sat down before it, they asked Satyavan why he had arrived so late. He related how he had fallen into a deep sleep and woke up much later. Then the Brahmins asked Savitri if she knew how her father-in-law had recovered his eyesight. She explained how Satyavan had died, how Lord Yama had come to take away her husband's soul, and how she had complimented the lord of death for his exalted character. Next she explained how he in turn had granted her five blessings, and what those blessings were.

The Brahmins replied, "Savitri, the king was drowning in a sea of misfortune and darkness, but you've rescued him." The ascetics applauded and revered her. Then, after saying good night, they peacefully and happily departed for their ashrams.

The next day, after the sun had risen and the holy men had observed their morning rituals, they gathered together. Repeatedly, they spoke to Dyumatsena of Savitri's good fortune, but they were not completely satisfied. For they wondered about the blessings she had obtained from Lord Yama that were yet to be fulfilled.

Soon a large number of people from Shalwa arrived there and went to King Dyumatsena. They informed him that his enemy, who years ago had usurped his throne, had recently been assassinated by his own minister. They further said that the minister had also slain the usurper's friends and allies, and when his troops heard about it, they fled. After this, all the citizens unanimously exclaimed, "Whether our former king can see or is blind, he will again become king!"

The spokesman for the group then said to Dyumatsena, "As a result of that decision, we have been sent here. Your chariot and your army have come to take you back. May good fortune be yours! Please come. Kindly reassume the same position your father and grandfather had."

When they saw that the king had regained his eyesight and was able-bodied, they opened their eyes in astonishment and bowed their heads. The king paid his respects to all the elderly ascetics living in the sanctuary, and they in turn reciprocated. Then, after mounting his chariot, the monarch proceeded to his city, his wife and daughter-in-law trailing in a palanquin.

When Dyumatsena arrived at his capital, the happy-hearted priests installed him on the throne and Satyavan as prince regent. As the years passed, Savitri gave birth to one hundred sons; they were all stout hearted and fearless—never would they flee from battle—and they enhanced the renown of Shalwa's people. Also, Savitri's mother, Malavi, bore for Savitri's father, Ashwapati, one hundred sons. Thus, from a pathetic tragedy, Savitri elevated herself, her father and mother, her father-in-law and mother-in-law, and her husband's family line to the highest fortune.

* * *

It is said that whoever listens to this account of Savitri reverently achieves happiness, success in all pursuits, and never experiences anguish.

Ganga took her baby to the river, threw it in, and as it drowned, said,
"This is for your benefit."

CHAPTER TWO

BHISHMA'S TERRIBLE VOW

A perfect example of selflessness, Bhishma took a lifetime vow that enabled his father to become free of sorrow and full of joy. If we want to attain wisdom and virtue—as Bhishma so amply did—we have to develop this quality of selflessness, for it helps us to stay peaceful amidst life's disturbances.

In the dynasty of Ikshavaku there was once a king named Mahabhisha. He ruled the entire earth, spoke the truth, and was verily heroic. Because he had satisfied the king of heaven by performing one hundred horse sacrifices and one hundred *Rajasuya* sacrifices, he finally attained the heavenly realm.

One day the gods gathered together in the heavenly realm to worship Lord Brahma. Numerous royal saints, such as King Mahabhisha, and Ganga, the queen of rivers, also attended. As Ganga offered Brahma her respects, a strong wind suddenly blew, lifting up her white gown and exposing her lovely body. Out of respect for her, all the celestials lowered their eyes and heads—except Mahabhisha. Instead, he gazed at her person irreverently.

When Lord Brahma saw this, he cursed Mahabhisha: "You rascal! You have forgotten yourself in front of Ganga. Therefore you shall take birth again on earth. And Ganga, too, shall take such a birth, but she will hurt you. And when you become angry, you will be free from my curse."

After reflecting upon all the kings and holy men on earth, Mahabhisha desired to be born as a son to the powerful King Pratipa. Ganga, who had seen Mahabhisha lose his self-control, went away and thought about him wistfully. On her way, she beheld the eight Vasus going in the same direction. They were gods, personifications of various natural phenomena over which they had control. Their names and functions were Apa—water, Dyu (or Dhruva)—pole star, Soma—moon, Dhara—earth, Anila—

wind, Anala—fire, Prabhasa—dawn and Pratusha—light. Seeing that they were distressed, she asked, "Why do you look so hopeless?"

The Vasus explained why, and then made a secret agreement with her.

***

King Pratipa was kind to all beings. He had spent many years at the source of the Ganges River performing spiritual austerities and was still absorbed in them. One day the beautiful and gifted Ganga rose from her waters, approached the royal saint, and sat down on his powerful right thigh.

The king smiled and said, "How friendly. Is there something I can do for you?"

"Yes," replied Ganga. "I would like you to marry me."

"Marry you? Well, I've vowed to never consort with other men's wives or with women who are not of my caste."

"But I'm unmarried, a virgin, and a goddess."

"Nonetheless, I've also vowed to avoid sex for awhile. It would be a sin for me to violate this vow—and I would surely be killed. Now you've hugged me while sitting on my right thigh. But that thigh is the seat reserved for daughters and daughters-in-law. The left thigh is for the wife. Therefore, it would not be proper for me to marry you now. Instead, why don't you become my future son's wife and thus my daughter-in-law?"

"All right. But please understand that when I become your daughter-in-law, your son must not judge the ethics of my actions. As his wife, I will benefit him and enhance his happiness. By the sons I bear him and by his excellent behavior, he will ultimately achieve the Divine realm."

Ganga then vanished.

***

Because King Pratipa wanted to have children, he and his wife were performing austerities. When they had become elderly, she gave birth to a son who was none other than the reincarnation of King Mahabhisha. He was named Shantanu.

As Shantanu grew up, he learned that imperishable bliss can be gained only by devotional service to God. He therefore became dedicated to righteousness. When he attained young manhood, Pratipa said to him, "Shantanu, a heavenly maiden once approached me for your welfare. If you should meet that lovely young woman privately and she should ask you for children, accept her as your wife. However, you must never judge the propriety or impropriety of her actions, or ask who she is or who she belongs to or where she comes from. My order is that you just accept her as your wife."

Pratipa then installed his son as king and repaired to the forest to practice austerities. King Shantanu had a high intelligence and was equal in glory to Indra, the lord of the celestials. Like most warriors, Shantanu became habituated to hunting, so he spent a good deal of time in the forest.

One day, as Shantanu was roaming along the bank of the Ganges, he came to a spot that was often visited by Siddhas and Charanas. There, he saw a maiden whose beauty was as ravishing as that of the goddess of fortune. Her teeth were pearly and perfect, she wore heavenly adornments, and the fine texture of her clothes was magnificent, like the filaments of the lotus. As the king saw her, he was surprised and joyful, his hairs instantly standing up. He gazed at her unwaveringly and appeared to be imbibing her charms; however, as many drinks as he took, they failed to fully satisfy his thirst.

The young woman saw the resplendent king pacing about in great excitement. She herself was stirred, and she experienced tender feelings for him. The more she gazed at him, the more she wanted to gaze at him forever.

Then, in gentle words, the king said, "Oh lovely one, whether you are a goddess, a Gandharva, an Apsara, a Yaksha, a Naga or a human being, I would like you to become my wife."

Listening to those tender and honeyed words of the smiling king, Ganga remembered her promise to the Vasus and replied, "I will be glad to be your wife. But you must not hinder me in anything I do, whether pleasing or displeasing to you. And you must never speak to me harshly. As long as you treat me gently, I agree to stay with you. But the moment you hinder me or speak harshly to me, I shall surely leave you."

"So be it," promised Shantanu.

When Ganga obtained that admirable king for her husband, she became very satisfied. Shantanu likewise fully enjoyed her companionship. Abiding by his agreement, he never hindered her in anything. He became highly pleased with her behavior, loveliness, thoughtfulness, and concern for his comforts. Ganga, too, receiving the result of her good deeds, lived joyfully as Shantanu's wife. She satisfied him with her beauty, caring, wiles, love, music and dance—and thereby satisfied herself as well.

Taking her child with her, Ganga vanished and went to a heavenly planet.

The king was so transported by his lovely wife that months, seasons and years passed without his being aware of them. While so enjoying himself with Ganga, the monarch produced eight children, whose beauty was indeed heavenly. But after each one was born, his wife took it to the river, threw it into the water and said, "This is for your benefit!" The children sank and never surfaced!

This bizarre behavior did not please the king. Nevertheless, he remained silent lest his wife abandon him. However, after the eighth child was born and Ganga was about to smilingly fling it into the river, the king's face became sad. Then, yearning to save it from death, he shouted, "Stop! Don't kill it!" He gazed at her searingly. "Who are you? And why do you kill your own children? Oh, murderess! The burden of your sins is great!"

Ganga cooly replied, "Since you want to have children, I won't kill this boy. But you've broken your promise to me, so I will not live with you any longer. My name is Ganga and I'm the daughter of Jhanu. The great ascetics always worship me. I've remained with you this long to achieve the purpose of the eight Vasus. Those powerful gods were cursed by the sage Vasishtha to assume human bodies. And on earth there was no one more worthy of the honor of being their father than you. Nor was there any woman on earth besides myself—a goddess in human form—to be their mother. By fathering them, you will eventually attain continuous heavenly joy. I once promised the Vasus that as soon as they'd be born, I'd free them from their human bodies. Thus, I've liberated them from Vasishtha's curse. May you be blessed. I'm leaving now."

"But—what offense did the Vasus commit, and who was Vasishtha? What was the wrong of this eighth child—that he will have to live among human beings? And why were the Vasus, who are masters of the three worlds [heavenly, earthly and nether], damned to take birth among humans?"

"The son of Varuna, the ocean god, is named Vasishtha. This sage was later called Apava, and he had his ashram on Mount Meru. It was very holy and teemed with birds and animals. All year, flowers of every season bloomed there and the place contained sweet roots and water. Varuna's son practiced ascetic disciplines there.

"Daksha, one of the first human beings, had a granddaughter named Surabhi. She desired to benefit the whole world. Marrying the sage Kashyapa, she gave birth to a daughter in the form of a cow called Nandini. She was the best of cows, for she was able to fulfill any desire one might have. Vasishtha obtained Nandini for his *homa*, or fire-sacrifice rituals, and she wandered about that forest sanctuary without any fear.

"But one day the Vasus entered those holy precincts. They roamed about with their wives and delighted themselves. Then one of the wives spotted Nandini. After noting her large eyes, full udders, fine tail, nice hoofs and other good features, she showed her to Dyu, her husband. Dyu looked at her, appreciated her many virtues and said, 'This wonderful cow belongs to the sage of this hermitage. Any mortal who quaffs her sweet milk will stay youthful for ten thousand years.'

"His pretty wife said, 'On earth, I have a friend named Jitavati. She is very beautiful and youthful, and is King Ushinara's daughter. I would like to get this cow and her calf for her. Would you please bring her so that when my friend drinks the milk, she may become free from weakness and old age?'

"Dyu wanted to pacify his wife, so with the help of his brothers, he stole the cow and her calf. He forgot the mighty ascetic power of the sage and never thought that by this sin he would fall down.

"In the evening, when Vasishtha returned to his ashram with the fruits he had gathered during the day, he didn't see his cow or her calf. Thus, he looked for them in the forest. When he couldn't find them, he saw by inner vision that they had been stolen by the Vasus. This made him very angry, so he cursed them: 'For this sin, they shall take birth on earth!' The sage then became absorbed in ascetic meditation.

"When the Vasus learned of the curse, they quickly went to the sage's ashram and pleaded with him to withdraw it. Although he wouldn't, Vasishtha said, 'You'll be free of the curse within a year of your human birth. But Dyu will have to live on earth for some time. However, he'll be righteous and knowledgeable in the scriptures and submissive to his father.'

"This child previously was Dyu." Taking him with her, Ganga vanished and went to a heavenly planet.

Shantanu, with a sad heart, then repaired to his capital.

***

King Shantanu was the monarch most admired by the gods and royal saints, and he was known the world over for his wisdom, virtues, intelligence, modesty, forbearance and great energy. He was knowledgeable in both religion and economic development, and he protected not only the Bharata race but all human beings. There had never been a king like Shantanu, and because all the kings of the world saw him as so dedicated to righteousness, they conferred on him the title "King of Kings."

During Shantanu's rule, the kings of the world did not have any sorrow, fear, or worry; they slept peacefully and had happy dreams. They, too, became righteous and dedicated to charity, spiritual deeds, and sacrifices. The spiritual merits of every caste increased enormously. The Kshatriyas, or administrators and warriors, served the Brahmins; the Vaishyas, or merchants and farmers, attended the Kshatriyas; and the Shudras, or laborers and artisans, waited on the Brahmins, Kshatriyas, and Vaishyas.

While Shantanu lived in Hastinapura, the Kuru capital, he held sway over the entire earth. He was truthful, straightforward and, like the king of the gods, learned in the rules of ethics. His generosity, spirituality, and austerity enabled him to achieve a tremendous fortune. He was devoid of anger and malice. Extremely handsome, he shone like the sun and moved quickly and bravely like the wind god.

Shantanu's righteous indignation was like Yama's, the lord of death, and his forbearance like Mother Earth's. During his reign, deer, boars, birds, and other animals were not needlessly slaughtered. In his territories, people practiced kindness to animals, and the king himself, whose soul was merciful and free of anger, provided equal protection to all beings.

When sacrifices honoring the gods, sages, and forefathers were held, no creature was killed sinfully. Shantanu was indeed the monarch and sire of everyone—the distressed, the unprotected, the birds and beasts, and every created being. During his reign, people spoke the truth and their minds were oriented toward generosity and righteousness.

Shantanu's son, the Vasu born of Ganga, was called Devavrata. In handsomeness, habits, conduct and learning, he resembled Shantanu. He was highly conversant in every field of knowledge, mundane or spiritual. He had extraordinary strength and energy, and he became an excellent charioteer. In fact, he was just like a king.

One day King Shantanu was hunting along the banks of the Ganges River. He struck a deer with his arrow and hastened after it. Noticing that the river had become unnaturally shallow, Shantanu wondered why. Then he saw that a youth—handsome, muscular and friendly— had stopped the flow of the river with his sharp celestial arrow. This greatly surprised the king.

The youth was actually Shantanu's son. Having seen his son only once—for a few seconds after the boy was born—he could not recognize him. But the youth knew immediately that Shantanu was his father. However, instead of revealing himself, by his mystic power he clouded the king's vision and vanished from his sight.

The king reflected seriously on what he had just beheld and imagined that the youth might be his son. Gazing at the river, he exclaimed to it, "Please show me that youth!"

Ganga then assumed a lovely form, and was decked in ornaments and a fine white gown. She held the youth under her right arm and presented him to Shantanu. But though he had known her before, Shantanu failed to recognize her. "Shantanu," she said, "he's the eighth son you produced in me sometime ago. This wonderful child has knowledge of all weapons. I have brought him up with care. He has exceptional intelligence and has studied with Vasishtha the complete Vedas and their branches. He's competent with all weapons, a powerful archer and resembles Indra when fighting. Both the gods and the demons regard him with esteem. He knows completely all the branches of knowledge the sage Brhaspati knows and is thus a master of those scriptures. Every weapon that Jamadagni's son, Parashurama, knows, your illustrious son knows. He is also learned in the interpretation of all essays on a king's responsibilities. Take him now and return to your capital."

Complying with Ganga's request and considering himself very fortunate, Shantanu arrived at his city. He then assembled all the Pauravas [descendants of Puru] and proclaimed his son as his successor. After this, the prince, by his conduct, pleased his father and all members of the kingdom. Thus, the mighty king lived happily with his son.

***

One day, four years later, the king entered the forest and ambled along the bank of the Yamuna River. He suddenly smelled a sweet fragrance coming from an unknown direction. Driven by a desire to determine its source, the king walked here and there. Finally, he saw a maiden with black eyes and heavenly beauty. "Who are you?" he asked. "And whose daughter? What is your business here?"

"I'm the daughter of the chief of the fishermen. He's asked me to work for religious merit by rowing people in my boat across the river."

At that moment, enchanted by her beauty, friendliness and fragrance, Shantanu desired to marry her. The king proceeded to her father and asked for his consent.

The chief fisherman replied, "O king, I know you are truthful. If you wish to marry my daughter Satyavati, I would like you to make a promise."

"A promise?"

"Yes. If you do, I will surely give her to you."

"What do you want me to promise?"

"That my daughter's future son will be your successor."

On hearing this, though the fire of Shantanu's desire burned intensely, he was not disposed to make such a promise. For he knew that there would never be anyone more qualified to rule the kingdom than Devavrata. The king, with his heart still yearning for Satyavati, returned to Hastinapura.

At home, the king spent his time brooding about. One day Devavrata approached his sad father and remarked, "You have prosperity. All the leaders obey you. So why are you sorrowing?"

"Sorrowing?"

"Yes. You're so absorbed in your thoughts—you don't even answer me. You don't ride horses now. And you look pale and thin."

"I do?"

"Yes. And you seem to have no life. I would like to know what sickness you're suffering from so that I can try to find a cure."

"Well, my sickness is that—should you be overcome by some danger, I would have no son or heir. And, since I don't plan to marry again, our family line might not be perpetuated. Let's face it—you're a hero with an explosive disposition, and you're always using weapons. Therefore, it's quite possible you'll be killed on the battlefield...That's the reason I'm so gloomy."

After the highly intelligent Devavrata heard this, he thought about it for some time. Then he proceeded to the elderly minister who was committed to his father's well being and inquired further about the king's sorrow. The minister informed him of the monarch's desire to marry Satyavati as well as the sole condition under which her father would offer her, which Shantanu had rejected.

Devavrata, escorted by a number of aged warrior leaders, then went to the fishermen chief, who received him with proper respect. Devavrata then entreated him to bestow his daughter on the king.

But the chief said, "I have just one objection. He already has a son. Therefore, if Satyavati married your father and he produced a son from her, even if the son were a god, what security would he have with you as his rival?"

Devavrata replied, "Chief, for the benefit of my father and to fulfill your condition, I will now take a vow, as follows: If your daughter marries my father and she gives birth to a boy, *he*, and *not I*, will become our next king!"

The fishermen chief said, "Prince, the vow you have just taken in the presence of these leaders for the welfare of Satyavati is truly worthy of you. And I have not the slightest suspicion that you will breach it. But I do have doubts regarding the children you may father. Suppose they felt that, although *you* had relinquished the throne, *they* had a just right to it. What then?"

Perceiving the doubts of Satyavati's father, Devavrata said to him, "To fully satisfy you, I will take another vow, as follows: From today on, I shall remain celibate for the rest of my life. And even if I die without a son, I shall still achieve the higher world of eternal bliss!"

When Ganga's son said this, the fishermen chief was delighted and the hairs of his body stood on end. "Then I gladly give my daughter to your father!"

Then the gods, heavenly sages and Apsaras showered down blossoms from the sky on Devavrata's head, shouting, "He is bhishma!" meaning one who has taken a terrible or arduous vow.

Devavrata helped the lovely maiden into his vehicle and drove to Hastinapura. When he reached the capital, he told his father what had happened. The leaders assembled there complimented his exceptional sacrifice and said, "He is truly bhishma!" Shantanu was also highly pleased and conferred a blessing on him: "My son, as long as you desire to live, you will never die. In other words, you will die only when you desire to."

***

From that time on, Devavrata was called Bhishma. King Shantanu married Satyavati and fathered two children from her, Chitrangada and Vichitravirya. And these two, respectively, became the next kings of the Kurus.

As Amba's body was consumed, she cried out, "This is for Bhishma's death!"

CHAPTER THREE

AMBA'S REVENGE

Although Amba's vengeful desire was foolish and virtually impossible to fulfill, she nonetheless satisfied it by maintaining her steadfast resolve. Similarly, in trying to acquire virtue and wisdom, we must remain firm in our resolve, otherwise we may fall prey to the allurements of evil and ignorance.

1

In the grand outdoor arena, numerous kings from all over India were sitting on thrones and waiting impatiently. For they had been invited by the king of Kashi to participate in his beautiful daughters' *swayamvara*, or marriage-selection ceremony. Hoping that one of the three teenaged princesses would choose him over the other candidates, each king gazed at the girls with eager longing: Amba, the oldest; Ambika, second; and Ambalika, the youngest.

Behind the kings, the stands were packed with many of Kashi's citizens, all of them wondering and speculating about which of the sovereigns each princess would select.

The master of ceremonies then began announcing the names of the illustrious monarchs, when suddenly there was an unexpected interruption. From the entrance of the arena, a horse-drawn chariot, bearing a driver and a warrior, sped across the dusty field and halted just in front of the princesses. Surprised and curious, almost everyone recognized the warrior, who appeared to be in his forties. For he was none other than the world-famous General Bhishma of Hastinapura.

Bhishma stood up in his car and, in a thundering voice, enumerated the various kinds of marriages mentioned in the Vedic scriptures. Then he concluded, "But the best type for a warrior is to kidnap the bride-to-be, challenge the aspiring kings, and prove his prowess over theirs.

Thus—I'm ready to fight with any of you. Either defeat me or be defeated!"

Bhishma quickly seized each of the young ladies, carefully placed each one on his chariot, and then ordered his charioteer to quickly drive off.

Angered, all the kings stood up. They hurriedly discarded their ornaments and grabbed their flashing weapons. When their charioteers brought their shiny cars, which were harnessed with fast horses, the princes jumped onto them. Brandishing their weapons, they ordered their drivers to chase Bhishma.

When the kings drew fairly close to him, they simultaneously shot numerous arrows. However, Bhishma, rapidly shooting his own shafts, checked their onslaught. The monarchs then besieged and showered arrows at him the way rain clouds pelt a mountain top. Bhishma not only intercepted these but pierced each king with many of his own darts.

This horrendous battle lasted for some time. But finally, with his blazing arrows, Bhishma knocked down the kings' horses and charioteers, split apart their bows, flagstaffs and breast plates, and shot off some of their heads. His skill was so astonishing and captivating that even some of his enemies applauded him.

After vanquishing all the princes, without even a scratch on his body, Bhishma happily proceeded towards his capital. Passing through many forests, rivers and hills, he treated the young ladies as if they were his own daughters-in-law, younger sisters, or daughters. And when they arrived in Hastinapura, he presented them to his stepmother Satyavati and told her about how he had won them. Her eyes welled up with tears and, out of gratitude, she smelled his head affectionately.

However, Bhishma had won the princesses not for himself but for Satyavati's son, Vichitravirya, who was the king and still a young man. Had Vicitravirya himself attempted to kidnap the girls, he, having neither the skill nor the experience of Bhishma, would surely have been slain.

As the time for the nuptials approached, Amba, fair complexioned and lovely, approached Bhishma and anxiously said, "Before you had arrived at my *swayamvara*, I had already chosen the king of Shalwas for my husband. And he, without my father knowing, had privately asked me to be his wife. Do you still think it's right for me to become Vichitravirya's wife?"

Bhishma was surprised by this.

"I believe the king of Shalwas is waiting for me. Would you please be merciful—and let me go to him?"

Bhishma consulted with Satyavati, the counselors and the priests. After considering their advice, he allowed Amba to leave and travel to King Shalwa.

When she reached his kingdom, she approached him and gladly said, "My lord, I've come back—you're the only man I want to marry."

Shalwa laughingly replied, "Really?"

"Yes."

"Well, I'm not interested anymore."

Amba was incredulous.

"Bhishma touched you, so it would be better if you returned to him."

"But it was against my will!"

"Was it? Then why didn't you resist or jump off the chariot?"

"I was shocked and sobbing."

"Well, by staying with him, you married him."

"No!"

"Yes. I'd be a disgrace if I married you now."

"But he kidnapped me for his brother."

"So?"

"So now that his brother knows I love you, he's not interested in me."

"And I'm not either. So please—go. You're wasting your time."

"But—"

"No!" His voice was firm and final.

Choked with angry tears, Amba exclaimed, "All right, throw me away! But wherever I go, the good will protect me. For truth can't be destroyed!"

Wailing like a female osprey, Amba sadly left the city. As she wandered about, she reflected, "I'm the most miserable woman in the world. Alas! I have no friends. I've been rejected by Shalwa. And I can't return to Hastinapura. Who is to blame for this? Me? Bhishma? Or my foolish father, who arranged my *swayamvara*? Maybe it's my fault. During the battle, I should have jumped off Bhishma's chariot and run to Shalwa.

"May Bhishma be cursed!" she continued irrationally. "May my terrible father be cursed! May I be cursed! May King Shalwa be cursed! And may my creator also be cursed! May everyone be cursed who is responsible for my misery!"

Her eyes narrowed in hatred. "But the real cause—is Bhishma. Therefore, I should avenge myself against him—by acquiring power through ascetic disciplines; or by having someone defeat him in battle." Then she wondered, "But what king would attempt to defeat Bhishma?"

Having made her decision, she went to an ascetics' retreat and stayed there for the night. In minute detail, she explained to the holy men everything that had transpired. An advanced spiritual master named Shaikavatya lived there. He had immense ascetic merit and was extremely learned in the scriptures. After hearing her lament, he said, "How can we renunciates help you? We live here in the forest and are always engaged in penance."

"I've given up the world and wish to live here also. My suffering, I realize, is the result of my past-life sins. I have no desire to return to my relatives—for I've been humiliated by Shalwa. And I feel unwanted and depressed. All of you, by your penances, have washed away your sinful reactions and tendencies. You are all godlike and I want you to teach me ascetic disciplines. Oh please, show me your mercy!"

The sage consoled Amba by referring to examples and reasons in the scriptures. Then he and the other Brahmins promised to help her.

Those virtuous recluses proceeded with their usual activities, considering what they should do for Amba. Some suggested that she should be taken to her father's palace. Others hinted that Bhishma should be reproached. Some stated that King Shalwa should be petitioned to accept Amba, while others disagreed because she had already been rebuffed by him.

After a while, the ascetics approached her and one of them said, "Young lady, do not give up the world and spend your life in the forest. Better go to your father's palace. Your father will know what should be done next. There, you will have every comfort and live happily. You are a woman and your father is your only protector now. When a woman is married and comfortable, her husband is her protector; but when she is unmarried and miserable, her father is. You are a princess and very delicate. But life in the forest is very harsh. It has so many difficulties and discomforts. But in your father's palace, you will not have to bear any of them."

Another ascetic remarked, "Kings who might be passing through these lonely woods might see you alone and want to consort with you."

But Amba replied, "I can't return to my father's palace. For I have no doubt that all my relatives will scorn me. I just want to live under your protection and practice ascetic disciplines. Then I won't have to suffer as miserably in my future life. Please help me to engage in asceticism."

As the holy men considered her response, the saintly King Hotravahana entered the retreat. The ascetics honored him with courtesy,

welcome and worship, and then offered him a seat and water. After he
was comfortably seated and had rested for a while, the ascetics continued
their conversation with Amba. Overhearing it, the saintly king became
anxious and sympathetic. He recognized her as his granddaughter, and
thus he went and comforted her. She then narrated her story in full,
arousing compassion and grief in him.

When she finished, he knew what she would have to do and said,
"Do not return to your father's palace. I'm your grandfather and I will
drive away your grief. You can depend on me. How great your sorrow
must be, for you are so thin now. I advise you to go to Parashurama, the
son of Jamadagni. He will help you. Bhishma is his disciple. If he doesn't
obey his guru, Parashurama will slay him in battle."

Shedding tears, Amba bowed her head reverently to Hotravahana
and said, "I will go to him. But how will he relieve my grief? And how
can I reach him?"

"Parashurama is always engaged in severe austerities in the forest of
the Mahendra Mountains. Many sages, Gandharvas and Apsaras live
there. Go and find him, offer him your obeisances, and tell him what
you want. If you refer to me, Parashurama will do everything for you,
as he is my friend. He likes me and always wishes me well."

As King Hotravahana was speaking, who should wander into the
retreat but the sage Akritavrana, a close companion of Parashurama.
Everyone there, including the king, stood up respectfully. They offered
him all the rites of hospitality and then sat around him. Then, with
satisfaction and pleasure, they began to speak on various charming,
praiseworthy subjects. And after their discussion ended, King Hotravahana
asked Akritavrana, "Where can one see Parashurama now?"

Akritavrana replied, "Parashurama always talks about you. He says
you are his dear friend. I believe Parashurama will be here tomorrow
morning. You will see him then. But—this young woman. What is she
doing here? Who is she related to? And what is your interest in her?"

"She's the favorite daughter of the king of Kashi—and my daughter's
child. Her name is Amba." He then described all that had recently
happened which had led her to this retreat; and also stated that she was
ready to do whatever Parashurama would suggest.

Akritavrana asked Amba, "Do you want Parashurama to urge Shalwa
to marry you? Or do you want to see Parashurama defeat Bhishma in
battle? Whichever is your wish, Parashurama will satisfy."

Amba replied, "My wish is that whatever is proper should be done—
to either Bhishma or to Shalwa or to both of them."

"What you have said is worthy of you," said Akritavrana. "But listen. If Bhishma had not taken you to Hastinapura, and if Parashurama had asked Shalwa to accept you, he certainly would have. It's because Bhishma kidnapped you that Shalwa has suspicions about you. Bhishma is proud of his manliness and is crowned with success. Therefore you should take vengeance on Bhishma and only Bhishma."

"Yes, that is what my heart desires—I want to cause Bhishma's death in battle. But whether it be Bhishma or Shalwa—just punish the man who you think is guilty and has made me miserable."

The next day Parashurama, beaming with energy and resembling a blazing fire, arrived there. He was wearing matted locks and deerskins, and was encircled by his disciples. Carrying his bow, he bore a sword and a battle-axe. As he approached King Hotravahana, the king, the ascetics, and Amba stood up with folded palms and waited. Then they gladly worshiped him with honey and curds. Afterwards, Parashurama sat down and they all sat around him. Parashurama and Hotravahana sat together and conversed. But after a while, Hotravahana introduced Parashurama to his granddaughter and said, "She would like you to do something for her."

Parashurama turned to Amba and asked, "What would you like?"

After Amba worshiped his lotuslike feet, she wept aloud.

"Tell me what's bothering you?" asked Parashurama. "I will do what you want."

"I beg your protection. Lift me from this bottomless sea of sorrow."

"Yes, but explain yourself."

Amba reiterated her story of woe, and then said, "Please slay Bhishma. For he's the root of my suffering. He is greedy, mean and proud. Even while he was kidnapping me, I wanted to cause his death. Please satisfy my desire."

But Parashurama replied, "Princess, I do not fight with anyone now except to protect holy men. However, both Bhishma and Shalwa are obedient to me. Therefore, don't sorrow. I will fulfill your wish."

"But Bhishma has made me miserable! Therefore, kill him immediately!"

"Princess, although Bhishma deserves respect from you, he will, at my word, place your feet on his head."

"No, just kill him! If you want to please me and fulfill your promise to me, then kill him!"

Akritavrana interposed, "Lord, you once made a vow that you would not desert those who come to you in fear and beg for your protection;

and that you would kill the proud warrior who would defeat all the warriors on earth. Well, Bhishma has done this. Therefore, challenge him to battle!"

"Yes, I recall that vow," said Parashurama. "But this matter is very serious. Thus, I will first try to negotiate and reconcile it. If Bhishma doesn't satisfy my request, then I will kill that proud creature. This is my resolve."

Parashurama spent the night there with his disciples. The next day, along with his followers and Amba, he proceeded towards Kurukshetra to reach Bhishma. Upon arriving there on the banks of the Saraswati River, they established their camp. Three days later Parashurama sent Bhishma a message announcing his presence and informing him that there was something he wanted him to do. Bhishma, accompanied by many Brahmins, family priests, and others, went there quickly.

When Bhishma and all the others arrived at Parashurama's camp, Bhishma worshiped him devoutly. After accepting the worship, Parashurama said, "You kidnapped Amba and then later dismissed her. Since you touched and contaminated her, what prince will marry her now? Therefore, I order you to take her back. Let her be married. She should not have to suffer such humiliation."

"Brahmin," Bhishma began, "I can't give her to my brother, for when she told me she was Shalwa's, I allowed her to go to him. How can I take her back now?"

Parashurama angrily exclaimed, "If you don't do as I say, I will kill you this very day—along with all your advisors." Parashurama repeated his threat several times.

Though Bhishma tried to pacify him with sweet words, Parashurama remained inflamed. "Why do you want to fight with me?" asked Bhishma. When I was a child, you instructed me in the military arts. I'm your disciple."

"You call me your guru and yet you refuse to please me—by accepting Princess Amba."

"But I can't do it. For what man would welcome into his house a woman whose heart belongs to another? Such a woman would be like a poisonous snake. Thus, your request is improper."

"What?!"

"According to the scriptures, a preceptor's order may be rejected when the teacher is filled with vanity, doesn't know right from wrong, and is treading a devious path. You're my guru, and because of this, I have accorded you great respect. But you, however, don't know the duty of a guru. So yes, I will fight you."

Parashurama glared at Bhishma.

"Normally," Bhishma continued, "I would not fight with a Brahman, especially one like you, with ascetic merit. But the scriptures clearly say that a warrior is not sinful or guilty if he kills a Brahman who has assumed the position of a warrior. Though you are difficult to defeat, I will curb your pride."

Parashurama's anger blazed.

"For many long years you've boasted that you single-handedly defeated all the warriors on earth. Do you know why you beat them? Because neither I nor any warrior like me had yet been born. The warriors you conquered were mere heaps of straw—nothing to boast about. The warrior who has been born to quell your pride is none other than myself. And that is exactly what I intend to do!"

Parashurama laughingly shouted, "Oh, really? Then let's go to the battlefield! Let your mother Ganga see you dead there—pierced by my arrows and eaten by vultures, crows and other carnivorous birds. Yes, let her weep today at the sight of your miserable corpse, no matter how undeserving she may be to see that. But enough talk. Let's get ready for battle."

Bhishma respectfully bowed his head to Parashurama and said, "So be it!"

2

As Parashurama headed for the battlefield, Bhishma returned to Hastinapura. He revealed to Satyavati all that had happened and she gave him her blessings. Then the Brahmins performed a victory ceremony, showering Bhishma with benedictions. Next, he dressed himself in white garments, a white coat of mail, and a white helmet. Taking his white bow, he mounted his silver chariot to which were yoked white horses. The vehicle was spacious and covered on all sides with tiger skins. Equipped with many great weapons and furnished with everything necessary, the car was driven by a brave, expert driver.

As servants fanned Bhishma, the Brahmins honored him by chanting glorious hymns and wishing him victory. The charioteer then quickly drove the vehicle to the battlefield of Kurukshetra. There, both combatants, eager for battle and yearning to display their prowess, saw each other. Then Bhishma blew his conch loudly.

Many spectators had arrived to view this colossal fight. There were Brahmins, forest ascetics, as well as gods, headed by Indra, standing around the field. The celestials wore heavenly garlands and played various kinds of divine music.

Just then, Ganga, Bhishma's mother, appeared before him and said, "My son, you're a warrior—so why are you about to fight with Parashurama, a Brahman? And don't you know that, in the past, he single-handedly destroyed every warrior on earth?"

Bhishma explained to his mother all the facts that had led to this conflict and how he had tried to avert it.

Ganga then hastened to Parashurama and said, "Don't fight with Bhishma—he's your disciple."

"Go and tell Bhishma to stop. He's not done what I asked him. Therefore, I've challenged him."

Out of affection for her son, Ganga returned to Bhishma and asked him to desist. But Bhishma's eyes were rolling in anger and he refused to obey her.

At that moment Bhishma saw Parashurama—standing on the ground and wearing no armor—and Parashurama dared him to fight.

But Bhishma said, "Hero, if you want to fight with me, first get yourself a chariot and then encase yourself in armor."

Parashurama replied, "The earth is my car, the Vedas are my horses, the wind is my charioteer, and the three great Vedic mothers—Gayatri, Savitri and Saraswati—are my armor. With these as my covering, I will fight you." Then he showered Bhishma with a thick covering of arrows.

Suddenly, by a mere act of will, Parashurama materialized a wonderful, well-equipped chariot containing every kind of weapon. It was yoked to celestial horses, decked with golden ornaments, and covered all around with tough skins. He was armed with a bow, equipped with a quiver, and wore leather gloves. And his charioteer was Akritavrana. Then Parashurama said repeatedly, "Come! Come! And gladden my heart!" He shot three showers of arrows at Bhishma and curbed his horses.

Bhishma jumped off his chariot and hastened to Parashurama. There, he worshiped and saluted him, and then said, "Parashurama, whether you are equal or superior to me, I'll fight with you. You're my virtuous guru. Master, please bless me and wish me victory."

Parashurama, deeply pleased with his disciple's respect and humility, said, "If one wants good fortune, he should act like you. That's the duty of any warrior about to fight with a combatant more famous than himself. Had you not done this, I would have cursed you. You should fight carefully and patiently. But I can't wish you victory because

I'm here to defeat you. Go—and fight fairly. I am pleased with your behavior."

Bhishma bowed to Parashurama and quickly returned to his chariot. Blowing his gold-plated conch again, Bhishma began the combat. He shot a sharp, broad-headed arrow and cut off one of the horns of Parashurama's bow, which fell to the ground. Then he discharged a hundred straight arrows into Parashurama's body, and streams of blood gushed out of it.

But Parashurama, filled with anger, released numerous sharp, golden-winged arrows at Bhishma's vital organs and made him tremble. This enraged Bhishma, and thus he pierced Parashurama with a hundred arrows. Afflicted by their impact, Parashurama seemed to lose his senses. Bhishma became filled with pity, stopped fighting and said, "Shame on me! I've committed a great sin. I've harmed my guru, who is a Brahman endowed with virtue!"

As the sun went down, the battle stopped. Bhishma's charioteer then removed the arrows from his own, Bhishma's and his horses' body.

The next day, when the sun rose, the battle recommenced. Bhishma overwhelmed Parashurama with a thick shower of arrows, and Parashurama, too, covered Bhishma with a similar downpour. Parashurama shot many more arrows, but Bhishma, with his own shafts, repeatedly hit and deflected them in mid-air before they reached him. Parashurama then hurled celestial weapons, but Bhishma repelled all of them. The latter hurled a wind weapon, but Parashurama neutralized it with a Guhyaka weapon. Then Bhishma discharged a fire weapon, but Parashurama neutralized it with a water weapon.

Thus, they continued shooting and neutralizing each other's celestial weapons. But suddenly Parashurama shot an arrow into Bhishma's chest and the latter fainted. As Bhishma's charioteer drove him off the battlefield, Parashurama's followers, Akritavrana and Amba were filled with delight.

After Bhishma recovered, his charioteer drove him back to Parashurama, and he angrily overwhelmed him with a storm of shafts. However, Parashurama, shooting three arrows for every one of Bhishma's, split apart in mid-air the latter's shafts before they reached him. In this way, as Parashurama intercepted hundreds and thousands of Bhishma's arrows, all his followers were filled with delight.

Then Bhishma, yearning to slay his opponent, shot a powerful death arrow at him. The impact was so shocking that Parashurama fell unconscious and toppled to the ground.

People all over exclaimed, "Oh! Alas!" In fact, everyone in the universe was filled with confusion and alarm, as they would be if the sun fell from the sky. All the ascetics, along with Amba, anxiously proceeded to Parashurama. Holding him with their hands, they began to soothe him and assure him of victory.

Thus relieved, Parashurama awoke, stood up, fixed an arrow to his bow and shouted, "Stay, Bhishma! You're finished!" When he released the shaft, it penetrated Bhishma's left side, and the latter trembled like a tree in a tempest. Next, Parashurama showered Bhishma's horses with darts and then pierced Bhishma with a terrible swarm of arrows. But Bhishma recovered and released countless of his own shafts to obstruct Parashurama's. Then suddenly, all those shafts stopped moving and remained suspended in the air! The sky was so covered with arrows that neither the sun nor the wind could pass through them. And as a result of this intense friction, a huge fire erupted. But after a while, the arrows turned into ashes and fell to the ground.

It was then that Parashurama, thoroughly incensed, discharged thousands of arrows at Bhishma. But before they could touch him, Bhishma intercepted them with his own shafts and they fell to the earth.

When the sun set, the warriors desisted from further combat and returned to their camps.

In this way, the battle raged for many days. Though neither warrior defeated the other, their wrath and determination increased daily.

Then one day various evil omens appeared. In the sky, masses of clouds formed and they showered down blood. As hundreds of meteors fell, peals of thunder shook everything. The planet Rahu eclipsed the blazing sun and harsh winds began to blow. When the earth quaked, vultures, crows and cranes flew joyfully. Jackals repeatedly howled and the points of the horizon flared. And drums—unpounded by human hands—produced a harsh thumping.

On the twenty-second night, while Bhishma was asleep, he had a strange dream. Eight effulgent look-alike Brahmins surrounded him and one of them said, "You need not fear for we'll protect you. Parashurama will never be able to defeat you. Rather, you'll defeat him. In your former life, you had control over a weapon called praswapa. No one on earth, including Parashurama, knows about it. Just recall it and then use it. You will not incur any sin. For all it will do is put Parashurama to sleep. Defeating him in this way, you can then awaken him with the samvodhana weapon." The Brahmins then mysteriously vanished.

On the twenty-third day, as the combatants were skirmishing on the field, Parashurama, full of anger and vengeance, invoked the great Brahma weapon. But Bhishma checked it with his own Brahma weapon. As the two weapons collided in the sky, they blazed like a supernova. The whole sky appeared to be burning and all creatures became highly disturbed. The earth, with her mountains, oceans and trees, started shaking. And all beings, feeling the heat of those weapons, were sorely distressed. The horizon became so filled with smoke that birds could not fly in the sky.

Seeing all this distress and wanting to end the battle, Bhishma desired to use the praswapa weapon. And sure enough, as soon as he desired this, he recalled the mantra for releasing it. Just as he was about to do so, he heard the tumultuous voices of the gods booming in the sky: "Don't release the praswapa weapon!"

But as Bhishma aimed the weapon at Parashurama, the great sage Narada suddenly appeared there and checked him. "The gods are forbidding you, so don't aim the praswapa weapon. Parashurama is not only an ascetic with Brahminical merit, but he's also your guru. Therefore, don't humiliate him!"

Bhishma then saw the eight effulgent Brahmins—whom he had seen in his dream—in the sky. They said, "Bhishma, do what Narada says. For that is beneficial to the world."

Bhishma then withdrew the praswapa weapon. Noticing this, Parashurama angrily exclaimed, "Wretch that I am, I'm defeated, Bhishma!"

Suddenly Parashurama's deceased venerable father, Jamadagni—and his father's fathers—appeared there and surrounded him. His father said, "Parashurama, never show such recklessness again—in fighting with Bhishma or with any warrior. To fight is the duty of a warrior. But you're a Brahman. Therefore it's your duty to study the Vedic scriptures and undertake vows. These are the riches of the Brahmins. Let this fight with Bhishma be your very last, for you have done enough fighting. Throw your bow aside and practice ascetic disciplines. The gods are forbidding Bhishma to defeat you, his guru, in battle. And as we are your superiors, we likewise forbid you to fight with him. You are lucky to still be alive. How can you defeat him? He is a celebrated Vasu, a god."

Parashurama replied, "I can't give up the fight, for I've made a solemn vow. Up to now, I've never fled the battlefield. Father and grandfathers, if you wish, please ask Bhishma to stop fighting. As for myself, I can't."

The ascetics, along with Narada, went to Bhishma and said, "Please stop fighting and honor this topmost Brahman."

But Bhishma replied, "I can't stop fighting. This is my solemn vow. I've never run from the battlefield. And I can't, out of temptation, distress, fear, or greed, ever leave my duty."

Though they all pleaded with Bhishma, he was determined to keep fighting.

They next returned to Parashurama and one of them said, "Parashurama, please stop fighting. You can't slay Bhishma, nor can he slay you."

Parashurama then laid down his weapons.

***

When Bhishma saw that Parashurama had disarmed himself, he did the same. Although heavily bruised, Bhishma approached Parashurama and worshiped him. Parashurama smiled with great affection and said, "On earth, there is no warrior equal to you. And in this battle, you have greatly pleased me."

Then Parashurama summoned Amba and sadly said to her, "I have fought Bhishma to the best of my ability. But I could not defeat him. Therefore, Amba, go wherever you like. But seek Bhishma's protection."

Amba replied, "No, I won't return to Bhishma. I'll go where I can obtain the means to kill him!" Full of hostility, she left the area.

Parashurama bid Bhishma farewell and left for the mountains; then Bhishma ascended his vehicle and returned to Hastinapura.

Amba entered a forest retreat and began to practice extremely harsh austerities. Her hair matted, her body thin and dirty, she lived only on air and remained in one spot for six months. She fasted from all food and stood in the Yamuna River for a year. During the next year, she stood on her tiptoes and ate one fallen leaf. And for the next twelve years, she practiced such severe austerities that the heavenly planets became hot. Though her relatives tried to dissuade her, they failed.

Amba then spent her time roaming from one holy retreat to another, observing difficult vows and bathing in the sacred waters. She was relentless in her determination to kill Bhishma.

Then suddenly, Lord Shiva, holding his trident, appeared before her. Pleased with her austerities, he asked her to request a blessing.

"Please let me slay Bhishma."

"So be it," he replied.

"But how? I'm in a woman's body now."

"You'll become a man—in your next life.

"A man?"

She discovered that her 'husband' was a young lady like herself.

"Yes. And you'll recall all the incidents of this life." Lord Shiva then disappeared.

Elated, Amba gathered a heap of wood and made a funeral pyre on the banks of the Yamuna River. After lighting the sticks, she sat down angrily in the blazing flames. As her body was consumed, she cried out, "This is for Bhishma's death!"

3

King Drupada was the king of Panchala, and for a few years his eldest queen was childless. For the sake of acquiring a son, the king went to the forest, worshiped Lord Shiva and practiced harsh austerities. Then one day, Lord Shiva appeared to him and said, "You will have a child—who will at first be a female and then become a male. It can't be otherwise."

The king returned to his capital and informed his wife. And in due course of time, she became pregnant and gave birth to a beautiful girl. But she told everyone that she had delivered a son. Consequently, the king had rites performed for a male child and named her Shikhandi. Thus no one in the city, except the king and queen, knew the actual sex of the infant. And they guarded their secret vigilantly.

King Drupada, as his daughter grew up, educated her in writing, painting, and all the arts. After a while, the queen asked Drupada to find a wife for her (as if she were a son). The king was worried about this because she was still a female. But the queen said, "Lord Shiva's words can never prove untrue. I'm sure of it."

The royal couple chose the daughter of the king of Dasarnakas. This king, Hiranyavarman, who was Drupada's brother, was very powerful, not easily defeated, and had a large army. He welcomed the marriage.

Sometime after the wedding, Hiranyavarman's daughter attained her youth and Drupada's daughter also reached hers. It was then that the former discovered that the latter—"her husband"—was a young lady like herself. She shyly told her nurses, and they in turn sent emissaries to inform her father of the deceit.

King Hiranyavarman was furious. He immediately sent a message to King Drupada, which read: "You have humiliated me. That was not very wise—to request my daughter for your daughter. Evil one, you will now reap the fruit of your deception. For I will now kill you, along with your relatives and counselors."

Hiranyavarman immediately left his city. He informed his friends of the deception and soon mobilized a large army to fight against Drupada. But he first held a conference with his ministers. It was then settled that if Shikhandi were really a female, they would bind Drupada and drag him from his city. Then, after installing a new king, they would kill Drupada and Shikhandi.

King Drupada's city was naturally well protected. But now that danger loomed, his warriors began to defend and fortify it more painstakingly. The king and queen, filled with grief, wondered how they might avert a war with his brother. His wife advised, "Pay homage to all your superiors, worship all the gods, offer large gifts to the Brahmins, and pour oblations on the fire to pacify Hiranyavarman. Then think of how to appease your brother to avoid a war."

* * *

Their helpless, humiliated daughter, Shikhandi, reflected, "It's because of me that my parents are grief-stricken. Therefore, I will kill myself."

Firmly resolved, Shikhandi sadly left home and trekked to a thick, lonely forest. This was the haunt of an exceedingly dreadful Yaksha named Stuna. Fearful of him, men never entered that forest. There was a mansion in it that had high walls and a gateway, and these were plastered over with powdered earth. Shikhandi went into the mansion and began fasting from food, her body gradually becoming emaciated.

It was then that the Yaksha Stuna, who happened to be kind, appeared before her and said, "Why are you fasting? I can quickly help you achieve your purpose."

"No, you can't help me," she replied.

"Yes, I can. I'm a follower of Kuvera, the treasurer of the gods. And I can give blessings. I can bless you with the impossible. Just tell me what you want."

She then informed Stuna about all that had happened and the danger her father and she were in—because she was a female. Then she said, "Please show me your grace—and make me into a perfect man!"

"I'll surely do what you ask. But on one condition."

"Which is?"

"I'll give you my manhood for a certain amount of time. But when the time elapses, you must return it to me."

"All right."

"Promise?"

"I promise. As soon as King Hiranyavarman leaves my city, I'll come back here—and give you back your manhood."

By the mystic power of Stuna, he became a woman and Shikhandi became a man.

Shikhandi returned to his city with great delight and approached his father and mother, telling them everything that had occurred. Becoming ecstatic, the king and his wife recalled Lord Shiva's earlier prophesy. The king then sent a message to Hiranyavarman that read: "My child is a male. Please believe me."

Meanwhile, Hiranyavarman arrived at the outskirts of Kampilya, Drupada's capital. Having never received Drupada's message, he sent his envoy to Drupada with a threatening message: "I plan to kill you, your counselors, your sons and your relatives today!"

Drupada immediately sent a Brahman agent to Hiranyavarman. When he arrived, he relayed the king's message: "My child is truly a male. You may send a witness to confirm this. Somebody has lied to you. Don't believe it."

Filled with sorrow, King Hiranyavarna sent several beautiful women to determine whether Shikhandi was a male or a female. After the women examined him, they joyfully reported back to Hiranyavarman that Shikhandi was indeed a male—and a rather powerful one at that. Fully elated, Hiranyavarman went to his brother Drupada and honored him. When he saw Shikhandi, he gave him much wealth and many elephants, horses and cows. Then he scolded his daughter for lying about Shikhandi's sex.

Meanwhile, a spaceship descended from the sky and hovered just above Stuna's mansion. In it was the god Kuvera, along with a small entourage. Kuvera noted the beautiful flowers, fragrant grass, and sweet scents, as well as the canopies, flags, and banners there. Seeing all kinds of food and drink, jewels and gems, and flowers and trees, he said to his followers, "Stuna's house is well adorned. But how disrespectful he is. He knows I'm here, yet he's failed to welcome me. Therefore, I will punish him."

But a Yaksha friend of Stuna, standing on the ground, explained, "In order to save some lives, Stuna has given away his manhood to King Drupada's daughter Shikhandi and has assumed her womanhood."

"So?"

"Well, he feels too embarassed to show himself to you in his—female form."

Kuvera ordered his driver, "Park the ship here and bring Stuna to me. I will punish him for his insolence!"

Stuna, shamefaced, was brought before lord Kuvera, who angrily said, "You've disrespected us. Therefore, from today on, you'll remain a woman and Shikhandi, a man!"

The Yakshas tried to appease Kuvera, and one of them said, "Please place a time limit on this curse."

After Kuvera considered this, he concluded, "All right. After Shikhandi's death, Stuna will recover his manhood."

Stuna offered Kuvera proper respect, and then the spaceship, with Kuvera and his followers aboard, boomed up into outer space.

Shikhandi, to keep his promise, again journeyed to the forest mansion—to return Stuna's manhood. But Stuna, pleased by Shikhandi's truthfulness, explained that it was no longer necessary because of Kuvera's curse. He also said, "I think your coming here and then Kuvera's coming here were preordained. What has happened could not be prevented."

***

Shikhandi, filled with delight, returned to his city. There, he paid his respects to the Brahmins, Deities, large trees and crossways with various scents, flower garlands and expensive gifts. King Drupada, very happy to hear about what had transpired, then encouraged his son to further his education in military science and become an expert warrior.

Shikhandi, who had been Amba in his previous life, had reincarnated mainly to slay Bhishma. But how could he—or anyone, for that matter—slay Bhishma? For Bhishma appeared to be invincible. And why had Shikhandi been born first as a female? Could this, in some strange way, be related to his wish to slay Bhishma?

4

Many years later, the Great War or the Battle of Kurukshetra ensued—a fratricidal war between cousins, the Pandavas and the Kurus. Every state of India became irresistibly involved, some siding with the Kurus, others with the Pandavas. Bhishma became commander in chief of the Kuru army, while Shikhandi allied himself with the outnumbered Pandavas. But what was the cause of this colossal conflict?

Dhritarashtra and Pandu were brothers in the Kuru dynasty, and they descended from King Bharata, a former ruler of the earth. The elder brother, Dhritarashtra, was born blind; thus, instead of him ruling, his younger brother Pandu did. But Pandu died at a fairly young age, so his five children—Yudhishthira, Bhima, Arjuna, Nakula and Sahadeva—were then cared for by Dhiritarashtra, who temporarily governed under Bhishma's direction.

Both Pandu's and Dhritarashtra's sons were raised in the same royal household. The military expert Drona trained them, and Bhishma, their venerable "grandfather," counseled them in statesmanship. However, Dhritarashtra's oldest son, Duryodhana, always envied the Pandavas' prowess and thus hated them. His father wanted him and not Pandu's sons to eventually rule the kingdom, notwithstanding that the Pandavas alone were entitled to the throne.

Duryodhana, with his father's approval, tried to slay Pandu's sons several times. However, because their uncle Vidura and their cousin Lord Krishna carefully protected them, they always escaped. Finally, they became the rulers of the whole world—but not for long. For Duryodhana challenged them to a gambling match and, with the crafty aid of his uncle Shakuni, cheated them of all their wealth and kingdom.

***

Consequently, the Pandavas were exiled to the forest for twelve years and then had to live for one year incognito in a city. However, both sides had agreed that at the end of the thirteen years, the Pandavas' kingdom and wealth would be returned to them. But when that time arrived, Duryodhana flatly refused to surrender any of it. This breach of ethics soon led to a declaration of war—the eighteen-day battle of Kurukshetra—in which the Pandavas, under Lord Krishna's direction, would try to recover their kingdom and re-establish righteousness.

During the first nine days, the chief heroes of the war were Bhishma on one side and Arjuna on the other. Both extremely proficient in the use of ordinary and mystical weapons, they were implacable and invincible. Each was doggedly determined to win, and each easily killed thousands and thousands of their opponents. However, near the end of the ninth day, Bhishma, now well over a hundred years old, became furious and relentless. Breaking through the Pandava ranks, he defeated and slaughtered hundreds of thousands of them.

Bhishma looked like the mid-day sun blazing in its own brilliance as he performed superhuman feats. Many of the Pandava troops, overwhelmed with fear, helplessly fled from Bhishma's devastating darts. But soon the sun set—announcing the end of the day's warfare—so the warriors, many mangled from combat, retired to their respective camps. While the Kurus loudly rejoiced, the Pandavas sorely lamented. They knew that unless they defeated Bhishma, they would lose the war. But how could he be conquered?

The Pandavas held a conference, trying to determine how to accomplish this. King Yudhishthira then asked Lord Krishna for His advice. Krishna said that if Arjuna did not wish to slay Bhishma, He Himself would. "For anyone who is your enemy, is my enemy also," He declared. "Therefore, just command Me and I'll do it."

Yudhishthira acknowledged that, without a doubt, Krishna could slay Bhishma. But he refused to order Him because Krishna had already vowed that while He was Arjuna's charioteer, He would not fight. Thus Yudhishthira refused to allow Krishna, for the Pandavas' glorification, to break His promise. However, he remembered that Bhishma had earlier agreed to give him counsel if he needed it. "Therefore, let us go to him and find out how we may defeat him."

The five Pandavas, along with Lord Krishna, proceeded to Bhishma's tent. There they asked him the all-important question. Bhishma replied, "As long as I have my weapons, I can't be defeated. Nor can I be killed unless I want to be. Those blessings I received from my father. But if I lay my weapons aside, I can be slain. And there are certain situations that would make me do that." He then enumerated them, but elaborated on one which could serve the Pandava's well, namely, that he would not fight with a female. This was because it was against the ethics of a warrior and would subsequently induce other warriors to condemn him.

"I would not fight with the brave chariot fighter Shikhandi. He was at first a female but later transformed into a male. Therefore, let Arjuna, keeping Shikhandi in front of him, shoot his arrows at me. I will not fight back. Once you defeat me, you'll be able slay all the Kurus."

The Pandavas, with Krishna, left Bhishma's tent. Arjuna wondered how he would ever be able to fight with his wise grandfather—the man who had raised him when he was a child and who had loved him as a father. But Krishna emphasized that it was necessary if righteousness was to be re-established in the world. He then cited the scriptural mandate that a warrior's eternal duty is to fight, protect subjects, and perform sacrifices, but without malice. "And you alone, Arjuna, are capable of slaying Bhishma."

Arjuna, with great difficulty, accepted his guru's and friend's counsel.

When the sun rose on the tenth day, the musicians in the Pandava camp beat drums, pounded cymbals and blew conches. Soon after, the Pandava host drove out for battle. Placing Shikhandi in the front and other great fighters around him, he was well protected.

The Kurus drove out to meet the enemy, placing Bhishma at the vanguard. The leaders were aware that Bhishma would not fight against Shikhandi, therefore they guarded him vigilantly. For if Shikandi broke through their ranks, Bhishma would become an easy target for him.

The Pandavas attacked and killed many Kurus, causing them to flee in all directions. But Bhishma could not brook this. Summoning his might and skill, he slew Shikhandi's division as a fire consumes a forest. Shikhandi became enraged and sent three arrows into Bhishma's chest. Bhishma was extremely angry but he laughingly shouted at Shikhandi, "Whether you strike me or not, I will never fight with you. For you're really a woman, despite your sex change!"

Shikhandi became furious and said, "I've heard about your battle with Parashurama. I've also heard about your super-human prowess. But I'll still fight with you today. And I'll surely kill you! This, I promise. So take your last look at this world!"

Recalling the hatred he had once felt as Amba, Shikhandi then pierced Bhishma with five straight arrows.

Arjuna, right behind Shikhandi, urged him, "Rush him—he won't be able to touch you. If you don't kill him today, the world will ridicule both of us. You must kill him!"

Although Shikhandi tried, he could not succeed. Nonetheless, the Pandavas, for a while, routed many of the Kurus—until Duryodhana incited Bhishma to defeat them. He attacked the Pandavas and killed numerous warriors, horses and elephants. The Pandavas then charged at Bhishma, even though a large force still protected him on all sides.

Arjuna exhorted Shikhandi, "Drive towards Bhishma! I'll be right behind you."

Shikhandi, joined by many other allies, rushed at Bhishma. But the Kurus resisted them valiantly, and a fierce battle between Arjuna and Duryodhana's brother Dushashana ensued. Arjuna shot a number of shafts at him, causing him to faint. But when he awoke, he continued to battle Arjuna.

Bhishma slew thousands and thousands of warriors. But then quite suddenly, he lost all desire to protect his life and reflected, "I no longer want to kill many great warriors." Seeing the oldest of the Pandavas nearby, he called, "Yudhishthira, if you want to satisfy me, please try to kill me."

Yudhishthira urged on his troops, promising them the protection of Arjuna and Bhima. "We'll defeat Bhishma today—with Shikhandi in front."

But as hard as they tried, they were repeatedly repelled by those guarding Bhishma. After a while, however, there was an opening in the ranks, and Arjuna and Shikhandi entered it. Shikhandi struck Bhishma in the chest with ten arrows, but Bhishma, remembering Shikhandi's femininity, just looked at him angrily. Then Arjuna shouted, "Rush Bhishma and kill him! Only you can!"

Shikhandi quickly covered Bhishma with various types of weapons. But Bhishma disregarded them and focused his attention on checking Arjuna. With his mighty skill, he dispatched numerous Pandava troops to the other world. But the Pandavas also began to overwhelm Bhishma. Shikhandi pierced Bhishma with many arrows; however, Bhishma just laughed at them, for he hardly felt any pain. Then Arjuna released various celestial weapons, killing numerous warriors just as fire swallows a swarm of insects. Indeed, a river of blood flowed between the two armies. And evil portents—vultures, crows, wolves, jackals, etc.—sounded everywhere.

Shikhandi rushed at Bhishma, and Arjuna, following him, slew all those warriors who were trying to protect him. The ranks open, many Pandava leaders charged at Bhishma, overwhelming him and piercing him in various parts of his body. But amazingly, although stabbed in every vital part, Bhishma felt no pain. Then the Kuru leaders entered the fray and tried to attack Arjuna. But the Pandava leaders protected him well.

Shikhandi pierced Bhishma with ten shafts, struck his charioteer with other arrows, and cut down his flag with one shaft. Then Arjuna and Bhishma fought strongly against each other, but neither of them could conquer the other. It was then that Bhishma said to himself, "I now wish to die, for this is the proper hour." The gods and sages who were stationed in the sky said to him, "Son, we approve of your decision. So withdraw your heart from this battle." However, no one but Bhishma could hear their words.

Suddenly, fragrant breezes blew, heavenly cymbals clanged, and a shower of flowers fell upon Bhishma.

Shikhandi, enraged, struck Bhishma in the chest with nine sharp arrows, but the latter did not even tremble. Arjuna hit him in every vital part with hundreds of arrows. As Bhishma tried to fight back, Arjuna repeatedly split apart his opponent's bows. Bhishma then no longer desired to fight with Arjuna. He said to Dushashana, "The thousands of arrows covering my body—they are all Arjuna's, not Shikhandi's." Bhishma then grabbed his sword and shield, but Arjuna shot the shield into a hundred fragments. Almost every space of Bhishma's body was penetrated by Arjuna's arrows.

Resembling a tired porcupine, Bhishma fell off his chariot, his head facing east. The gods and the kings cried out, "Alas!" and "Oh!" and everyone stopped fighting to watch him. Bhishma's body, not touching the ground, lay on a bed of arrows. The clouds poured a cool shower over him and the earth trembled. Noticing that the sun was in the southern solstice and considering this an inauspicious time to die— according to the scriptures—Bhishma decided to remain alive until the sun would begin moving in a northerly direction.

The Pandavas blew their conches. Everyone surrounded, applauded and praised Bhishma. But seeing him with his flag down and his armor cut open, the Kurus felt deep sorrow. The Pandavas and the Kurus offered Bhishma their salutations. Then Bhishma said to them, "Welcome, warriors. I'm happy to see you."

However, his head was hanging down uncomfortably, so he asked for a pillow. Though the kings fetched and offered him the finest, Bhishma rejected them. He smiled and said, "These are not fit for a hero's bed." He looked at Arjuna. "Please give me the kind of pillow you think suitable."

With eyes filled with tears, Arjuna said, "All right." He took out three arrows, charged them with mantras, and shot them into the ground: they perfectly supported his grandfather's head. Seeing that Arjuna had divined his thought, Bhishma was pleased and applauded him.

The Pandavas and Kurus saluted Bhishma, respectfully walked around him three times, and stationed guards all about for his protection. Then, with bodies drenched in blood and hearts plunged in grief, all the warriors repaired to their own tents for the evening.

***

Thus Amba—who, before reincarnating as Shikhandi, had prayed unremittingly for Bhishma's death—fulfilled her desire. Although her steadfast resolve was misguided by vengence, that same kind of determination can be used to attain virtue. And when it is, instead of experiencing only momentary gratification (as Amba did), we can experience long term inner happiness. It is only then that our lives become filled with true meaning, value and happiness.

"When your flesh weighs as much as the pigeon, you can give it to me.
That will satisfy me."

CHAPTER FOUR

KING SHIVI TESTED

1

King Shivi had so much compassion that there was nothing he would not do to save the lives of his subjects. To advance in wisdom and virtue, it is necessary to develop deep compassion—feeling the sufferings of others and acting to relieve them. This helps us overcome our selfishness and releases us from our false identification with our body.

One day Indra and Agni, the chief gods, went to the sacrificial ground of King Shivi of Ushinara. Their purpose was to test the king's virtue and to confer blessings on him. Indra assumed the form of a hawk and Agni, a pigeon.

The hawk was chasing the pigeon, and the latter, very fearful and seeking protection, landed on the king's thigh. The hawk said to the king, "All the monarchs of the world say you're a righteous king. Why then are you sheltering this pigeon and thus violating the scriptural injunction? I've been terribly distressed by hunger. Therefore, don't, under the notion you're being virtuous, deny me the food God has designated for me. By doing this, you're actually abandoning virtue."

"But this pigeon is afraid of you," replied the king. "It wanted to escape from your claws; thus, it landed on my thigh and appealed to me to save it. Why don't you realize that the highest virtue exists in my not giving the pigeon to you?"

"Highest?"

"Yes. Just look at it. It's shaking with fear, it's flustered, and it's asking me to protect it. For me to desert it would be sinful. One who kills a Brahmin or a cow—the mother of the earth—and one who abandons someone seeking his protection, are equally wicked."

But the hawk argued, "But all beings obtain their life from food, which nourishes and maintains them. A man can live for a long time even after abandoning what is dearest to him. But he can't do that after denying himself food. If I'm denied food, I will certainly die. And my wife and children will also—all because of your protecting this one pigeon.

"Thus," continued the hawk, "you will not be protecting *many* lives. When one virtue blocks the expression of another one, the former is no virtue at all but actually a sin. A virtue deserves to be called that when it doesn't conflict with another virtue. But when it does, the two virtues must be compared, their comparative merits weighed, and the one that doesn't conflict should be accepted. Therefore, you should consider both virtues and then adopt the one that's greater in importance."

The king replied, "Your words have much value; thus I suspect you to be Garuda, the chief of birds. And I don't have the slightest hesitation to say you're fully learned in the practice of virtue. You appear to know everything about it. But how can you consider as virtuous the abandoning of a creature asking for help? Since you're seeking food, you can satisfy your hunger with some other kind that's even more plentiful. I'm completely willing to obtain for you the type of food you enjoy most, whether it be an ox, boar, deer or buffalo."

"But I don't want the flesh of a boar or an ox or any other type of beast. They're not my natural food. But this pigeon—it's been provided for me by Providence. Therefore, please give it to me."

"You can have this rich province or any other thing you'd like—except this pigeon. What do I have to do to satisfy you and save this bird?"

"Well, you can cut off a piece of your own flesh, weigh it, and compare it to the pigeon's weight. And when your flesh weighs as much as the pigeon, you can give it me. That will satisfy me."

"Thank you. You shall have it."

The king placed the pigeon on one side of the scale, then sliced off a piece of his own flesh and placed it on the other side. But the pigeon was heavier. Therefore, he sliced off another piece of his flesh...and another...and another...repeatedly, till at last there was no more flesh left on his body. Then, totally devoid of flesh, he himself stepped on the scale.

Amazed and incredulous, the hawk and the pigeon decided to reveal their true identities. The hawk said, "I'm the god Indra and this pigeon is Agni. We've come here to test your spiritual merit. Because you've sacrificed your own flesh to protect a pigeon, you will shine with a glory greater than anyone else's in the world. And it will continue for as long as people talk about you. Eventually, you will reside in the higher regions."

Indra and Agni ascended to the heavenly realm. And the righteous King Shivi of Ushinara, after he filled heaven and earth with the splendor of his virtuous deeds, ascended to the higher realm in a luminous body.

2

When King Shivi was subjected to the most harrowing circumstances, he remained serene throughout his ordeal, always trusting in a higher power. Similarly, to acquire wisdom and virtue, we must learn to stay calm under the most disturbing conditions and depend on Divine guidance. This will elevate us to the transcendental level.

King Ashtaka, who was in the family line of sage Vishvamitra, held an Ashvamedha, or horse sacrifice. Many other kings, as well as the king's three brothers—Pratardhana, Vasumanas, and Shivi—had come to attend it. When the sacrifice was over, Ashtaka and his three brothers, traveling on his chariot, saw Saint Narada coming in their direction. They offered their respects to him and said, "Please come aboard with us."

Narada replied, "Surely," and mounted the vehicle.

Then one of the kings said to Narada, "I would like to ask you something."

"Go ahead."

"The four of us are blessed with long lives, and we possess every good quality. After we die, we'll be allowed to enter a heavenly planet and reside there for a long time. But which of us will be forced to return to earth first?"

"Ashtaka."

"Why is that?"

"I stayed at Ashtaka's house for a few days, and one day we rode on his chariot out of town. There I saw thousands of cows, and their varied colorings differentiated each one from the other. I asked Ashtaka whose cows they were and he said, 'I've given those cows away.' By answering in this way, he praised himself. For this answer, he will have to descend first."

Then another of the kings asked, "Of the three of us left in heaven, which will have to return to earth first?"

"Pratardhana."

"Why?"

"I stayed at his house for some time, and one day he drove me in his vehicle. As he did, a Brahmin said to him, 'Give me a horse.' And Pratardana answered, 'Yes, I'll give you one after I return.' But the Brahmin replied, ' But I'd like it soon.' The king then gave him the horse yoked to the right side of the car.

"Soon he encountered another Brahmin who wanted a horse. Pratardhana said, 'I'll give you one after I return.' But the Brahmin demanded, 'I'd like it soon.' The king thus gave him the horse tied to the left side of the car.

"As the king continued on his way, he met two more Brahmins at different junctures. They both wanted a horse soon. To the first, he gave the horse yoked to the left front of his car, and to the second, he gave the horse yoked to the right front. Since he had no more horses to pull the chariot, the king himself pulled it. And as he did, he grudgingly remarked, 'Now there is nothing for the Brahmins!' Although the king had given charity, he had done so reluctantly. Consequently, he will have to fall from heaven."

Another of the kings asked, "Of the two of us remaining, which will fall from heaven next?"

"Vasumanas."

"And why, he?"

"Well, one day I arrived at Vasumanas' house and I approached him. At that time the Brahmins were conducting the religious rite called Swastivachana to obtain from heaven a flowery car. When the Brahmins finished the ceremony, the car materialized before their eyes. After I praised it, Vasumanas said, 'You have praised this car, therefore please accept it for yourself.'

"At another time I went to Vasumanas when I needed a flowery car. As I admired the car he had, the king said, 'It's yours!' After that, I went to the king a third time and again admired the car. And once more, showing the car to the Brahmins, he looked at me and said, 'You've praised this flowery car enough!' However, the king said only these words but didn't offer the car as a gift to me. For this, he will be the third to fall from heaven."

One of the kings then said, "That leaves only Shivi. But between you and him, who will fall first?"

"I will."

"You? But—why?"

"Because I'm not Shivi's equal."

"You're not?" they asked, incredulous.

"No. You see, one day a Brahmin came to Shivi and said, 'King, I've come to you for food.' And Shivi replied, 'Tell me what you would like.' The Brahmin answered, 'You have a son named Vrihadgarbha. Please kill him and cook him for my food!'

"I waited to see what would happen. Shivi immediately slayed his son, properly cooked him, and placed the food in a bowl. Then he placed the base of the bowl on his head and began to search for the Brahmin. While Shivi was looking, someone said to him, 'The Brahmin you're looking for has entered the city and set your house on fire. And out of anger, he also set fire to your treasury, arsenal, stables for horses and elephants, and the female apartments.'

"When he heard this, Shivi remained unchanged in mood. And when he entered the city, he said to the Brahmin, 'The food you ordered has been cooked.' The Brahmin did not reply but, astonished, just looked at the ground. But Shivi, eager to satisfy the Brahmin, urged, 'Your Holiness, please eat this.' The Brahmin gazed at Shivi for a second and then exclaimed, 'Eat it yourself!' And Shivi replied, 'Certainly.' Shivi then cheerfully lowered the bowl from his head and was just about to proceed when the Brahmin seized Shivi's hand and said, 'You have conquered anger, for you're able to give Brahmins anything.'

"The Brahmin then worshiped Shivi. As Shivi looked at him, he saw his son standing there, like a child of the gods. The boy was adorned with ornaments and his body exuded a delightful fragrance. The Brahmin who had materialized all this then revealed who he truly was. He was none other than the Supreme Lord Vishnu Himself acting as a Brahmin. Having come to test the saintly king, He then vanished.

"Shivi's counselors next asked him, 'Since you know everything, why did you do all this?' Shivi replied, 'I did not do it to acquire fame, riches or pleasurable objects. There was no sin in what I did. I did it because it was the virtuous course, and my heart always leans towards virtue. For the way of the virtuous is praiseworthy.'"

When he was only six, he was so strong he would grab lions and tie them to trees in the retreat.

CHAPTER FIVE

SHAKUNTALA VINDICATED

Lying to his holy wife and denying that he was married to her, King Dushmanta was ultimately exposed by Divine arrangement. In pursuing virtue and wisdom, it is essential that we learn to be truthful. For when we lie, we naturally become anxious, fearful and sometimes guilty, all of which keep us gravitating to lower levels of consciousness.

King Dushmanta, along with his troops—which consisted of infantry, chariots, cavalry, and elephants—were on a hunting expedition. As they were traveling through a beautiful forest, the monarch beheld the lovely and enchanting retreat of the great sage Kashyapa. It was filled with tall trees, colorful blossoms, various fruits, soft grasses, warbling birds, humming bees, and gentle breezes. There were also monkeys, bears, elephants, deer, peacocks, tigers, and snakes wandering about. And the holy and clear Malini River, inhabited by all types of waterfowl, flowed by the picturesque ashram. On its banks many ascetics were seated, each tending his own sacrificial fire.

Adoring this incomparable, sacred retreat, the king desired to see the glorious sage Kanwa, who had descended in the line of Kashyapa. He possessed every good quality, and because of his splendor, it was difficult to gaze at him. At the entrance to the sanctuary, the king halted his army and said, "I am going to see the powerful, self-illuminated Kanwa. Remain here till I return."

The king, accompanied only by his minister and priest, and laying aside all signs of royalty, entered the retreat. Looking about, he thought it resembled the charming garden of the god Indra. Gratified beyond estimation, the monarch soon forgot his hunger and thirst. At various spots he heard learned Brahmins chanting the *Rig, Yajur, Sama,* or *Artharva Vedas,* or the *Samhitas,* or other kinds of *mantras* based on the established rules of intonation. Indeed, that holy sanctuary resembled the abode of Lord Brahma.

There were other Brahmins there who were adept at making sacrificial platforms; they were conversant in logic and the mental sciences, fully knowledgeable of the Vedas, cognizant of the meanings of all types of expressions, familiar with all special rituals, and followers of the path of liberation. Others were proficient in establishing propositions, rejecting the dispensable and inferring proper conclusions; still others knew the science of words—grammar, meter, and etymology—astrology, the results of sacrificial rites, causes and effects, the screechings of birds and monkeys, and various other sciences. And some were engaged in the vow of *japa*, or reciting God's names, and *homa*, or offering oblations into fire.

The sanctuary was auspicious and holy, protected by the sage Kashyapa's ascetic qualities, and had all the requirements of a sacred ashram. The more the king saw it, the more he wanted to see it. He was not satisfied with just his brief glimpse.

The king, leaving his minister and priest at the hermitage entrance, proceeded inside. But he did not see Kanwa. Noticing the ashram was empty, he cried out, "Is anybody here?"

The sound of his voice echoed back.

Then a maiden, who was as gorgeous as the goddess of fortune, emerged from one of the rooms. She was clothed as a holy man's daughter.

As the black-eyed maiden saw King Dushmanta, she welcomed and received him properly. Reverently offering him a seat and some water to bathe his hands and feet, she asked about the king's well being and peace. Then she respectfully inquired, "Your Highness, what would you like done? Just tell me."

"I've come to worship the holy sage Kanwa. Where has the famous rishi gone?"

The maiden, Shakuntala, replied, "My father left the hermitage to collect fruits. But he should be back soon."

As the king gazed at her, he noticed she was exceptionally lovely and endowed with perfect proportions, what to speak of her honeyed smile. In the fullness of her youth, she exuded beauty from her perfect features, her holy austerities, and her humble manner.

The king asked, "Who are you? And why have you come to live in the forest? You're invested with so much charm and such good qualities. Where do you come from? You've stolen my heart at first glance! I want to know all about you. Please tell me everything."

"King, I'm the daughter of the pious, wise and ascetic Kanwa."

This puzzled Dushmanta. "But—the glorious sage is known to be celibate. So how could he be your— Even Dharma, the personification of virtue, might fall down, but a holy man of firm vows like Kanwa— he never can. Therefore, how could you have taken birth as his daughter?"

"Once a sage came here and asked Kanwa about my birth. This is what he told him: In the past, the sage Vishvamitra was absorbed in the severest of austerities. This frightened Indra, the chief of the gods. He imagined the yogi would, as a result of the power he'd acquired, dethrone him. Indra then called one of the heavenly courtesans and said, 'Menaka, you're the best of the dancing girls. Please help me. I want you to tempt Vishvamitra and stop him from practicing his austerities.'

"'Stop him?' she asked, surprised.

"'Yes. Entice him with your beauty, youth, friendliness, arts, smiles, and words.'

"But Menaka replied, 'Indra, you know that he's very quick-tempered. His power, austerities, and anger have made even you fearful. So why shouldn't I also be fearful?'

"'Please don't worry,' said Indra.

"'Don't worry?' she asked in disbelief. 'He caused even the famous sage Vasishtha to suffer the pain of seeing his children die prematurely. Though originally born as a warrior, he later became a Brahmin through the practice of severe asceticism. And for the purpose of bathing, he materialized a deep river that can be crossed only with difficulty. Yes, it was Vishvamitra who angrily created another world and many stars. And you say I shouldn't worry?'

"'No, you shouldn't.'

"'Then tell me how I can tempt him without being burned by his fury. Just by his effulgence, he can burn up the three worlds. By just stomping his foot, he can make the earth tremble. He can fling the great Mount Meru any distance he wants. And he can circle the earth in a second. Thus—how can a woman like me even touch such a person—when great spiritual personalities, just thinking of him, become petrified?'

"'I'll figure out a way to make it safe for you. But just go—and now!'

"Menaka left for Vishvamitra's ashram. When she arrived, she saw him still practicing austerities. She offered him her respects, and then started frolicking in front of him. At that moment, Indra had the wind god blow her white gown off her body. Feigning bashfulness and apparently annoyed with Vayu, she hastened to retrieve it.

"Vishvamitra, seeing her naked, noted that her features were flawless. Extremely beautiful, she showed no signs of age on her body. As he gazed at her beauty and qualities, Vishvamitra was seized by lust. When he indicated that he wanted her company, she seductively joined him. They spent a long time there—though it seemed like only a day— playing with each other in whatever way they wished.

"Menaka soon became pregnant. So she went to the banks of the Malini River, which flowed along a valley of the enchanting Himalaya Mountains. There she gave birth to a daughter, but soon abandoned it. When a bevy of vultures saw the helpless infant lying there without human care, they clustered around it to protect it from the danger of lions and tigers. Consequently, no carnivorous animals or man-eating Rakshasas killed it.

"On that day, Kanwa proceeded there to bathe and saw the baby surrounded by the vultures. He brought her to his ashram, adopted her, and named her Shakuntala [bird protected]. Never having met her real father, she has regarded Kanwa as her father."

"So—you're Shakuntala?" asked the king.

"Yes."

"O lovely one, I would like you to become my wife."

"Your wife?"

"Yes. This very day I will give you golden garlands, gowns, golden earrings, lovely white pearls from different countries, golden coins, and the best carpets. Please marry me according to the Gandharva rite."

"I think it would be better if we wait till my father returns. Then he can properly offer me to you."

"But why wait? Our religious law allows you to make your own decision and offer yourself to me. Oh Shakuntala, I'm full of longing. And if you are too, then let us unite in this Gandharva rite. This very moment."

"All right. But only on one condition."

"Condition?"

"Yes. I want the son you produce in me to succeed you on the throne."

"The next king?"

"Yes. If you agree, then we can unite in marriage."

"I agree. Fully."

They then engaged in sexual activity and regarded each other as husband and wife. Shortly after, the king said, "Oh sweet one, I shall later send my troops here to escort you to my capital." After thus assuring her, he departed with his troops.

Soon after the king left, Kanwa approached the hermitage.

Feeling remorseful, Shakuntala did not go out to greet him.

But the mighty sage, by his spiritual power, was aware of everything that had occurred. Gratified, he entered the ashram and said, "My daughter, what you have done today in secret, without first getting my approval, has not harmed your virtue. For union between a willing woman and a desirous man is said to be best for warriors. King Dushmanta is noble and righteous, and you've accepted him as your husband."

Smiling affectionately, Shakuntala went to her tired father and bathed his feet. She took the load of fruits from him, arranged them in the right order, and said, "Please bless King Dushmanta and his ministers."

"In your interest, I bless him."

After some time, Shakuntala gave birth to a boy of prodigious energy. When he was only three years old, he shone like a blazing fire. He was handsome, considerate and had all good traits. Kanwa performed all the religious rites for that intelligent child. Growing in beauty and strength, the boy was endowed with pearly teeth, a broad forehead, glistening hair, every favorable sign on his palms, and enough strength to kill even lions.

Like a heavenly child in glory, he grew up quickly. When he was only six, he was so strong he would grab lions, tigers, bears, buffaloes and elephants and tie them to the trees in the retreat. In a playful mood, he would ride on some animals and charge after others. Because he was endowed with valor, energy and power, the ashram residents called him Sarvadamana [the subduer of all].

When Kanwa saw the boy's extraordinary deeds, he told Shakuntala the time had arrived for him to be installed as successor to the throne. He thus ordered his disciples to immediately escort Shakuntala and her son to her husband's palace. They then proceeded toward Hastinapura. On reaching it, they entered the palace gardens where King Dushmanta was conversing with priests, teachers, and ministers. Kanwa's disciples presented the boy's mother to the king and then started back to the sanctuary.

Shakuntala paid her respects to the monarch and then said, "Here's your godlike son. It's time to install him as your successor."

"My what?"

"Your successor. Don't you remember?"

The king looked perplexed.

"Yes, we made an agreement before we were married."

"I'm sorry but I think you have the wrong king."

"What?!" Shakuntala was surprised.

"I never made any agreement with you."

"You most certainly did. That was my condition for marrying you."

"Marrying me? You must be mad. I never saw you before in my life."

The innocent Shakuntala was stunned. She stood there for a while like a wooden post, humiliated and aggrieved. Soon, however, her eyes became as red as copper and her lips trembled. She appeared to burn the king with her fiery glances. Nonetheless, by a remarkable effort, she extinguished her rising anger and ascetic fire. Collecting her thoughts, she glared at the monarch and said, "O King, you know what I'm talking about. Stop pretending."

"I'm not pretending. Now if you'll please excuse me, I have other—"

"You *are* pretending—and degrading yourself! Now stop it!"

"No, you stop it! I've had enough of your fancy!"

"Fancy?

"Yes, fancy! Now please—"

"It's not fancy. It's fact. And you know it. And the Lord in your heart also knows it. So stop sinning before all these people."

"How can you accuse me of sinning?"

"Because you are: Denying that I'm your wife and treating me as though I were a common woman." She then launched into an impassioned speech about the glories of a wife and a son, emphasizing that life was virtually useless and empty without them.

"All right," said the king exasperatedly, "I've heard enough."

"Just look at your son—how can you neglect him so? Don't you see that he wants to play with you and hug you?"

"No, what I see is that both of you should leave this place—right now!"

"I'll be glad to. But your son—you should not abandon him. For he's come from your body and is a reflection of you."

The king remained adamant.

She took hold of her son's hand and said to him, "Let's get away from here—before we become further contaminated."

But just as they began walking away, a disembodied voice from the sky boomed down, "King Dushmanta, Shakuntala has spoken the truth!"

Everyone looked up, astonished.

"Yes," the voice continued, "she's your lawfully wedded wife, so stop offending her. And the boy is your son, so you should begin cherishing him."

When the voice stopped speaking, everyone looked at the king critically. But Dushmanta began to smile gladly. "Did you all hear the heavenly voice?"

They nodded, wondering why the king was smiling. Shouldn't he have felt ashamed of himself?

Apparently not, for he obviously had a plan, which he now revealed to them: "I knew all along that this child was my son. But had I accepted him as such only because Shakuntala said he was, all my subjects may have become suspicious and thought that he was the result of an illicit affair I had had with her. And had I subsequently installed him on the throne as my successor, everyone might have regarded him as a prince of impure birth. Thus, I waited for Divine intervention to counter my false rejection of them. And now that it's come, everyone here knows that Shakuntala is my wife and that my son's birth is pure. No one should have any doubt about that now, right?"

Everyone nodded, then began looking at each other and laughing.

Next, the king happily administered to his son the customary rituals, smelled the boy's head affectionately, and embraced him with love. Then the Brahmins blessed him and the poets applauded him. And the king felt the intense joy a father feels when he touches his son.

King Dushmanta, with love, accepted Shakuntala as his wife. He apologized to her for the distress he had just caused her and confessed that she was extremely dear to him. He then offered her perfume, food and beverage, gave his child the name Bharata, and officially installed him as the heir apparent.

Years later, Bharata, seated on his rattling chariot, journeyed to every country. Reducing all the kings to subjection, he reigned righteously and acquired great renown. He also became known by the names Chakravarti and Sarvabauma. Like Indra, he conducted many sacrifices, such as that of the cow and the horse, and made great offerings to the Brahmins. Bharata gave Kanwa, who presided over these sacrifices, a thousand gold coins as his fee.

He is this same Bharata who was responsible for many magnificent attainments and after whom the glorious Bharata dynasty developed. In that race there were born many godlike kings who, like Lord Brahma, were highly energetic and devoted to truth and honesty [such as Shantanu, Pandu, and the five Pandavas].

"By taking the milk foam, you're preventing the calves from enjoying a full meal."

CHAPTER SIX

GURU AND DISCIPLE

1

By devotion to his enlightened spiritual master—even though he had to suffer great distress—Aruni received great blessings from his teacher for further spiritual advancement. Likewise, if we have a self-realized guru, we should cultivate devotion to him/ her and try to fulfill his/ her wishes. By earning the good favor of such a person, we can quickly awaken to the higher joys of wisdom and virtue.

Ayodha-Dhaumya was a saint, and he had three disciples—Upamanyu, Aruni, and Veda. One day the sage asked Aruni to go to a particular field and plug up a break in a dam there. When he reached the spot, Aruni realized he could not do it by ordinary means. Unable to carry out his guru's order, he was disturbed. He considered the problem for awhile, and when he finally solved it, he said to himself, "Yes, I will accomplish his desire in this way." He approached the breach, lay himself down against it, and stopped the water from flowing through.

Later on, Ayodha-Dhaumya asked his other disciples where Aruni was.

One said, "I thought you had sent him to plug up the break in the dam."

"Yes, I did. Let's all go there."

Arriving in that area, Ayodha-Daumya cried out, "Aruni! Aruni of Panchala! Where are you? Come here, my child."

Hearing his preceptor's voice, Aruni quickly left the dam, came before his guru, and said, "Master, I could not think of any other means of plugging up the breach, so I used my own body to do it. However, because you just called me, I left it and allowed the water to again seep through. Master, please accept my obeisance and tell me what you would like me to do."

"You have gotten up from the dam and opened the water way. Thus, from here on, you will be known as Uddalaka as a sign of your guru's affection. And because you obeyed me, you will have good fortune. All the Vedic scriptures will shine in you.

2

Because Upamanyu failed to practice moderation in eating—always thinking of gorging himself—a terrible tragedy befell him. If we want to acquire wisdom and virtue, we must cultivate the practice of moderation, otherwise we will be dragged down by the degrading feelings of lust, anger and greed.

Ayodha-Daumya had another disciple known as Upamanyu. One day his preceptor said to him, "Go, my son, and tend the cows."

After looking after the cows all day, he returned to his guru's house in the evening and saluted him reverentially.

Seeing that Upamanyu's body looked very plump, his guru asked, "My child, how do you sustain yourself? You look extremely well-fed."

"Gurujee, I sustain myself by begging."

"Begging? But you have not given me your donations. Out of respect, whatever you collect, you must first give to me. And then only that part which I return to you, you may use for yourself."

Upamanyu collected alms the next day and immediately offered them to his guru, who accepted them. After that, Upamanyu went to look after the cows. At the day's end he returned to his master's ashram, went before him, and offered obeisance. Ayodha-Dhaumya noted that Upamanyu continued to look very well-fed. He thus said, "Upamanyu, my child, earlier, I took all your donations. How have you sustained yourself today?"

"Gurudeva, though I gave you all my donations, I went out begging a second time. And whatever I received, I used for myself."

Ayodha-Dhaumya shook his head and replied, "That is not the way to obey your guru. By doing that, you are reducing the amount of donations that other needy beggars may receive. That is very greedy conduct."

Upamanyu agreed completely with his preceptor. The next day, after watching the cows till sundown, he returned to his guru's hermitage. Standing before his master, he bowed his head low. The guru again noted that Upamanyu was still quite plump. "My child," he said, " I take all your donations. And you don't go begging twice in one day anymore. Yet you still look stout. How are you feeding yourself?"

"Master, I drink the milk of the cows I tend."

"The milk? But it's not proper for you to take the milk without my permission."

Upamanyu agreed and accepted his teacher's instruction. The next day, after tending the cows, he approached his guru in his usual respectful way. Ayodha-Dhaumya, observing that Upamanyu was still quite fat, said, "My child, you no longer keep your donations, nor do you beg twice a day, nor do you drink the cow's milk. How then do you stay so plump?"

"Master, while the calves suck on the cow's udders, they throw out some foam. I sip that."

"But those calves are being compassionate to you. They see that you're hungry, and therefore they spit out large amounts of foam. Thus you're preventing them from enjoying a full meal. Is that what you want? Upamanyu, it's not proper for you to drink that foam."

Upamanyu completely agreed with this instruction. The following day while Upamanyu was tending the cows, he became very hungry. But remembering his guru's instructions, he would not beg for donations, drink the cows' milk, or sip the calves' foam. However, while passing through the forest, he decided to eat the leaves of the Arka tree. As he did, because of their bitter and salty properties, he became blind. And while crawling about, he fell into a deep well.

When evening came, Ayodha-Daumya mentioned to his disciples that Upamanyu had not returned home.

One of them replied, "Upamanyu went out earlier to tend the cows."

"Yes, I know. And I forbade him to eat anything. Consequently, he may feel weak and not arrive here till late. Let's go and search for him."

The guru, with his disciples, went into the forest. Looking for his student, he cried out, "Upamanyu, where are you? Where are you?"

Upamanyu, hearing his teacher's voice, answered loudly, "Over here, Master! Over here! At the bottom of this well!"

Arriving there, the preceptor asked him how he happened to be inside. Upamanyu explained what had occurred. His guru then advised him, "Begin praising the twin physicians of the gods, the Ashwins."

"And what will that do?"

"You'll see."

The guru then withdrew from the immediate area.

Upamanyu proceeded to praise the two celestial physicians using words from the Rig Veda. After completing the glorification, he begged, "Honorable Ashwins, please restore my sight to protect my life!"

The Ashwins materialized their handsome forms and said, "We are very pleased with you. Here is a cake for yourself. Take it and eat it."

"Your words have always proved to be true, honorable Ashwins. However, unless I first offer this cake to my guru, I do not dare eat it."

One of the Ashwins replied, "In the past, your teacher once called for us. We appeared before him and offered him a cake like this. And he accepted it without first offering it to his teacher. Therefore, you should follow his example."

"Please pardon me, but unless I first offer this cake to my guru, I do not dare eat it."

"We're gratified by your devotion to your master. His teeth are made of black iron, but yours will be made of gold. Your sight will be restored and you will have good fortune."

Upamanyu immediately regained his sight. He then went to his guru, offered him respects, and related everything that had just occurred. His spiritual master was indeed satisfied with him and said, "Yes, just as the Ashwins have said, you will acquire prosperity. And all the Vedic scriptures shall gleam within you."

3

Utanka could not have fulfilled the wish of his spiritual master's wife if, when he encountered various obstacles, he had not had such strong determination to overcome them. Similarly, to attain wisdom and virtue, we must have indomitable determination to conquer the many difficulties that may descend on us.

One day Ayodha-Dhaumya called his other disciple, Veda. "My child," he said, "stay in my house for some time and serve your guru. You will be benefited by this." Veda agreed and remained for a long time in his preceptor's house, serving him. He always bore heat and cold, hunger and thirst—whatever burdens his master loaded on him—without a whimper. In a short while, his guru was satisfied and bestowed on him good fortune and transcendental knowledge.

After Veda finished his studies and obtained his guru's permission, he left the ashram and entered household life. Soon, at his own residence, he became the teacher of three students. Because his own guru had subjected him to harsh disciplines and caused him much distress, he never ordered his pupils to do any work or to obey his requests unquestioningly.

In a short while, two young men of the warrior caste arrived at Veda's ashram and employed him as their preceptor. One day as Veda was about to leave on some business connected with a sacrifice, he appointed his disciple Utanka to manage his household. He said, "Utanka, if anything has to be done in my house, please do not neglect it." He then set out on his trip.

Utanka moved into his guru's house and followed his instructions. One day the women of this house got together and one of them said to him, "Utanka, your teacher's wife is now in her fertile period. And he's away. Why not take his place and do what's necessary?"

"Because it's not proper for me to do that at the urging of women. And I've not been instructed by my guru to do anything improper."

Sometime later Utanka's preceptor returned from his trip. When he heard what had occurred, he became extremely gratified and said, "Utanka, my child, how shall I bless you? You have served me properly. Thus our friendship has increased. You have my permission to leave now. Go, and may your desires be fulfilled!"

Utanka replied, "Master, allow me to do something for you that you'd like. For it has been said that if one gives instruction that contradicts custom, or if one receives instruction that contradicts custom, hostility will arise between the two and one of them will die. Now, on the one hand, you haven't asked me to give you the customary appreciation payment for having taught me; you have merely given me leave. And on the other hand, though I'm ready to leave, I haven't yet given you the customary appreciation payment and would very much like to. Thus, to respect this *dakshina* custom, would you please ask me to do something you would like?"

"Utanka, please wait a while."

Shortly after, Utanka again said, "Master, please ask me to do something that you would like."

"My dear Utanka, you have asked me this once before. Therefore, please go and ask my wife what she would like. If she wants you to do something, then do it."

Utanka went to his guru's wife and explained to her that he did not want to leave the ashram and return to his own home without first having discharged his debt to his teacher. "Please tell me what you would like me to do for you."

She answered, "I would like you to go to King Paushya and beg him for the pair of earrings that his queen wears. Then bring them to me. In four days it will be a holy day and Brahmins will be invited here to dine. At that time I want to appear adorned with those earrings. Please accomplish this, Utanka. If you succeed, you will be blessed with good fortune. But if you don't, then what favor can you hope for?"

Utanka departed. As he was traveling along the road, he saw a huge bull and a tall man riding on it. The man cried out to him, "Hey, eat the dung of this bull!"

But Utanka refused.

The man said, "Utanka, eat it without inspecting it. In the past, your spiritual master ate it."

Utanka wanted to follow his master's example, so he ate the dung and drank the bull's urine. Finished, he stood up respectfully, washed his hands and mouth, and proceeded to King Paushya's palace.

When Utanka arrived there, he saw King Paushya sitting on his throne. Approaching him, Utanka offered his respects by blessing him. Then he said, "I've come to ask you for something."

Having reciprocated Utanka's respects, the king asked, "What would you like?"

"I've come to beg for a pair of earrings which I'd like to present as a gift to my guru. I'd like the ones your queen wears."

"Surely. Please go to the ladies quarters and ask the queen for them."

Utanka went there but he could not find her. He therefore returned to the king and said, "I couldn't find your queen in the women's quarters."

The king deliberated a few moments, then answered, "Sir, please try to recall whether you're in an unclean state as a result of eating impure food. My queen is a chaste wife and can't be seen by anyone who is impure from eating impure food."

After considering this, Utanka said, "Yes, that must be true. When I last washed myself after eating, I was in a hurry, so I washed while standing."

"That is a violation. One cannot properly purify himself while standing or moving along."

Utanka agreed. Thus, he seated himself, faced the east, and washed his face, hands, and feet completely. Taking some water, which was free from scum, foam, and warmth, and was just enough to reach his stomach, he drank it. Then he wiped his face two times and dabbed water on his eyes, ears, nose, etc.

After he finished, Utanka again went to and entered the women's quarters. But now he did see the queen. When the queen saw him, she offered him reverence and said, "Greetings, Sir. Is there something you would like?"

"Yes. I would like you to give me your earrings, which I want to offer as a gift to my guru."

The queen was gratified with Utanka's behavior. Realizing that as an object of charity he should not be ignored, she removed her earrings and donated them to him. "Please bear in mind that these earrings are greatly desired by Takshaka, the king of the Naga race. Those beings have human faces, serpent tails, and cobralike necks, and they dwell under the earth. You should carry the earrings with maximum care."

"My dear queen, there's no need to worry because Takshaka can't catch me."

Utanka returned to the king and said, "King Paushya, I'm very satisfied."

"Good. You're an honored guest. Therefore, I'd like to sponsor a *shraddha* ceremony. Please stay a little longer."

"All right. But please bring me some pure food soon."

When the food was set before Utanka, he noted that it had hair in it and was cold. He considered it impure, which was highly offensive to a Brahmin. He said, "You've given me impure food. Therefore, I curse you to lose your sight!"

But the king angrily replied, "No, the food is pure. But because you've called pure food impure, I curse you to not be able to have any children!"

Utanka replied, "You shouldn't have, after offering me impure food, cursed me in return. See for yourself if it's not impure."

After the king scrutinized the food, he understood it to be truly impure. It had obviously been prepared by a woman with unbraided hair. King Paushya therefore attempted to placate the Brahmin and said, "Sir, you're correct. The food does contain hair and is cold. It wasn't prepared with enough care. Please excuse me—and retract your curse."

"What I've said must come true. However, though you'll become blind, you'll soon regain your sight. But—please grant that the curse you pronounced on me doesn't come to pass."

"I'm unable to stop my curse. For even now my anger hasn't subsided. But you wouldn't know this. For the heart of a Brahmin is as soft as newly churned butter, even though his words are like a keen-edged blade. However, it's just the opposite for a warrior. A warrior's words are as soft as newly churned butter, but his heart is like a keen-edged blade. Because my heart is so hard, I can't neutralize my curse. Therefore, be on your way."

"You cursed me to not be able to have children because you believed that the food was pure when I said it was impure. But since what I said was true, your curse can't touch me. I'm certain of this." Utanka then left with the earrings.

* * *

As he was ambling along the road, Utanka saw, coming in his direction, a nude, idle beggar; sometimes he could see him and at other times he could not. Then Utanka, deciding to bathe, laid the earrings on the ground and went into the water. Meanwhile, the beggar hastened to the spot, picked up the earrings, and ran away.

After Utanka finished his bath, purified himself, and respectfully offered obeisances to the gods and his gurus, he very rapidly pursued the thief. With some trouble, he caught up to and arrested him. But at that moment the thief transformed his beggar form into that of his true snakelike form, namely, that of Takshaka, who then slithered into a large open hole in the earth. From there he hastened to his home in the serpent region.

Remembering the queen's warning, Utanka tried to pursue the Naga by digging open the hole with a stick. But he made little progress. However, Indra, chief of the gods, seeing the Brahmin's difficulty, hurled his thunderbolt into the stick and enabled it to widen the hole.

Utanka then hurried through the hole till he came to the Naga locale. He saw that the place was extremely large. It contained hundreds of palaces and ornate mansions with turrets, domes and gateways, and was filled with magnificent sites for sports and entertainment. Utanka began to glorify the serpent race as follows:

"O Nagas, subjects of King Airavata, you are excellent in battle and discharge your weapons like lightning-charged clouds propelled by the winds. O children of Airavata, you are beautiful, multiformed, adorned with colorful earrings, and you glow like the sun in the sky. On the Ganges' northern bank are many serpent abodes. I continuously admire the glorious serpents there. Who else but Airavata would want to move in the scorching rays of the sun? When the huge many-headed powerful serpent Dhritarashtra [Airavata's brother] goes out, 28,008 Nagas follow him as his servants. You who go near him or who remain at a distance from him, I admire all of you who have Airavata as your older brother.

"And I also admire you, O Takshaka, in order to regain the earrings. You formerly lived in Kurukshetra and the forest of Khandava. You and Aswasena are steady friends who live on the banks of the Ikshumati River. I also admire the famous Shrutasena, Takshaka's younger brother, who inhabited the sacred spot called Madhadyumna for the purpose of gaining the kingship of the Nagas."

After Utanka completed his eloquent greeting, he still did not recover the earrings. He then began to think about this. As he did, he looked around and saw two women sitting at a loom with a fine shuttle. There were black and white threads in the loom. Utanka also saw a wheel with twelve spokes that was spun by six boys. And he also saw a man with a beautiful horse. He began to recite the following prayer to them:

"O Indra, dispenser of thunder, protector of the earth, slayer of Vritra and Namuchi, displayer of truth and untruth in the universe, owner and rider of the white horse that arose from the ocean when it was churned—I bow to you, O king of the gods and lord of the three worlds!"

The man with the horse said to Utanka, "I am pleased with your worship. What can I do for you?"

"Enable me to control the Nagas."

"All right. Just blow onto this horse."

Utanka did. Suddenly, smoky flames shot out of every opening of the horse's body and were about to devour the Naga kingdom. When Takshaka saw this, he was exceedingly surprised and frightened by the fire's heat. Consequently, he hastened from his home, came before Utanka holding the earrings and said, "I beg you, Sir, to take back these earrings."

Utanka accepted them. Then he remembered, "Today is the sacred day of my guru's wife. But I'm far away. How can I show my respect to her?"

As he thought about this, the man with the horse said, "Utanka, ride this horse, and in one second he'll carry you to your guru's residence."

Utanka agreed, climbed onto the horse, and was instantly taken to his master's abode.

His guru's wife, after bathing that morning, was now sitting and dressing her hair. She was thinking that if Utanka did not return soon, she would curse him. But at that moment he entered his teacher's ashram, offered his reverence to her, and gave her the earrings.

She said, "Utanka, you've come at the right time and to the right place. Greetings, my child. You are faultless and thus I will not curse you. Rather, you shall have good fortune. May all your desires be fulfilled!"

Utanka then went to his spiritual master, who said, "Welcome! Why have you been away so long?"

"Master, as I tried to satisfy your wish, I was impeded by Takshaka the Naga king. I had to follow him down to his kingdom. There, I saw two ladies sitting before a loom. They were weaving a cloth with black and white threads. I also saw six boys perpetually turning a wheel with twelve spokes. I likewise saw a man with a large horse. Earlier, when I was on the road, I beheld a man sitting on a bull. He cordially asked me to eat the dung of his bull, and said you had also eaten it. So I ate it. Master, I would like to understand what all those things mean."

Utanka's guru explained, "The two ladies you saw signify the two weavers of fate; the black and white threads represent night and day; and the twelve-spoked wheel turned by the six boys denotes the year, which consists of the six seasons [in India]. The man was Parjanya, the rain god, and the horse was Agni, the fire god. The bull on the road was Airavata, the elephant king; the man riding him was Indra, and the bull's dung was *amrita*, the nectar of immortality. Because you had eaten it, you were not killed in the Naga region. Indra happens to be my friend and, by his mercy, he blessed you. This is why you have returned home safely with the earrings. Utanka, you now have my consent to depart. You shall surely have good fortune."

Sharyati immediately gave his young daughter to the aged, high-souled Chyavana.

CHAPTER SEVEN

CHYAVANA REGAINS HIS YOUTH

Although Sukanya was tempted to forsake her decrepit husband, she showed how rewarding and satisfying faithfulness can be. If we wish to acquire wisdom and virtue, we must manifest faithfulness to our dear ones— otherwise we will remain stuck on the mundane plane. Such faithfulness is the training ground for developing faithfulness to the Divine.

The great saint Brighu had a son named Chyavana. The son had a splendid body and began practicing asceticism on the bank of a distant lake. He sat on his heels with his hands on his knees in the posture called *virasana*. Silent and still, like an inanimate object, he remained there for a very long time. After a while, ants began to swarm over and cover his body, making him appear exactly like a lump of earth. But he continued practicing this austerity without interruption.

One day King Sharyati, accompanied by his numerous troops, four thousand wives, and his only daughter, visited this superbly enjoyable lake for recreation. His daughter's name was Sukanya. In the prime of youth, she wore a single piece of cloth and exquisite jewelry, and she looked very beautiful. Accompanied by her maids, she began to enjoy herself by looking at the tall trees and lovely scenery. Meandering about, she wandered away from her companions and approached the anthill that had enveloped Chyavana. She felt lustful and inclined towards playing, so she snapped the twigs of flower-bearing trees.

When Chyavana saw her through a hole in the anthill, he was seized with sexual desire. He called out to her, but because he had a low voice, she did not hear him. However, as she approached the anthill, she noticed something glowing inside the hole. Confused and curious, she said, "Oh, what's this?" Then, grabbing a thorny branch, she poked it into the hole and pierced the sage's eyes.

Feeling intense pain, Chyavana became angry. Thus, he cursed her father's troops to be unable to urinate or defecate.

When the men discovered they were unable to answer their calls of nature, they became sorely distressed. The king, surprised and perplexed by the situation, proceeded to study it more carefully. He soon realized that Chyavana was covered by the anthill and that he alone, if provoked, could cause such a calamity by his mystic powers. He thus shouted, "Which person has offended the famous sage Chyavana, who is old, always absorbed in asceticism, and of angry temper? If anyone knows, tell me immediately!"

One of the men replied, "We don't know if anyone has offended the sage. We suggest you inquire further into the matter."

The king, using threat and appeasement, asked his friends about the situation, but they also knew nothing. However, when Sukanya saw the soldiers in anguish and her father disturbed, she explained to him, "As I neared the anthill, I saw something shining in it. I thought it was a glowworm, so I poked it with a branch of thorns."

King Sharyati quickly went to the anthill. He joined his palms reverently and begged, "O great saint, please forgive my daughter for what she did to you. It was done out of ignorance and innocence."

Chyavana replied, "Because she's puffed up with pride, she has disregarded me and poked at my eyes. Though she's beautiful, she lacks reason due to ignorance and lust, and will have to pay a price. And the price is—she'll have to become my wife! On no other condition will I forgive her!"

Sharyati immediately gave his young daughter to the aged, high-souled Chyavana, who was then satisfied with the king. Having gained the sage's favor, the king, along with his troops and wives, returned to the capital. But Sukanya stayed with the ascetic and began to serve him, observing austerities and following the rules of marriage. Sincerely worshiping Chyavana, she also cared for his guests as well as the sacred fire.

One day the celestials known as the twin Ashwins happened to see Sukanya when she had bathed in the nude. Having beheld her exceptional legs, they approached her and asked, "O lovely one, whose daughter are you? And what are you doing in the forest? Please tell us."

Sukanya bashfully replied, "I am Sharyati's daughter and Chyavana's wife."

The Ashwins smiled, and one said, "Why did your father give you to a person who is about to die? Your beauty flashes in this forest like lightning. Not even on the heavenly planets have our eyes feasted on beauty like yours. Even without your adornments and robes, you decorate this forest admirably. But why are you serving such an old, feeble husband—one who can't even enjoy pleasure or support you? Goddess, renounce Chyavana and instead accept one of us for your husband. You should not spend your youth wastefully."

Sukanya grimaced and said, "I'm devoted to my husband, so don't harbor any doubts about my faithfulness."

"We are the famous celestial physicians. We can and will make your husband young and handsome. But if we do, you must choose only one of us three for your mate. Please bring your husband here now."

After Sukanya told Chyavana what had transpired, he said, "Yes, you may do it." When the holy man and his wife reached the twins, they told him to enter the lake. As he did, they accompanied him. The very next moment, all three emerged from the lake in handsome, youthful bodies, wearing shining earrings. Resplendent to look at, they all looked exactly alike! One said to Sukanya, "Now choose one of us for your husband."

This obviously would not be easy. Before selecting, Sukanya meditated deeply on each of them. When she intuitively knew which one was her husband, she picked him. Very pleased, Chyavana said to the Ashwins, "Since, with your help, I've regained my youth and beauty, as well as my wife, after some time I'll enable you to drink the coveted, exhilarating *soma* juice in front of the king of the gods himself."

Having heard about the ecstasy that such a beverage could arouse, the twins were delighted and returned to the celestial world. Chyavana and Sukanya also spent their days joyously, like the gods.

***

When King Sharyati learned that Chyavana had regained his youth, he was overjoyed. Therefore, accompanied by his wife and troops, he went to the sage's ashram. As he and his wife saw the couple, who looked like two divine youths, their ecstasy was as great as it would be if the monarch had won the whole world.

The saint received them respectfully. The king sat down near him, and they conversed pleasantly on auspicious topics. Then Chyavana said, "O King, I shall soon officiate at a sacrificial ceremony to be undertaken by you. Please procure the necessary articles for this."

This made the king extremely happy, and he expressed his approval of the idea. So, on a favorable day fit for the start of a religious ceremony, Sharyati ordered the building of a sacrificial shrine. When completed, it was beautiful to look at and excellently furnished with all requisites. There, Chyavana served as the king's chief priest.

As the ceremony proceeded, Chyavana took up a certain amount of soma juice to offer to the Ashwins. But Indra, the chief god, indignantly said, "In my opinion, the Ashwins have no right to receive the soma juice! They're celestial physicians, mere servants of the gods. This alone disentitles them."

But Chyavana argued, "But they do great things, have glorious souls, and are especially gifted with handsomeness and kindness. It is they who've transformed me into an everlastingly youthful person, just like the gods. Thus, why should you and the other gods be entitled to the soma juice and not they? My opinion is that they also qualify as gods."

But Indra insisted, "These two practice the healing art, so they're only servants. At their will, they assume various forms and wander about in the world of human beings. Therefore, how can they justly lay claim to the soma juice?"

Indra continued to argue, but Chyavana decided to disregard him altogether. He was just about to take up a goodly portion of soma juice to offer to the Ashwins when Indra exclaimed, "If you give them the soma juice, I'll hurl my thunderbolt weapon at you!"

Glancing and smiling at Indra, Chyavana took up a considerable amount of soma juice to offer to the twins. Then Indra displayed a terrible-looking thunderbolt and was just about to hurl it when Chyavana paralyzed his throwing arm. The sage next recited some holy chants, made an offering into the fire, and prepared to kill Indra.

By his mystic power, the ascetic suddenly materialized an evil spirit. His name was Mada, and he was huge, powerful, gigantic—so big that he appeared immeasurable. His mouth was terrible, his teeth sharp, and one of his jaws rested on the earth while the other one touched the heavens. He had huge fangs that resembled palace towers, and his two arms were like hills that extended many miles. His two eyes looked like the sun and the moon, and his face vied with the colossal fire at the end of the world. His mouth was open, his lightning-like tongue licking it, and his gaze was so terrifying that he looked as though he were about to swallow the cosmos.

The demon, roaring loudly and hideously, then charged at Indra with the intention of eating him alive.

When Indra saw Mada's open mouth coming towards him, looking like the death god himself, he fearfully licked the ends of his mouth repeatedly. Horrified and tormented, he shouted, "O Chyavana! O Brahmin! Please believe me. From today on, the two Ashwins may drink the *soma* juice. I swear it! By your power, you've entitled them to it. Please be merciful and try to understand. I've deliberately acted this way to provide you with an occasion to display your power and spread your glory. I've also done it to spread the renown of Sukanya's father. So please—be merciful to me."

Chyavana's anger was quickly pacified, and he freed Indra from the demon. He then demolished Mada [which means "intoxication"] and distributed particles of him throughout the world in drinks, women, gambling, and sporting events. He further satisfied Indra with a drink of the *soma* and helped King Sharyati worship all the gods, spreading his fame all over the world.

After this, Chyavana spent his days joyfully in the forest with his devoted wife, Sukanya.

"Yes, please go to King Nala and tell him I would like to marry him."

CHAPTER EIGHT

NALA AND DAMAYANTI

Damayanti, after being abandoned by her husband and encountering immense troubles, never lost hope that she would one day find him and reunite with him. In striving to achieve wisdom and virtue, we, also, must never lose hope. Rather, we must realize that to gain something valuable and important can sometimes take us a long time of effort.

Once there lived a king named Nala who ruled over the country of Nishadha. He was handsome, powerful, adept in horse lore, and had attained every desirable accomplishment. A king of all kings, he was like Indra, lord of the gods. His glory resembled the sun's, and in attractiveness he was peerless, like Kandarpa, the love god. Moreover, he was heroic, a leader of a powerful army, conversant in the Vedic scriptures, and desirous of the Brahmins' well being. Though he enjoyed playing dice, he spoke only the truth and restrained his passions. A topmost archer, he protected all his subjects, and thus they loved him dearly.

In another kingdom, known as Vidarbha, there reigned a monarch named Bhima. Like Nala, he was valiant, fearsome, virtuous, and friendly toward his subjects. Nevertheless, although he had tried his best to produce children, he was unsuccessful. Then, one day, a Brahmarishi arrived at the palace as his guest. King Bhima and his queen so greatly pleased the saint with gracious hospitality that he blessed them to have four children—three boys and one girl.

The girl's name was Damayanti. When she grew up and became a young woman, she became famous throughout the world for her beauty, intelligence, reputation, grace, and good fortune. Her eyes were large, her features faultless, her waist slender, and, bedecked with many ornaments, she glowed like lightning. Never before, neither among the gods nor humans, had such beauty ever been seen or heard of. With hundreds of lovely maidservants to attend her every need, she looked like Lakshmi, the goddess of fortune.

The heralds, filled with admiration, repeatedly proclaimed the glories of King Nala to Princess Damayanti, and those of Damayanti to Nala. Although the king and the princess had never seen one another, by frequently hearing each other's praises, they developed an attraction towards one another. After a while the attraction materialized into an intense affection, one which Nala found impossible to control. Therefore, in the gardens bordering the inner apartments of his palace, Nala began to spend much time alone mooning over Damayanti.

One day, while in the garden, Nala saw several golden-winged swans wandering about. Curious, he reached out his arms and caught one. And as he held it firmly, the swan began to speak. "King Nala, I don't deserve to be killed by you. Allow me to do something for you that you'll like. I'll go to Damayanti and talk about you in such a way that she'll never want anyone else for a husband."

Pleased, the king released the swan. All the swans then flew into the sky and headed toward Vidarbha. When they arrived, they landed in front of Damayanti and her maidservants. Seeing the swans' rare golden plumage, Damayanti was charmed and hastened to catch one of them while the maidservants ran after the others.

The swan that Damayanti was chasing led her to a solitary place and said, "Damayanti, in Nishadha there is a king known as Nala. He's equal in beauty to the gods Ashwin and Kandarpa, and he has no rival among men. If you, with your fair complexion and slender waist, become his wife, your life and beauty will have some meaning. Though we have seen magnificent men, celestials and gods, never before have we seen anyone like Nala. As you are a gem among young women, Nala is first among men."

Damayanti replied, "Yes, please go to Nala and tell him I would like to marry him."

The swan soared into the sky, flew to Nishadha, and disclosed to Nala what Damayanti had said.

From that day on, Damayanti lost all equanimity. She was struck by the god of love; dwelling on Nala and often sighing, she became anxious, depressed, wan, and thin. Abstracted, she frequently glanced upwards and looked deranged. She ceased using beds, seats and pleasure objects, and refused to lie down during the day or night. She was always weeping and exclaiming, "Alas!"

When Damayanti's maidservants noticed her morose condition, they hinted to her father that something was amiss. After observing her, the king realized the matter was grave and wondered why his daughter looked so ill. The only conclusion he could come to was that because

Damayanti had reached the age of puberty, she now needed a husband. But who? To find out, he decided to arrange for her a *swayamvara* ceremony, wherein she would select a husband from numerous eligible suitors.

King Bhima invited all the monarchs of the world to participate in Damayanti's *swayamvara*. Gladdened by his message, the kings soon arrived at Vidarbha amidst the clattering of their chariots, the roaring of their elephants, the whinnying of their horses, and the marching of their splendid-looking soldiers. Then, after King Bhima properly honored them, they repaired to their designated quarters.

At this particular time, the celebrated saints Narada and Parvat— men of prodigious wisdom and vows—arrived on the heavenly planet of Indra and entered his jeweled palace. After Indra duly welcomed and worshiped them, he inquired about their welfare in all respects.

"We are filled with peace," Narada replied. "And so are the kings of the world."

"Yes," said Indra, "but where are those kings who are my favorite guests? Those virtuous sovereigns who are ready to sacrifice their lives by fighting, who never flee from the battlefield, and who eventually reside here permanently and satisfy all their desires—where are they?"

"They are all going to the *swayamvara* of Damayanti, the daughter of the king of Vidarbha. She is the most beautiful young woman—a true pearl of the earth—and will be selecting a husband soon. Every one of those kings ardently wants to be chosen."

As the conversation continued, other important gods arrived there, such as Agni, Yama, and Varuna, and they listened to Narada's words seriously. Delighting in the possibility of becoming Damayanti's lord, all of them finally decided to attend her *swayamvara*. Then each god, accompanied by his servants, mounted his respective vehicle, which flew into the sky and soared toward Vidharba.

As the gods drew near to Bhima's kingdom, they saw King Nala walking cheerfully in the same direction. Having planned to attend the *swayamvara*, he was filled with intense love for Damayanti. The gods were amazed by his exquisite beauty, for he shone like the sun and looked like the love god. Leaving their vehicles in the air, they descended to the ground and approached Nala. "O king of Nishadha," said one, "you are the topmost of monarchs and devoted to truth. Please help us by becoming our messenger."

"Certainly," replied Nala. Joining his palms respectfully, the king asked, "But who are you? And what else can I do for you?"

"We are the gods of this universe," Indra returned, "and we've come here for Damayanti's sake." He then introduced him to the other gods. "We would like you to tell Damayanti that Indra, Agni, Varuna and Yama would like to marry her, and that she should pick one of us."

Nala was surprised and stunned. "But—I've come here with the very same purpose. Therefore, I don't think you should send me to tell her. For if I'm in love with her, how will I be able to speak on your behalf?"

"But King, you promised. You said you would become our messenger."

"Yes, I know, but—the palace, the women's quarters—they're very well guarded. How will I be able to enter them?"

"We'll arrange for that. You just go there—and enter."

Nala realized he had no other choice. "All right, I'll go."

When Nala reached the palace precincts, he saw that the area was ringed with powerful-looking guards. Nevertheless, as he approached some of them, he noted that they appeared to be completely unaware of his presence. This, he realized, was caused by the mystic power of the gods. He thus walked right past the guards through the gates and into the palace, then through the large portals and into the women's quarters.

Arriving in Damayanti's apartment, Nala saw her surrounded by her handmaids. She was ablaze in beauty—her body symmetrical, limbs exquisite, waist thin, eyes bright, and smile sweet. As Nala gazed at her, his love for her increased. But wanting to keep his promise to the gods, he restrained his desire.

When her maidservants beheld him, they were astonished, fascinated, and conquered by his effulgence. Springing up from their seats, they mentally offered him respect and praise. Who was this handsome, gentle, modest hero? they wondered; a god? A celestial? They were too bewildered to address him.

Although Damayanti was equally impressed by Nala's valiant looks, she smilingly asked, "What *are* you—a man, celestial, or god? Your features are flawless and you've aroused my—interest."

Nala smiled gently at her.

"You appear sinless and angelic," continued Damayanti. "I'm eager to know who you are and why you have come here. How were you able to escape notice of the guards surrounding my apartment? My father's orders are very strict in this regard."

"O lovely one," began the king, "my name is Nala."

Damayanti's eyes opened wide.

The Nishadha king explained the purpose of his visit, the mystery of his unperceived entrance, and concluded, "Just do what pleases you."

Damayanti offered obeisances to the gods, and then, smiling, turned to

Nala. "I want only your love—and no one else's. For I love you. Just tell me how I may serve you. The words of a swan, who told me all about you, are burning me now. You're the only man I desire to marry. All the kings have been invited here to learn of this. But—if you abandon me now, I'll have no other alternative but to take poison, burn, drown, or hang myself."

Nala was confounded. "How can you choose me, a mere mortal, when the chief gods have come here to marry you? They're high souled administrators of the world, and I'm not even equal to the dust of their feet. Therefore, you should turn your heart towards them."

Damayanti began to weep.

"If you displease the gods on my account, they'll surely kill me. Therefore, save me by choosing one of them. Then you'll enjoy splendid robes, multicolored garlands, and superb ornaments. What woman would not choose Indra—chief of the gods and punisher of the demons—for her husband? Why, the fear of his mace alone causes creatures to act virtuously. Or, you could even choose Varuna. But please—accept this friendly advice."

Damayanti's palms were still folded and her eyes were bathed in tears. "Though I bow to all the gods, still I choose you for my husband. I say this in all truth."

"You may do as you like, my dear. But how can I, who have given my word and come as the gods' messenger, seek my own interest? It's not ethical. But if I could seek my own interest in an ethical way, I would. And you should do the same."

Damayanti falteringly replied, "But there is an ethical way."

The king listened intently.

"Just come to the *swayamvara* with the gods, and there, in their presence, I'll choose you. Then you can't be blamed."

Having agreed with Damayanti, King Nala returned to the place where the gods were waiting. They anxiously questioned him about what had transpired. He told them he had delivered their message, but Damayanti had already chosen him for her spouse; and she had also requested the gods to come to the *swayamvara* where she would, in their presence, formally make the choice. "This is all that occurred," Nala concluded. "The outcome is now in your hands."

The gods were not pleased by the turn of events; thus they decided, by a very clever device, to foil Damayanti's plan.

***

At a sacred hour of the day on which the *swayamvara* was to be held, King Bhima summoned the kings to the arena. Filled with desire for Damayanti and eager to possess her, they quickly left their quarters and headed for it. Entering the amphitheater, which was decorated with golden pillars and a high gateway arch, the monarchs looked like powerful lions. Their arms were muscular, their hair attractive, and their faces, graced with well-shaped noses, eyes and brows, shone like the stars. Adorned with scented garlands and gleaming jeweled earrings, they eagerly took their seats.

Damayanti, holding a lovely flower garland, entered the arena. Her gorgeous face and attractive form stole the hearts of the kings. Whichever part of her person they first happened to glance at, their eyes became riveted there.

Soon the names of the monarchs present were loudly announced. When Damayanti heard Nala's name, she looked in the direction of where he was seated. But instead of seeing only one form of King Nala, she saw five—and each looked exactly like the other! This sight filled her with doubt and confusion. For she could not ascertain which was the true King Nala. Then Damayanti remembered, from descriptions given by the elders, that the four gods had specific discernible characteristics. But when she looked for them, they were not evident. She thus became filled with grief.

After deliberating on the matter for awhile, she realized it would be impossible for her to select the actual King Nala. Feeling completely helpless, she decided to petition the gods themselves for help. Trembling, she folded her hands, bowed her head, and prayed: "Ever since a swan spoke to me about the king of Nishadha, I chose him as my husband. Since that day, I have never thought of anyone else. Please, in the interest of that truth, make him known to me. O gods, you yourselves have preordained the Nishadha king to become my lord. Please, in the interest of that truth, make him known to me. Moreover, because I desire to honor King Nala, I have committed myself solely to him. Please, in the interest of that truth, make him known to me. O illustrious lords of the world, I beg you to assume your own actual forms so that I may now see the virtuous King Nala."

By Damayanti's poignant words, the gods perceived how steadfast was her determination, how ardent was her love, and how pure was her heart and affection for Nala. Convinced of her deep sincerity, they revealed to her their specific characteristics, which she had been looking for a few moments ago: For example, their bodies did not perspire, their eyelids did not blink, their garlands remained unfaded, their clothes stayed dust-free, and their feet never touched the ground. But Nala's characteristics were just the opposite.

As soon as Damayanti knew which of the five candidates was Nala, to signify her choice she bashfully clutched at his robe and placed the beautiful flower garland around his neck.

When the other kings realized they had lost, they cried out in dismay, "Oh, no!" But the gods and sages, applauding the king, admiringly exclaimed, "Bravo! Bravo!"

Nala, with a joyous heart, said assuringly to Damayanti, "You have selected an earthling in the company of the gods. As your husband, I will always serve your wishes. And I say this with all my heart—that as long as there is life in my body, I shall be yours and yours only!"

Damayanti, with palms folded, offered him similar words of respect. The happy couple mentally asked the gods for protection. In response, the gods cheerfully conferred on Nala eight blessings: Indra blessed him with the ability to see his lordship during sacrifices, and with the assurance that, after death, Nala would reach the heavenly planets. Agni granted Nala the blessing of his personal presence whenever Nala desired it, as well as admission into the bright heavenly planets. Yama bestowed the power to perceive subtle tastes in food and achieve supremacy in righteousness. Varuna conferred his own presence anytime Nala desired it, as well as floral wreathes with heavenly fragrance.

When the gods finished benedicting Nala, they returned to their celestial regions. The kings also returned to their capitals.

Soon after, King Bhima, very satisfied, celebrated the wedding of Nala and Damayanti. After remaining there for some time, Nala took leave of the king and returned with his wife to his own kingdom.

As the gods were traveling through outer space, they chanced to see, moving towards them, the celestials Dwapara and Kali, the personifications of the copper and iron ages. [It is through their influence that righteousness in the world is gradually reduced.] Indra cried out, "O Kali, where are you and Dwapara going?"

"To Damayanti's *swayamvara*. I intend to make her my wife. My heart is set on her."

Indra smiled. "But the *swayamvara* is over. Damayanti has chosen Nala as her lord."

"What!" exclaimed Kali angrily. "Well, since she's taken a mortal for her husband in the presence of you gods, it's only proper that she be severely punished."

"But wait, Kali. She did it with our approval. What woman would not choose him? King Nala possesses every good quality. He's conversant with his responsibilities, is always acting with virtue, and has meditated on all the Vedic scriptures. He doesn't injure any creature unnecessarily, he tells the truth, he's steadfast in his commitments, and he always pleases the gods by performing sacrifices. In fact, he resembles us gods, for he's truthful, forbearing, learned, austere, pure, self-disciplined, and serene. Kali, considering Nala's sterling qualities, whoever curses him would actually be cursing and destroying himself; for he'd fall into a bottomless hole of hell and suffer its countless tortures."

The gods departed for their heavenly abodes. But Kali, sorely frustrated, said to Dwapara, "I'm unable to hold back my anger. So I will enter Nala's body and possess him, take away his kingdom, and stop him from further enjoying Damayanti. And you, Dwapara, must help me—by entering a set of dice."

***

In Nishadha, King Nala spent his days happily, and, ruling his people, made them very content. He undertook many sacrifices, including that of the horse, and generously donated gifts to the Brahmins. In the enchanting forests and groves, he frolicked with Damayanti, and after a while, she bore him a son and a daughter named Indrasena and Indrasenah respectively. The king, living in opulence, reigned over his country.

After the evil Kali had secured a promise from Dwapara that, at the proper time, he would enter a set of dice—in an attempt to deprive Nala of his kingdom—he went to the monarch's palace. Kali knew that in order for him to enter Nala's body and influence his mind, he would first have to catch Nala in the act of violating some scriptural ordinance or injunction. He waited and watched for a long time. Finally, after twelve years, he beheld it—a flaw in Nala's behavior.

The king had just urinated, and was then supposed to wash his feet. But he had forgotten. Instead, he immediately proceeded to recite his twilight prayers while touching water. Kali then entered his heart and possessed him.

To fulfill his plan, Kali appeared before the king's brother Pushkara and suggested, "Why don't you play dice with Nala? With my help, you'll surely beat him. Yes, you'll win his kingdom and become the ruler of Nishadha!"

Convinced by Kali, Pushkara approached Nala and slyly suggested, "Let's play a game of dice."

Although Nala was disinclined, Pushkara urged him repeatedly in front of Damayanti. As a warrior, Nala was obliged to accept the challenge; to refuse, would have brought disgrace and dishonor to him. A time was thus fixed for the game to start.

When the game began, Nala became completely possessed by Kali's influence. He lusted after victory, felt divinely favored, and was certain he would win. But instead, he lost. He lost gold, silver, chariots, horses and robes. The more he lost, the more he wanted to play—and win! Without a doubt, he had become mad.

Though Nala's friends tried to dissuade him from playing, they failed. The citizens and councilors heard of the monarch's huge losses and, urged by loyalty, came to the outer gate to plead with him to desist. The king's charioteer informed Damayanti of this, emphasizing that it had become extremely painful for them to bear their virtuous king's misfortune.

In faltering tones and kindly glances, she sadly conveyed this news to the king and asked him if he would please give them an audience. But Nala, influenced by Kali, completely ignored her. When the councilors and citizens heard about this, they became even more grievous and disappointed. Returning home, they exclaimed, "The king is dead!"

The dice game continued for many months and, as always, King Nala was defeated.

When the king had lost almost everything, Damayanti became extremely apprehensive. She then asked her devoted maidservant Vrihatsena to summon the councilors in Nala's name and inform them of what wealth had been lost and what still remained. The councilors, receiving the summons, considered this a good sign and hastened to the palace gate.

But when Damayanti disclosed their presence to Nala, he again completely ignored her. Embarrassed by this, Damayanti returned to her quarters. Because she considered the matter extremely serious, she asked her maidservant Vrihatsena to once more go in the king's name and bring back Nala's charioteer, Varshneya. Vrihatsena, using reliable servants, had him fetched and brought to the queen's apartment. After reminding him of how considerately the king had always treated him, and of how grave Nala's present difficulty was, Damayanti appealed to him for help.

She explained, "The more wealth the king loses, the more eager he is to continue playing. But the dice always favor Pushkara. Because the king is attached to the game, he has ignored the words of his friends, relatives, and even me. However, I don't think my good lord is at fault. Charioteer, I need your help, so please do what I ask. I fear that the king may soon lose everything. Therefore, please yoke to your chariot Nala's favorite horses—the ones that travel at the speed of the mind. Then transport my son and daughter rapidly to Kundina and leave them there with my family. You can also leave the horse and chariot there. As for yourself, you may either stay there or go wherever you wish."

Varshneya reported Damayanti's instructions to the king's chief officer. After consulting with him and receiving his consent, he departed with the royal children for Vidarbha. There, he delivered them to their grandparents. Leaving the chariot and horses at the palace, Varshneya said goodbye to King Bhima and went on his way. Sorrowing for Nala and journeying for some time, he finally reached the city of Ayodhya. There, he went to King Rituparna and was hired by him as a charioteer.

Meanwhile, as the dice game continued, Pushkara won all of Nala's kingdom and wealth. "Let us keep playing," urged Pushkara laughingly. "But what can you stake? I've won everything you own—except Damayanti. If you would like, you can stake her."

When Nala heard these words, he felt as if his heart would explode in fury. But he remained silent. Gazing at Pushkara in agony, he removed all his ornaments and clothes—except his loincloth. Then he renounced his wealth and, to the grief of his friends, set out to leave the city. And Damayanti, wearing a single piece of cloth, followed him closely.

Throughout the city, Pushkara proclaimed, "Whoever in any way shows concern for Nala—gives him food or shelter—will be put to death!" Because of this and Pushkara's hostility towards Nala, the citizens restrained themselves.

When Nala and Damayanti reached the city limit, they passed three nights there living only on water. Tormented by hunger, Nala, followed by Damayanti, began searching for fruits and roots. But after many days they had found none and began to starve. Then one day, upon seeing some golden-feathered birds, Nala said, "They will become my meal today as well as my wealth."

He removed his loincloth and held it in an aggressive manner. Stealing up behind the birds, he threw it over them. But as he reached down to grab the birds, they flew up into the sky bearing his loincloth. As Nala, naked and gloomy, stood gazing at the ground, the birds cried out, "Fool! We are the dice. We came here to take away your loincloth. For it displeased us to see you leave your capital with even a shred of clothing."

When the birds flew away, Nala said to Damayanti, "My enemies, in the form of those birds, have deprived me of my kingdom, my sustenance, my friends, and now, my loincloth. They have made me sad and senseless. As your husband, I'll tell you something for your own good. Please listen."

Nala raised his arms and began pointing in various directions. "These paths lead to the south and they pass by the city of Avanti and the Rakshavat mountains. Here are the great Vindhya mountains. There, the Payaswini River runs toward the sea, and in that direction are the hermitages of ascetics. This road goes to Vidarbha, and that one to Kosala. And past these to the south is the southern country."

Wanting her to leave his side and return to her family, Nala repeated those directions to Damayanti again and again. But all they did was increase her grief. Finally, with tear-filled eyes and a trembling voice, she said, "The very thought of leaving you makes my heart quiver and my limbs weak. How could I leave you alone in the woods—when you've lost your kingdom and wealth, when you're without clothing, when you're weary from hunger and walking? No, my lord, I would prefer to stay at your side and soothe away your fatigue. Even the doctors say that for a man's sorrows, there is no medicine equal to a devoted wife. Oh Nala, I am speaking the truth."

Nala replied, "Yes, what you've said is true—for a grief-stricken man there is no medicine or friend like a devoted wife. But I'm not renouncing you, my dear, so why are you afraid of this? I can forsake myself, my love, but I can never forsake you."

"Well, if you don't intend to forsake me, why have you pointed me toward Vidarbha? I know that normally you would not forsake me. But now that your mind is troubled, you might. You repeatedly pointed out to me the way to my family home, and this has increased my anguish. If it's your wish that I go to my family, then, if you like, let us both go to Vidarbha. There, my father will receive you with honor. And respected by him, you'll dwell there in happiness."

"Yes, your father's kingdom is like my own. But I would not go there in this condition. At one time I appeared there in honor and augmented your happiness; how can I now go there in distress and increase your sorrow?"

Nala repeated this argument several times and finally consoled Damayanti. Then, wrapping half of her garment around his body so that both of them were wearing the same cloth, they slogged on. After some time, feeling exhausted from hunger and thirst, they arrived at a shelter for travelers. Dirty, stained, and overcome with weariness, they lay down on the ground and fell asleep.

Damayanti, very distressed, fell into an extremely deep slumber. But Nala, whose mind was troubled, could not sleep peacefully. Awakening, he thought about the loss of his kingdom, the defection of his friends, and the agony of his forest life. "What is the use of my going on like this?" he wondered. "And what if I ended it all? Would it be better to be dead or to just abandon my wife? She's so devoted to me and is tolerating all this misery on my account. If she continues to stay with me, her misery will only remain. But if I leave her here, she might travel back to her family home and become free of this distress. Yes, she might even become happy some day."

Repeatedly mulling over this, and under the influence of the evil Kali, he finally decided that it would be best to abandon Damayanti. "Because she has excellent qualities and is very faithful to me, she has acquired mystical power. Therefore, no one along the way could ever harm her."

Keenly aware of his own nakedness and need for clothing, Nala gazed at the piece of cloth covering Damayanti. He wanted to tear it in half, but how could he without waking her? Standing up, he began pacing back and forth, wondering what to do. Suddenly, he saw an unsheathed sword lying near the shed. He picked it up, returned to Damayanti and, very slowly and quietly, cut her loose garment in half. Wrapping the sheared piece around his loins and discarding the sword, he left the shelter.

No sooner had he left than his heart began to ache. He hastened back to the shed and, looking at Damayanti, began to weep. "O God!" he thought. "My dear chaste wife is sleeping on the bare earth like a deserted person. Wearing a torn piece of cloth, she lies there as if tormented. How will my lovely wife react when she wakes up? How will she roam through the forest, filled with beasts and snakes, without me?" Then he silently said to her, "My dearest, may the gods protect you, though your best protection is your virtue."

Again, prevailed upon by Kali, he left the shed. And again, drawn back by love, he returned. He did this again and again and again—many times. Nala's heart soon felt as though it were broken in half. But at last— dazed, irrational, sad and pathetic—the king wandered away.

***

After awhile Damayanti woke up and felt refreshed. She looked around for Nala but all she saw was the dense, lonely forest. Filled with grief and sorrow, she fearfully cried out, "Nala! Nala! Have you abandoned me? I'm lost, helpless and afraid in this forsaken place. You speak the truth and know morality, and you vowed to protect me. So why, while I was asleep, have you abandoned me? I've always been devoted to you and have never harmed you, though others have.

"You're supposed to be faithful and do what you promised before the gods on our wedding day. That I'm alive for even one second after you abandoned me is only because human beings are predestined to die at a set time. Nala, enough of this play! I'm very much afraid. Please, let me see you. Let me—"

Imagining that she saw him, she shouted, "Oh, there you are. I see you! Yes, I see you, hiding behind those bushes. But—why don't you answer me? You see how sad I am in this predicament. It is unkind of you not to come and comfort me. I'm wondering—how will you spend your days alone? And at night, underneath the trees, when you're very hungry, thirsty and fatigued, how will you manage without me?"

Damayanti, filled with pain and sorrow, began to run here and there. Weeping, she fell down in a stupor; then she jumped up and cringed in terror. Sighing, fainting and burning with grief, she wept and wailed aloud, "The person who cursed Nala to suffer this anguish will suffer anguish even greater than ours. May that evil person who has caused my sinless husband this misery lead an unhappier life with even greater miseries!"

Having cursed the evil Kali, Damayanti continued searching for Nala through the forbidding forests, where many beasts of prey lurked. Sobbing intensely and wandering here and there maniacally, she cried out, "How horrible! Horrible! Oh Nala!" Unknowingly, she moved within the range of a huge hungry serpent. When she was close enough, the serpent sprang and coiled itself around her body, making it impossible for her to escape.

Thinking of Nala, Damayanti shouted, "Why don't you hasten here to protect me? Why have you deserted me here in the forest? When you remember me, how will you get along? When you regain your mind, senses and wealth someday, how will you feel when you think of me? When you're tired, famished and fainting, who will comfort you?"

As she was wailing, a hunter nearby heard her cries and hurried to the spot. Seeing Damayanti in the serpent's deadly coils, he lunged towards it and, with his long, sharp knife, chopped off its head. Then he freed Damayanti, sprinkled water over her, and provided her with food.

"You have eyes like a young gazelle," he smiled. "Who are you? Why have you entered this forest? And how have you come upon this extreme distress?"

Damayanti told him everything that had occurred.

He looked at her beautiful body and noticed it was covered with only a small piece of cloth. Listening to her honey-sweet voice, he gazed at her ample breasts, curvaceous hips, perfect delicate legs, moonlike

The serpent sprang and coiled itself around her body, making it impossible for her to escape.

face, and long curved eyelashes. By the time Damayanti finished her story, the hunter was afire with lust.

To try to attract her, he began to speak in a soft, soothing, captivating voice. But as soon as Damayanti knew his intentions, she became extremely angry. Seeing this, the hunter also became inflamed and tried to force her to yield to him. But he had no idea of the power of her chastity.

Damayanti was already aggrieved from the loss of husband and kingdom. And now, feeling even more aggrieved from this attempted rape, she wrathfully cursed the hunter: "I've never even thought of any man other than my husband. Therefore, low-minded demon, may you die now!"

No sooner had she uttered the curse than the hunter collapsed to the ground, dead—like a tree burned down by fire.

Damayanti wandered on through the dreadful and lonely woods, which teemed with lions, leopards, tigers, buffaloes, bears, and deer, as well as thieves and low-born tribes. It also abounded with many varieties of birds and trees, such as bamboo, mango, cane, banyan and palm. She saw numerous mountains—which contained different kinds of ores—and groves, rivers, lakes, ponds, brooks, fountains, as well as snakes, goblins and demons. Nonetheless, she was not frightened by any of this; rather, she felt safe in her virtue, glory and patience. Only her separation from her husband distressed her.

She sat down on a stone and, trembling with sorrow, cried, "Oh Nala, where have you gone? And why have you left me alone in this solitary forest? You've performed many sacrifices and have given numerous gifts to the Brahmins, but why have you acted falsely with me? Don't you remember what you vowed and what those golden-winged swans said to each of us? You should live up to that vow.

"Alas, I'm about to die in this terrible forest. Oh, why don't you answer me? Don't you think you should save me? You always used to say, 'No one is dear to me but you.' Please live up to these words. Although you love me and I love you, why don't you answer me? I want to know where you're lying or sitting or standing or going. Whom shall I ask about you? And who will tell me that you're here?"

Then, seeing a tiger nearby, she fearlessly accosted it. "Oh king of the forest, I'm Damayanti, King Nala's wife. I'm searching for my husband. If you've seen him, please console me with the news. But if you haven't any news, then please swallow me and free me from this unhappiness!"

When the tiger did not eat her, Damayanti turned toward the nearby mountain. After praising it for its manifold characteristics and occupants, she bowed down to it. Identifying herself and describing in detail Nala and his glories, she related how his kingdom had been lost and how he had abandoned her. "Have you seen my husband?" she asked it. "He's intelligent, long-armed, energetic, powerful, patient, courageous and famous."

But the mountain did not answer.

"You see how I'm weeping and grief-stricken; why don't you speak and soothe me, as you would your own daughter?"

Again, feeling lost, forlorn, and hopeless, she cried out, "Nala! My love! If you're in this forest, please show yourself to me! Oh, when will I hear you calling me again—with your sweet, soft, deep, rich, melodious voice, which can soothe away all my grief. Oh, please comfort me."

Damayanti then headed in a northerly direction and journeyed for three days and nights. Soon she saw a beautiful grove of hermitages that were occupied by holy ascetics, such as the illustrious Vasishtha, Bhrigu and Atri. Dressed in tree bark and deerskins, some of them were subsisting on water, some on air, and others on leaves. With their minds controlled and passions restrained, they were pursuing the Supreme Eternal.

When Damayanti entered the retreat, she humbly offered obeisance to the recluses.

"Welcome," they replied respectfully. "And please sit down. Tell us what we may do for you."

She informed them of all that had happened to her and Nala. Then she desperately cried, "If I don't find him in a few days, I'll just give up my life. For without him, my life has no value or meaning. I can't go on without him."

After one of the sages foretold her future, he, the other sages, the sacred fire and the hermitages suddenly vanished from sight.

Damayanti was wonderstruck. "Was that a dream I just saw? Where did they all go—the holy men, the retreat, the sacred river and the blossoming trees?"

Becoming pale and sad again, Damayanti proceeded to another part of the forest and saw an ashoka [evergreen] tree. Its orange and red flowers, its dark green, shining foliage, and the chirping of the birds sporting on it were all very charming. With tears in her eyes and her voice faltering, she said to the tree, "Oh beautiful Asoka tree, have you seen my husband around here? Your name means destroyer of grief, so please live up to it."

She reverentially circumambulated the tree three times and wandered away into an even more fearsome part of the forest. Again she saw many wonderful-looking trees, brooks, rivers, mountains, cliffs, caves, animals, and birds. As she moved on, she suddenly saw a sight that amazed her. She beheld a wide opening in the woods where a river flowed; and in and around it, she observed cane bushes, cranes, other birds, tortoises, alligators, fish, and speckled islets. She also noted—wonder of wonders!—a caravan of merchants, with horses and elephants, landing on the bank. As soon as she saw it, she hastened to the travelers.

Damayanti looked like a crazed person—grievous, thin, pale, dirty, and scantily clad. When they saw her, some of the merchants fearfully ran away, some became very apprehensive, some cried out, others laughed at her, and still others detested her. But there were some who, feeling compassionate, said, "Who are you? What are you seeking in this forest? We are frightened by seeing you here. Are you a human being? Or are you a goddess of this forest or of this mountain or of one of the stars in the sky? Or are you a demoness? Please protect us and enable us to move on in prosperity and security."

Damayanti, scanning the caravan leader, merchants, youths, elders and children, informed them who she actually was and why she was roaming through the woods. "If by chance any of you have seen my husband, please tell me!"

The caravan leader, whose name was Suchi, replied, "I've not seen any man named Nala. There are only wild animals in this vast forest. Except for you, I've not encountered any man or woman here."

Damayanti nodded sadly, then asked, "Where are you headed?"

"We are bound for the city of Chedi—to sell goods and make a profit."

Anxious to find Nala, Damayanti joined the caravan and traveled with it through the terrible, dense forest. The group came to a large beautiful lake, whose water was pure, sweet, cool and fragrant with lotuses. Its banks abounded with grass, fuel, fruits and flowers, and were inhabited by various kinds of birds and fowl. When evening arrived, the caravan was tired from the day's journey. They thus decided to halt and camp there.

At midnight, as the group lay sleeping, all was quiet and still.

But soon the silence was broken by the sound of wild elephants nearby thundering toward a mountain stream to drink. The elephants were in rut—their period of sexual excitement. When they saw the many elephants of the caravan, they became infuriated. With juice trickling down their temples, they rushed toward the domesticated elephants to kill them. As they stomped through the camp, they carelessly slayed and injured—with their feet, tusks and trunks—many of the sleeping merchants, horses and camels. All around, the dying and wounded cried out helplessly.

Damayanti awoke suddenly and saw the horrendous slaughter. Filled with fear and anxiety, she jumped to her feet and breathlessly raced for shelter in the brush.

When the other merchants woke up, they also ran in fear. Some of them accidentally killed each other; some climbed up trees; and some fled into the forest. Then a great fire broke out and spread rapidly.

After a while, when the wild elephants had departed, the remaining uninjured merchants assembled to discuss the calamity. Damayanti, still shaken, secretly watched them from her nearby hiding place.

"What have we done to deserve this?" asked one of the merchants.

"We must have failed to worship the exalted Manibhava, the god of travel, and the celebrated Vaishravana, the god of wealth," said another.

"Perhaps we failed to worship the gods responsible for calamities or failed to give them first respects."

"Maybe this misfortune is a result of the bad-luck birds we saw. What other causes could it have come from?"

Another merchant, who was aggrieved and deprived of his wealth and relatives, said, "I think it was the crazy woman who joined us that caused this—the one who looked weird."

Damayanti became even more frightened.

"Yes," the merchant continued, "I think she's a demon or an evil spirit. This entire misfortune is her work. I'm sure of it. When we see her again, we should kill her!"

Upon hearing this, Damayanti, feeling ashamed, afraid, and anxious, scurried into the forest to hide. She continuously reproached herself. "Alas! God's anger is on me, and it's cruel and heavy. There's no peace on my path. What sins did I commit that have resulted in this tragedy? I don't remember committing the slightest wrong to anyone in thought, word or deed—even since I was a child—that would cause this. So it must be the sins I committed in my past life."

Although some of the merchants, out of ignorance, blamed Damayanti for their misfortune, the Brahmins or priests did not. In fact, perceiving her purity, sincerity, and nobility, they were certain she was not responsible. When Damayanti learned of this, she approached and asked them if they would please guide and escort her to the city to which the caravan was traveling. They agreed.

Damayanti arrived at the mighty city of Chedi towards evening. When she entered it, the citizens saw she was wearing a half piece of cloth and looked thin, sad, pale, unkempt, dusty and crazed. A gathering crowd of boys curiously followed and annoyed her as she walked to and halted at the palace gate.

The king's mother, standing on one of the palace balconies with her maidservant, saw Damayanti surrounded by the crowd and said, "I want you to bring that woman here. She looks miserable and the crowd is irritating her. Obviously she's troubled and needs help." As the king's mother gazed deeply at Damayanti, she saw more than just a disheveled woman. "I find her to have a kind of beauty that brightens my palace. Though she appears to be crazy, she also looks like Shri, the goddess of fortune, with her large eyes. Bring her."

The maidservant went outside the gate, dispersed the crowd, and brought Damayanti upstairs to the lovely balcony. Highly impressed by her qualities, the maidservant said, "Though you're very troubled, you've got a beautiful form, and you glitter like lightning in the clouds. I'd like to know who you are and which family you belong to. Though you're not wearing any ornaments, you possess a beauty that's more heavenly than human. And though you had no defense, you weren't even shaken by the taunts of those boys."

Damayanti replied, "I'm a human being and I'm devoted to my husband. I'm a servant and come from a good family. My husband has many virtues and was always devoted to me. And I, too, was greatly devoted to him. I followed him like a shadow. One day he played dice and lost everything. Wearing only a loincloth, he went to live in the forest and I stayed with him. Though he was hungry, thirsty, and depressed, I tried my best to comfort him. And while he was trying to procure food, some birds stole his loincloth. I didn't sleep for many nights—till we found a shelter. While I was asleep, my husband cut off half of my garment. Then he abandoned me, though I had done him no wrong."

Tears began flowing down Damayanti's cheeks and she spoke in a faltering and choked voice. "I'm searching for my husband but haven't been able to find him. He has the traits of a god and is the delight and owner of my heart. Being unable to see him, I burn night and day in anguish."

The king's mother was convinced and moved by Damayanti's story. "Dear young lady," she said, "please stay with me. I like you. I'll send out a search party to find your husband. Or, during his wanderings, he may possibly come here. Thus, if you stay at this palace, you'll get back your lost husband."

Damayanti replied, "I will stay with you, but only under certain conditions, namely: That I will not have to eat the remnants from anyone's plate; nor will I have to bathe anyone's feet; nor will I have to converse with other men. And if any man pursues me to become his wife or mistress, he must be punished by you; and if he continues to pursue me, he must be punished by death. This is my vow. Also, before you dispatch the search party, I would like to interview each member of it." After pausing a moment, Damayanti concluded, "If you can do all this, I will surely stay here. If not, I'll have to leave."

The queen answered, "Yes, I will do it all. It's very noble of you to take such a vow." The queen summoned her daughter, and when she arrived, said, "Sunanda, regard this young lady as though she were a goddess. Since you're both the same age, let her be your friend—and you can happily play together."

Sunanda gladly received Damayanti and, accompanied by her friends, showed her to her own apartment. Because Damayanti was treated with dignity, she was very pleased. And with all her wishes properly satisfied, she continued to dwell there without any sort of worry.

***

After Nala had abandoned Damayanti, he saw in that dense forest a huge fire raging. From amidst the fire, he heard a voice repeatedly calling, "Virtuous Nala! Come here!"

As Nala hastened toward the voice, he shouted, "Don't fear!" Reaching it, he saw a mighty Naga [a snake-like creature], which generally dwells below the earth, lying on the ground. It had the head and arms of a human being, and the neck and trunk of a serpent. Trembling with joined palms, the Naga said, "My name is Karkotaka. In the past, I deceived the glorious spiritual master Narada. In return, he angrily cursed me, saying, 'Remain here immobilized until a person named Nala takes you away. Wherever he carries you, at that spot you will be freed from my curse.'

"Because of the curse, I can't take a single step. Therefore, you must save me. I will then guide you regarding your well being, and I'll also be your friend. There is no snake comparable to me. So pick me up and quickly leave this place."

As Nala wondered how he would carry the large snake, the Naga mystically shrunk its body down to the size of a thumb. Nala lifted him up and hurried to an open, fire-free area. There, he was about to drop the snake, but Karkotaka said, "Please keep walking and counting your steps. I will greatly benefit you."

Nala walked on and, as he counted his tenth step, the snake bit him. No sooner did this happen than Nala was transformed into an ugly-looking man with short arms. Nala was astonished.

The snake again assumed his normal size and said, "I've taken away your beauty so that people won't recognize you. Nala, the one who deceived you and made you suffer—namely, Kali—will continue to live in you, but he'll be tortured by my poison. As long as he doesn't leave your body, he'll have to experience pain there.

"King, I have saved you from Kali. Though you were perfectly blameless and undeserving of harm, out of anger and hatred he tricked you. But now, by my grace, you will no longer have any fear from hostile creatures with fangs and from Brahmins versed in the Vedic scriptures. Also, you will not experience any pain because of my poison, and you will always be triumphant in battle.

"Today, Nala, you should leave for the lovely city of Ayodhya. There, you should proceed to King Rituparna, who happens to be an expert in gambling. Just say to him, 'My name is Vahuka and I'm a charioteer.' "

Karkotaka next told Nala about his future—his prosperity and kingdom as well as his wife and children. Then he produced two pieces of mystical cloth and gave them to Nala, saying, "When you want to regain your original beauty, just remember me and wear these cloths. You'll recover it immediately." Having finished his instructions, the *Naga* vanished from sight.

Ten days later Nala entered King Rituparna's city. When he found the king, he said, "My name is Vahuka. In this world, there is no one who can compare to me in managing horses. I can also offer useful counsel in difficult matters and concerns. I am also unsurpassable in cooking. In whatever arts exist as well as whatever is hard to achieve, I'll endeavor to be successful. King Rituparna, please allow me to serve you."

"Yes, Vahuka, you may. And I extend to you my best wishes. You may do all that you've mentioned. I've always had a yen to be driven rapidly. Therefore, do whatever is necessary to make my horses run fast. In fact, I designate you as the supervisor of my stables. Your pay will be ten thousand coins. My charioteers, Varshneya and Jivala, will work under your guidance. In their company, I'm sure you'll live congenially. And I hope you'll stay with me, Vahuka."

Nala began to reside in King Rituparna's city. He was treated with honor, and Jivala and Varshneya—who had been his former charioteer—

were his friends. Every evening when Nala remembered Damayanti, he would recite: "Where does she lie, that helpless one who is troubled by hunger, thirst, and fatigue, and is thinking of that rascal? And whom is she serving now?"

One night as Nala was repeating those lines, Jivala asked him, "Vahuka, who are you sorrowing for every day? I'm curious. Whose wife are you grieving about?"

"A person who was lacking in sense had a wife whom many knew. The rascal did not live up to his vows. For some reason he was separated from her. He wandered about, overcome with distress. Burning with sorrow, he couldn't sleep during the day or night. And when evening came, he remembered her and sang those lines. He roamed all around and finally found a shelter. Not deserving the anguish he was experiencing, he spent his days dwelling on his wife."

Nala paused reflectively, then said, "When this man was defeated by tragedy, his wife followed him into the forest. But having little virtue, he abandoned her and left her in peril. Yes, he left her alone. She had no knowledge of survival, she couldn't bear suffering, she was weak from hunger and thirst, and she could scarcely defend herself against the wild animals."

Remembering Damayanti in this way, Nala continued to dwell incognito at the king's palace.

* * *

When King Bhima, Damayanti's father, learned that Nala had lost and left his kingdom, he wanted to see him. He summoned many Brahmins, gave them much wealth and said, "I would like you to search for Nala and Damayanti. To anyone who discovers where they are and brings them here, I will award a thousand cows, fields, and a village resembling a town. Even if he doesn't bring them here but discovers their whereabouts, I will still award him a thousand cows."

The Brahmins departed genially in all directions and journeyed to numerous cities and provinces. But they could not find the couple anywhere. However, after some time, a Brahmin named Sudeva began searching in the city of Chedi. And there, while the king was offering prayers, he saw Damayanti seated with her friend Sunanda. Her matchless beauty was slightly visible, like the brilliance of a fire covered by swirls of smoke.

"She's just as I saw her before," thought Sudeva. "She looks as beautiful as Shri, the goddess of fortune—with her large black eyes, full breasts, delicate frame and lovely limbs. Yet I notice that she's aggrieved and unhappy, probably because her husband isn't with her.

Due to this, it appears she's refused to wear ornaments and accept the comforts and luxuries of this household. Indeed, though she's gorgeous, without her husband beside her, she doesn't shine. It pains me to see her grieving when she deserves to be happy. I wonder when she'll be with her husband again. Since they're equal in nature, age and lineage, they certainly deserve each other. I must talk to her."

He approached Damayanti in private and said, "Princess, I'm Sudeva, your brother's close friend. At your father's order, I've come here looking for you. Your father, mother and brothers are well, and so are your son and daughter. Your relatives, though living, are nearly dead because of your loss. And hundreds of Brahmins are searching the country for you."

Damayanti, recognizing him, asked him about each of her relatives and friends. Then, because she had not expected to see Sudeva, Damayanti was filled with sorrow and began to cry heavily.

Sunanda, Damayanti's friend, was secretly watching this scene from a slight distance. Seeing Damayanti weeping, Sunanda became upset and hastened to her mother's apartment."Mother, Damayanti is sobbing terribly in front of a Brahmin. If you wish, you can see for yourself."

The queen mother immediately went to see them and said to the Brahmin, "Whose wife is this lovely lady? And whose daughter? And how has she become deprived of the company of her relatives and husband? And how have you come to know her? Tell me truly all the details."

Sudeva narrated Damayanti's actual history, and then said, "Between Damayanti's eyebrows there is an auspicious-looking birthmark that looks like a lotus. It's a sign of prosperity and wealth. Her forehead is covered with a layer of dust, so the birthmark is only faintly visible now. Her body is also covered by dust, yet her exquisite beauty still shines through. It is by these two features—her birthmark and beauty—that I've been able to discover her."

Sunanda then washed away the dust between Damayanti's eyebrows. And the birthmark became clearly visible, like the moon when it emerges from the clouds. Seeing it, Sunanda and the queen mother began to weep. After hugging Damayanti, they became speechless for a while. But soon the queen mother, still weeping, gently said, "By this birthmark—I know that—you're my sister's daughter. Your mother and I are daughters of King Sudamen, ruler of Dasharna. She was given to King Bhima and I, to King Viravahu. I witnessed your birth at my father's palace in Dasharna. Damayanti, my house is as much yours as your father's. And my wealth is as much yours as it is mine."

Damayanti bowed down to her maternal aunt and said, "Though you didn't know who I was, I still lived happily with you. You satisfied my every want and cared for me. And as happy as my stay has been, if I stayed here, it would become even happier. But I've been in exile for a long time. Therefore, I'd appreciate if you would allow me to leave. I sent my son and daughter to my father's palace, where they're now living. Without their father and mother, they must be passing their days sadly. If you'd like to please me, kindly engage a vehicle, as I want to go to my father's palace."

The queen mother warmly replied, "Yes, you shall have it."

Damayanti soon left Chedi in a beautiful palanquin that was borne by men, guarded by soldiers, and furnished with food, beverages, and the best of clothes. When she arrived in Vidarbha, her relatives were overjoyed, and they received her with honor. After Damayanti saw that her parents, children, relatives, and maids were well, she worshiped the gods and the Brahmins. Seeing his daughter, the king was delighted. Thus, he awarded Sudeva a thousand cows, a great amount of wealth, and a village.

The next day, having recovered from fatigue, Damayanti said to her mother, "Mother, if you want me to continue living, then please try to find Nala and bring him here."

The queen became sad and wept, unable to answer Damayanti. She went to the king and said, "Damayanti is grieving because of separation from her husband. She just revealed her mind to me. Please dispatch your men to try to find Nala."

The king requested many Brahmins to search for Nala in all directions. Before they left, they came before Damayanti and informed her of the journey they were about to embark on. Damayanti instructed them, "In every kingdom and in every assembly, I'd like you to cry out these words: 'My dear gambler, where have you gone? You cut off half of your dear and devoted wife's garment, and while she was sleeping, you abandoned her in the woods. That woman, wearing only a half piece of cloth and burning with sorrow, waits for and expects you. She constantly weeps for you, so please yield and respond to her.'

"To awaken his sympathy, you should also say: 'The wife should always be protected and supported by the husband. Then why, since you are virtuous and acquainted with your obligations, have you ignored both these duties? You have fame, wisdom, lineage, and goodheartedness. Then why are you so unkind? I'm afraid this is due to my loss of good fortune. Therefore, be compassionate towards me. You yourself have told me that the highest virtue is kindness.'"

Damayanti then said to the Brahmins, "After you say these words, if anyone answers you, you should try to find out who he is, where he lives, and tell me what he said. You should also act with such caution that no one may know that your words have been spoken at my request or that you will return to me. And you should also determine whether the person who responds to you is rich, poor, or powerless—everything about him."

***

The Brahmins proceeded in all directions to search for Nala. They looked in cities, kingdoms, villages, ascetic hermitages, and farms. Everywhere they went, they repeated the words Damayanti had spoken to them.

After a long period, a Brahmin named Parnada returned to the city and went to Damayanti. "Princess," he said, "when I arrived at Ayodhya and appeared before King Rituparna, I repeated your words. Although I recited them again and again, neither he nor his courtiers responded to them. But after the king dismissed me, I was accosted by the king's charioteer, whose name is Vahuka."

"Vahuka?"

"Yes. He was rather ugly looking, with short arms, but very skillful in driving a chariot rapidly and extremely conversant in the art of cooking. He began to sigh and weep, and then said, 'Although chaste women may fall into difficulty, they protect themselves; and thus, when they die, they certainly go to the higher regions. Although their husbands may abandon them, they don't become angry over this. Rather, they continue living by the protection of their virtuous conduct.'"

Damayanti's eyes became glassy as Parnada continued quoting Vahuka.

"'The woman you speak of should not be angry, because the man who abandoned her was overcome by tragedy and dispossessed of every joy. A woman who is beautiful and virtuous should not bear anger towards a man who, while trying to obtain food, was robbed by some birds of his only garment and who is now being devoured by sorrow. Whether such a wife is treated nicely or badly—since she's seen her husband deprived of kingdom, wealth and food, and overcome by tragedy—she should never be angry with him.'"

The Brahmin paused, then said, "After I heard those words, I came here quickly. I've told you everything. Please do what you think best and tell the king about it."

Damayanti, with tears in her eyes, went to her mother and spoke to her privately. "Mother, Parnada has found out where Nala is. He's in Ayodhya and is working for King Rituparna as a horse trainer. I have a plan to bring him back here, but I don't want Father to know about it. Oh Mother, if you value my well being, I beg you to keep my plan a secret."

After Damayanti revealed her plan, the queen agreed to co-operate with her.

* * *

When Parnada had recovered from the fatigue of his journey, Damayanti summoned him. After he arrived, she honored him with much wealth and said, "When Nala will come here, I'll give you much more. You've done me a great service, and as a result, I hope to recover my husband."

Parnada consoled Damayanti by bestowing words of blessing on her. Feeling he had accomplished his mission well, he went home.

After he left, Damayanti, overcome with sorrow and anguish, called Sudeva to her quarters. On his arrival and in front of her mother, she said, "Sudeva, please go to the city of Ayodhya immediately. Tell King Rituparna the following: The daughter of King Bhima—Damayanti—will hold another *swayamvara*. All the kings and princes are traveling there. The ceremony will occur tomorrow. King, if possible, please go there at once. Damayanti doesn't know whether or not her husband is alive. Therefore, after the sun rises tomorrow, she will select a second husband."

Sudeva proceeded to Ayodhya. Arriving there and meeting with King Rituparna, he related everything to him. The king said to Nala, "Vahuka, I would like to go to Damayanti's *swayamvara* and arrive there—it's about nine hundred miles away—within one day."

Hearing this, Nala's heart was overwhelmed with sorrow and he thought, "Perhaps Damayanti is doing this because she's blind with grief. Or maybe she's concocted this plan for my sake. Too bad! Though I acted sinfully by deceiving her, still, what she plans to do now is very cruel. How fickle a woman's nature is! But my sin was also grave."

Then another possibility popped into his mind. "Perhaps she's doing this because, due to our separation, she no longer loves me. Yet I know that even if she were overcome with sorrow and depression because of me, she wouldn't do anything like this, especially since she's the mother of the children I fathered. Well, I'll definitely find out whether this is true or false by going there. That way I'll accomplish Rituparna's as well as my own purpose."

With his mind resolved and his heart full of grief, Nala folded his palms and said to the king, "I respect your request and will drive you to Vidarbha in just one day."

"Good. Then ready the horses as we must leave soon."

Nala proceeded to the stables and scrutinized the horses. After mindful attention, he chose some horses that were lean, strong, energetic and docile; they were also devoid of unfavorable birthmarks, had wide

"The two branches of the tree have fifty million leaves and 2,095 fruits. I would like you to check this."

nostrils and swelling cheeks, were free of the fault of ten hairy curls, were born in Sindhu, and were as fast as the wind.

***

When the king saw those horses, he said irately, "How will such weak-looking, short-breathed horses carry us about nine hundred miles in one day?"

Nala explained, "Each of these horses has all the right markings. So I'm certain they'll be able to reach Vidarbha soon. But if you prefer others, please show me which ones and I'll yoke them."

"Vahuka, you're conversant in the science of horses and adept in driving them. Quickly yoke those which you know to be capable."

Nala joined to the chariot the four well-bred, prime horses, which were obedient and fast. After the horses were yoked, the king mounted the car. However, those excellent steeds then fell to their knees on the ground. For a few moments, Nala comforted them. Then, taking the reins, he lifted them to a standing position. After Varshneya and he mounted the chariot, Nala urged the horses to begin running. Once they started, they rose into the sky with the speed of the wind. Seeing this, King Rituparna was greatly astonished.

As Varshneya observed Nala directing the horses, he thought, "Is he Matali, the charioteer of Indra? I notice Vahuka has the same masterly skill. Or is he the sage Shalihotra—an expert in the science of horses? Or is he the celebrated King Nala—Vahuka and he are the same age. Or is it that Vahuka just knows the same science Nala knows, for his knowledge appears to be equal? Sometimes famous persons travel about in disguise as a result of some tragedy or as a consequence of following some scriptural regulation. Though Vahuka looks unattractive, this does not alter my opinion, for Nala may look different now. Vahuka, like Nala, has every accomplishment. Therefore, I believe Vahuka is Nala."

As Varshneya continued thinking about this, he and King Rituparna, seeing Nala's adept horsemanship, experienced great pleasure. Nala drove the chariot through the sky and over rivers, lakes, forests, and mountains.

While the chariot was coursing along, the King's shawl blew off his body and fell to the ground. Noticing this, the king said to Nala, "Vahuka, I'd like to recover my shawl. Land and halt the chariot now so Varshneya may retrieve it."

"The shawl is presently some distance away, for we've traveled nine miles since it fell. Therefore, we can't recover it."

Just then, King Rituparna saw in the forest a fruit-laden *vibhitaka* tree and said, "Vahuka, I'd like you to note my unusual calculating ability. Do you see that tree?" The king pointed to it. "There are 101 more leaves and fruits lying on the ground than there are on the tree. And the two branches of the tree have fifty million leaves and 2,095 fruits. I would like you to check this."

Vahuka suspended the chariot and replied, "King, I can't check this by merely glancing at them—as you have. But I can, by counting."

"All right, then count them. For only then will you be convinced."

Vahuka landed the chariot, hastily dismounted, and immediately cut down the tree. Then he began counting the fruits. And when he finished, he was absolutely amazed; for the king's claim was correct. "King Rituparna, your power is wonderful!"

"I'm also adept at dice-playing."

"Dice-playing?"

"Yes. I can never lose."

"Never?"

"Never."

"But—how?"

"It's a science."

"Oh. Well, would you teach it to me—if I teach you the science of horses?"

"Certainly. In fact, I can teach it to you right now. But we won't have enough time for you to teach me about horses now. You can do that later."

The king then taught Nala the science of dice-playing. And as soon as Nala learned it, something strange happened which only he could see and hear: The demon Kali stumbled out of Nala's body! And he vomited up the deadly poison the serpent Karkotaka had injected into Nala's leg. This brought to an end the burning sensation Kali had been experiencing since then.

A long time had passed since Kali had first influenced the king to become wicked. But now, seeing the demon, Nala became angry and was ready to curse him. But Kali, fearful and shaking, folded his palms and begged, "King Nala, please control your anger. I've already been cursed—by Damayanti—when you abandoned her. That's why Karkotaka injected his venom into your leg—to make me burn night and day. Please spare me. Please! If you do, I'll make you even more famous than you are. Yes, I'll bless everyone with fearlessness who recites your history!"

Nala restrained his anger and decided not to curse the demon. The fearful Kali hastily entered the *vibhitaka* tree. And from that moment on, the *vibhitaka* tree has been considered auspicious. Sometime later Kali left it and returned to his abode.

Now free of Kali and having counted the fruits of that tree, Nala was filled with great happiness and energy. He mounted the chariot and urged those excellent horses to proceed. They again leaped into the air like birds, and Nala drove the chariot toward the state of Vidarbha.

* * *

The chariot arrived at the outskirts of the city of Kundina in the evening. After the citizens informed King Bhima of this, he sent his ministers to greet King Rituparna and lead him and his charioteers into the city.

As the chariot wheeled in, it rattled loudly in all directions. When some of Nala's horses heard the loud rattle, they became as overjoyed as they previously had been in Nala's presence. When the peacocks on the terraces and the elephants in the stables heard the chariot's rattle, they turned toward it and cried out delightedly.

Damayanti also heard the sound and said to herself, "The rattle of that chariot gratifies my heart, so Nala must have arrived. But if I don't see him, I will surely die. If I don't receive Nala's thrilling embrace today, I will stop living." Thus moaning like a madwoman, Damayanti climbed to the terrace of her mansion to behold Nala. But in the courtyard of the central palace, on the chariot, she saw only King Rituparna, Varshneya, and Vahuka.

When they dismounted, Varshneya and Vahuka unyoked the horses and parked the car while Rituparna presented himself to King Bhima. As Bhima received Rituparna with great honor, the latter glanced all around but saw no indication that a *swayamvara* was about to be held.

King Bhima, not knowing that Rituparna had arrived to try to marry his daughter, said, "Welcome! What's the occasion of your coming here?"

Rituparna noticed that there were no other kings or princes present; that there was no one talking about the swayamvara; and that there was no gathering of Brahmins. After considering this for a few moments, Rituparna, with a strained smile, said, "Oh, I've come here just to offer you my respects."

King Bhima could scarcely believe this—that Rituparna would travel over nine hundred miles just to offer him his respects. No, there must have been some other reason, which he hoped to discover later. Realizing that the king must be tired from the long journey, Bhima assigned quarters to him so that he could rest. As Rituparna and Varshneya went to them, Nala took the chariot to the stable. There, he unyoked, tended, and soothed the weary horses and then sat down beside the chariot.

Meanwhile, the sorrowing Damayanti asked herself, "Then whose chariot rattle was that? It was as loud as Nala's, yet—I didn't see Nala there. Could Varshneya have learned the art from Nala when he worked for him? Or does Rituparna know how to make his chariot rattle in that way?"

Thinking thus, Damayanti summoned a lady servant. Pointing down at the stable, she said, "O Keshini, I want you to go and find out who that charioteer is—the one with short arms and an unattractive face who is sitting beside the car. Approach him and speak to him discretely and gently. Ask him the usual courteous questions and find out all the specifics. My mind and heart are experiencing satisfaction and delight, so I think he may be King Nala. After you ask him about his well being, I want you to repeat the words Parnada said to him and understand his reply."

While Damayanti observed from the balcony, Keshini went cautiously to Nala and said, "Welcome to our city. We wish you well. Princess Damayanti has instructed me to ask you—when did you begin your journey and why did you come here?"

"Why? Because King Rituparna learned from a Brahmin that Damayanti would be holding a second *swayamvara*. Thus, with the help of very fast horses that can run nine hundred miles, he's come here. And I'm his charioteer."

"From where does the third person hail, and who is his father? And who is your father, and how have you come to do this work?"

"The third person was once Nala's charioteer, and everyone knows him as Varshneya. After Nala had left his kingdom, Varshneya went to work for King Rituparna. I'm versed in the knowledge of horses, and therefore King Rituparna hired me as his charioteer. He also hired me as his cook."

"Does Varshneya know where King Nala has gone? And has he ever talked to you about his master?"

"Varshneya brought Nala's children here and then went away. He doesn't know where Nala is and no one else does. For Nala is roving about the world in disguise and without his good looks. Only Nala himself knows who he is." ·

"Some time ago a Brahmin went to King Rituparna's kingdom and repeated the following words: 'My dear gambler, where have you gone? You cut off half of your dear and devoted wife's garment, and while she was sleeping, you abandoned her in the woods. That woman, wearing only a half piece of cloth and burning with sorrow, waits for and expects you. King, she constantly weeps for you, so please yield and respond to her.' When you heard those words of the Brahmin, you responded to them. Damayanti would again like to hear the words you responded with then."

Nala's heart was breaking and his eyes were brimming with tears. But he suppressed his anguish and, in faltering words, said, "Although chaste women may fall into difficulty, they protect themselves; and thus, when they die, they certainly go to the higher regions. Although their husbands may abandon them, they don't become angry over this. Rather, they continue living by the protection of their virtuous conduct. The woman you speak of should not be angry, because the man who abandoned her was overcome by tragedy and dispossessed of every joy. A woman who is beautiful and virtuous should not bear anger toward a man who, while trying to obtain food, was robbed by some birds of his only garment and who is now being devoured by sorrow. Whether such a wife is treated nicely or badly—since she has seen her husband deprived of kingdom, wealth, and food, and overcome by tragedy— she should never be angry with him."

While speaking these words, Nala, overwhelmed with grief and unable to suppress his tears, began to weep.

Keshini returned to Damayanti and informed her of all that was said, as well as the outburst of sorrow. Damayanti, overcome with grief, suspected Vahuka to be Nala and said, "O Keshini, I want you to go again to Vahuka and study him carefully. Stay close to him in silence and scrutinize his behavior. Whenever he does anything skillful, observe this. And whenever he asks you for water or fire, try to hamper his purpose by bringing them slowly. Then, after observing his conduct, report it to me. Also, whatever superhuman traits you see him display, as well as anything else, you should inform me of them."

Keshini left and did everything she was ordered. After a while she returned to Damayanti and told her about all the activities she had witnessed. "Damayanti," she said, "I've never before seen or heard of anyone like him. He has such command over the elements. For example, whenever he approaches a low passageway, he never stoops down. Rather, the passageway grows taller to enable him to pass through it easily! When he approaches narrow, impassable holes, they open wider to accommodate him! When he gazes at empty jars, they instantly become filled up with water. And when he holds a handful of grass up to the sun, it instantly ignites into fire—and the fire doesn't burn him in the least! And when he squeezes some flowers in his hands, not only do they keep their original shapes but they become more colorful and beautiful than before!"

Damayanti now further suspected that Vahuka was Nala. But to be certain, she weepingly said to Keshini, "Please go to the kitchen and, without Vahuka's knowledge, bring me some food he's prepared."

Keshini hastened there, took a portion, returned, and gave it to Damayanti. Able to recognize Nala's unique style of cooking, Damayanti tasted it thoughtfully. After a few moments she had no doubt—Vahuka had to be Nala—and she wept loudly. Then she asked Keshini to bring her children to Vahuka.

When Vahuka saw and recognized his twin son and daughter, he hastily went to them, swept them up in his arms, and embraced them lovingly. Nala regarded them as though they were children of the gods. His heart grief-stricken, he began to weep audibly.

Lowering his children to the ground, Vahuka said to Keshini, "These twins—they look just like my own children. I didn't expect to see them, so the surprise has made me tearful."

Keshini returned to Damayanti and described what she had seen. Her heart breaking with eagerness to see Nala, Damayanti said to Keshini, "I want you to go to my mother and, on my behalf, tell her the following: I suspect Vahuka to be Nala. My only doubt is his appearance. Therefore, I want to personally study him. Mother, please allow him to come to me in the palace or allow me to go to him. You can arrange this with or without Father's knowledge."

After the queen received the message, she conveyed it to Damayanti's father, who gave his permission. Damayanti then had Vahuka brought to the terrace of her apartment. When he entered, he unexpectedly saw Damayanti there. She was wearing a piece of red cloth, her hair was matted in ascetic fashion, and her body was covered with dirt and dust. Recalling their painful days together in the forest, Vahuka, overwhelmed with grief, burst into tears.

Damayanti, also overcome with sorrow, said, "Vahuka, have you ever seen a dutiful husband abandon his sleeping wife in the forest? Who but the righteous Nala could do this to his devoted and fatigued wife? What offense had I committed since my early youth that he should abandon me while I was exhausted and asleep in the forest? I chose him over the gods as my husband, and I became the mother of his children. Why should he desert me, who was his ever devoted and loving wife? Before the sacrificial fire and the gods, he held my hand and vowed, 'I will be yours truly.' What happened to that vow when he abandoned me?"

Tears flowed profusely from both Damayanti's and Nala's eyes. Then, in a choked voice, he said, "My dear, I did not lose my kingdom nor desert you under my own power. It was under the power of the evil spirit Kali. Somehow he entered my person and overpowered my reason. But after I left you in the woods and you were sorrowing, you cursed Kali. This caused him to experience a constant burning sensation—as though he were on fire. Anyway, that sinful worm has now left me, and it is due to this that I've come here.

"Yes, my love, I have come here for your sake only, and I have no other motive. But can a woman who loves and is devoted to her husband ever choose a second husband, as you intend to? At your father's behest, messengers are traveling all over the world proclaiming, 'King Bhima's daughter will, of her own volition, select a second husband who is deserving of her.' As soon as King Rituparna heard this, he came here to try to gain your hand."

Hearing these sorrows and suspicions, Damayanti, fearfully trembling and joining her palms, said, "My dearest, you must not suspect me of any sin, for I chose you even above the gods as my husband. Yes, the Brahmins traveled to every kingdom and sang my words in the form of a ballad—but for one purpose only: To bring you here! Finally, the Brahmin Parnada discovered you. And after he related to me your reply, I hatched a plan to bring you here. I knew that there was no one in the world who, in a single day, could travel nine hundred miles—except you.

"I sincerely swear that I've not committed any sin—even in thought. If I have, may the all-seeing air that blows through the world strike me dead now; and may the three gods who sustain the three worlds either confirm this or forsake me now!"

Hearing her words, the wind god declared from the sky, "Nala, I say to you truly that Damayanti has not committed any sin. She has not only protected your family honor but has strengthened it. We gods are the witnesses of this, just as, during the past three years, we have been her protectors. It is for your sake that she has arranged this matchless plan, since no one in the world but you can travel nine hundred miles in one day. Nala, you have found Bhima's daughter and she also has found you. Do not harbor any doubt, but instead, re-unite with her."

Then flowers rained from the sky, kettle drums sounded from above, and favorable breezes began to blow. As Nala noticed these miracles, he divested himself of all doubts about Damayanti. And suddenly remembering the Naga Karkotaka, he took out the mystical cloths he had received, put them on, and immediately recovered his own true form!

Seeing Nala as she always knew him, Damayanti embraced him and began to cry aloud. Nala not only returned her embrace, but also hugged his children, experiencing intense joy. Damayanti buried her face in his chest and sighed heavily, recalling her past woes. Nala, overcome with anguish and clasping Damayanti, stood there for a while, speechless.

Later, Damayanti's mother cheerfully told Bhima everything that had transpired between her daughter and son-in-law. The king replied, "Nala may pass this day peacefully, and tomorrow, after his bath and prayers, I shall see him with Damayanti."

Nala and Damayanti spent that night congenially, telling each other about their past experiences in the woods. It had been four years since Nala had lost his kingdom, and now, with all his desires satisfied, he once again experienced great ecstasy. And Damayanti, having regained her husband, fulfilled her wish. With her anxieties and weariness gone, she shone with beauty and bliss, like a night that is illumined by the bright moon.

***

The next day Nala, wearing ornaments, with Damayanti beside him, presented himself at the proper time before the king. Nala and Damayanti saluted him with due humility. King Bhima joyously received him as a son, along with his devoted wife, and soothed them in befitting words. Accepting his father-in-law's respects, Nala offered him his services, as was proper.

When the citizens saw Nala arrive, they became joyful. And soon, throughout the city, there was an uproar of ecstasy. The citizens then decorated the city with flags, standards, and flower wreaths. They watered the streets and decked them with flower garlands and other adornments. They also heaped flowers at their gates and decorated the temples and shrines with blossoms.

When King Rituparna learned that Vahuka was really King Nala and that he had been re-united with Damayanti, he was happy. He then summoned Nala to his presence.

After Rituparna was honored by Nala, he wondrously said, "By good fortune you've gotten back your wife's company and have become happy. Nala, while you were living at my house in disguise, I hope I didn't offend you in any way. If I did, please forgive me."

Nala replied, "You didn't offend me in the slightest. Rather, you were my friend. From now on, I shall find even greater pleasure in you. I lived joyfully in your house—even more so than in my own—for all my wishes were satisfied. If you desire, I'll be glad to teach you the science of horses now."

Rituparna agreed; thus, Nala conveyed it to him with prescribed rites. After this, Rituparna, employing another driver for his charioteer, departed from Kundina to his own city.

Nala spent a month at his father-in-law's palace. Then, after taking King Bhima's permission, he proceeded, without Damayanti, to Nishadha. Driving in a white chariot, he was accompanied by sixteen elephants, fifty horses, and six hundred infantrymen. As he entered his own kingdom, the earth trembled.

Without losing a moment and filled with righteous indignation, Nala entered the palace, approached his brother Pushkara, and said, "I challenge you to another dice game."

"Are you serious?" Pushkar said condescendingly.

"Absolutely. In fact, I'll stake Damayanti and all my new wealth."

"Damayanti?" Lustful thoughts coursed through Pushkar's degraded mind.

"Yes. And you'll stake this kingdom, which you won from me. Besides this, we'll each stake our own lives."

Pushkar, certain he would win, snickered at Nala's supposed foolishness.

"Or, if you don't want to play with dice, we can play with weapons. And the winner will take all."

Pushkar laughed, "You're a fool, Nala! Really!"

"Take your pick—dice or combat."

"Your good luck is about to end."

"Dice or combat?"

"And your Damayanti is about to become mine."

"Dice or combat, Pushkar?" Nala's voice rose.

"And you know—I've always wanted to have her," he smiled.

Nala wanted to cut off his head with his sword. But he restrained himself. "Dice or combat?!" Nala exclaimed.

"Dice will be fine." Pushkar had a servant fetch the dice and hand them to Nala. "Since you're going to lose anyway, you can have the first throw."

"Thank you." Nala gazed at the dice, invoked the power that King Rituparna had conveyed to him, and commanded it to produce a winning number. He shook the dice in his hand, threw them on the table, and sure enough—the winning number appeared!

Pushkar's jaw dropped. He could hardly believe it.

"This entire kingdom, with all its riches, is mine now," Nala emphasized.

Pushkar was frightened. Would Nala now kill him?

"You defeated me in the past, not because you had any special talent. But because the evil spirit Kali favored you."

"Kali?"

"Yes. He told me this. Therefore, I can't blame you for his wrongs."

Instead of feeling satisfaction or pleasure in defeating Pushkar, Nala felt compassion and mercy towards him. For he realized that Pushkar was simply a helpless pawn and victim of Kali's vengeful scheme—to separate Nala from Damayanti. "Therefore," said Nala, "I grant you your life as well as your share of our ancestral kingdom, with all necessities."

Pushkar stared at Nala incredulously. It was too good to be true.

"And have no doubt about it," Nala continued, "my brotherly love for you now is no different from what it was before, and it will never become less. May you have a long life!" Nala hugged his brother again and again.

Pushkara, his heart touched with remorse, then realized how great Nala was. With his palms joined and head bowed, he humbly said, "O King, may your fame never die and may you live joyfully for many years—you, who have just granted me life and shelter."

For one month Nala entertained Pushkara. Then, with his heart overjoyed, the latter departed for his own town, followed by a huge army, many dutiful servants, and his own relatives. Nala had made him rich and free from worries. And as he proceeded, his beauty blazed like a second sun.

Nala comforted all the citizens and then entered his palace.

Their hair standing on end, the citizens and the country subjects were exceedingly happy. They, along with the state administrators, exclaimed, "Today, throughout the city and the country, we're truly joyful! For we've regained our king, as the gods once regained Indra, the performer of one hundred sacrifices!"

After the celebration in the city had begun, Nala led a huge army to King Bhima's realm to fetch Damayanti. The powerful, large-hearted Bhima duly honored his daughter, and then she and her children departed with Nala.

When they arrived at Nishadha, King Nala began to spend his days joyfully, like the king of the gods in the Nandana gardens. As he ruled his country, he once again became famous among kings. He performed many sacrifices and distributed numerous presents to the Brahmins.

***

This noble history of Nala and Damayanti destroys the evil influence of Kali. When people in distress listen to it, it is capable of greatly consoling them. Further, whoever repeatedly narrates or listens to this ancient story will never experience misfortune, will fulfill all his goals, and, if he wishes, acquire fame, sons, grandsons, animals, high rank, health and joy.

The prostitute led Rishyashringa to the boat that was disguised as an ashram.

CHAPTER NINE

RISHYASHRINGA THE RAINMAKER

Rishyashringa performed spiritual disciplines, became pure in heart, and ended a city's drought and starvation. By practicing spiritual disciplines, which purify and strengthen our mind, we can more readily remain focused on attaining wisdom and virtue.

Vibhandaka, son of the great sage Kashyapa, was a Brahmin saint. He had awakened his soul through religious disciplines, and his knowledge and brilliance resembled that of the Supreme Lord. His semen, if released, would never fail to produce children.

His eyes were light brown, like a lion's, and his hair hung down to his fingernails. He was devoted to studies suitable to his caste, and his pure life was spent in meditation on the Supreme.

Vibhandaka lived in Anga beside a large lake and performed austerities there for a long period. One day as he was washing his mouth in the lake, he saw the heavenly nymph Urvashi. She was so beautiful and captivating that he uncontrollably ejaculated semen into the water.

Shortly afterwards, a thirsty red deer lapped up the semen along with the water she was drinking and became pregnant. Actually, that very deer had been a daughter of the gods. Long ago she had been told by Lord Brahma, the creator, "You shall become a red deer. And one day, in that body, you will give birth to a saint. At that time you shall be freed."

As the word of Lord Brahma always proves true, the deer, in time, gave birth to a male baby whose soul was that of an illustrious saint. Because the infant had an antler on his head, he came to be known as Rishyashringa [deer antler]. Growing up, he practiced asceticism, always living in the forest. And except for his father, he had never seen any other person. Thus, his mind was completely dedicated to the duties of an abstinent life.

At this time King Lomapada was ruling over the kingdom of Anga, and he was a friend of the famous King Dasharatha. One day Lomapada, due to his love of pleasure, lied to a Brahmin; after that, all members of the priestly class avoided any association with him. Consequently, Lomapada had no priest to assist him in his religious rites. This led to the god Indra suddenly refusing to supply the king's territory with rain, causing much distress among his subjects.

Attempting to solve the problem, the king inquired about it from a group of holy men who practiced austerities, had advanced minds, and were knowledgeable in rain making. "I'd like to know what I have to do to make it rain. Please think of a way."

The sages offered their various opinions, and one of them—the best of the sages—replied, "The Brahmins are angry with you. Thus, you must do something to pacify them. I also suggest that you bring the young saint Rishyashringa here. He's the son of a great holy man and lives in the forest. Totally ignorant of the female sex, he enjoys simplicity. Although he's only a youth, he's performed a tremendous amount of austerities. Therefore, if he were to appear here, I'm absolutely certain that rain would fall."

Lomapada went away and atoned for his wrongs. Having pacified the Brahmins, he again returned, and as the people saw him coming, their hearts rejoiced. Lomapada called a meeting of his wise counselors who were competent in all fields of knowledge, especially in worldly and practical matters. With their help, the king, after painstaking efforts, finally decided on a plan for achieving his aim.

He summoned a number of clever prostitutes from the city. When they arrived, he said to them, "I want you charming women to think of some way to enchant and gain the confidence of the son of Saint Vibhandaka—Rishyashringa. Then, once you've done that, you must bring him over to my territory."

The courtesans, after considering this, became very fearful. If they refused to comply, the king would become angry; if they agreed, the saint would curse them. Baffled and somber, they told the king that the task was beyond their ability. However, one elderly woman said to the king, "Rishyashringa is rich in austerities and I will try to bring him here. However, in connection with my plan, you'll have to obtain certain things for me. Only then may I be successful."

The king ordered his ministers to obtain for her whatever materials she might ask for. He also donated much wealth and different kinds of jewels. Then, taking with her several youthful and beautiful women, she immediately departed for the forest.

In order to fulfill the king's wish, the elderly woman had a floating hermitage built. It was furnished with artificial trees decked with different blossoms and fruits, was encircled with various shrubs and creepers, and was able to provide the best of tasty fruits. Enchanting, pleasing and captivating, it appeared as if it had been fashioned by magic. She had the vessel anchored near Vibhandaka's hermitage. Then she dispatched scouts to ascertain when the saint would leave the retreat, where he would go, and when he would return.

With this information, the elderly woman hatched a devious plan. Knowing when the saint would be away from the ashram, she sent her clever daughter there. When the daughter, holding a filled bag, reached the hermitage, she saw the saint's son—alone. Approaching him, she smiled and said, "I hope all is well with the holy men."

"Everything is fine," he replied.

"And I hope you like this retreat and that you have a large supply of roots and fruits."

"Yes, it's very nice, and we have plenty of them here."

"Actually, I have come here to visit you."

"Me?" asked Rishyashringa, surprised. As she drew closer, he gazed at her lovely face and said, "You're glowing with light, like sunshine. So I consider you worshipable."

Never having seen or learned about a woman, he was unaware of their sexual differences. He gave her water to wash her feet as well as fruits to enjoy. Then he offered her a seat on a sacred grass mat that was covered with a black deerskin. "Tell me, where is your ashram?" he asked.

"On the other side of that hill," she said, pointing. "It's a lovely place."

"You look like a god. Perhaps I should worship you."

"I'm sorry, but my faith doesn't allow me to receive respects from persons like you."

"It doesn't?"

"No. However, it's my duty to offer *you* respects."

"Oh. And which religious vow are you observing?"

"My vow is that I must hold you in my arms."

"In your arms?" He had never heard of such a vow.

"But first I'd like you to have some sweets and a drink. You'll love them."

Because they were attractive and appealing, Rishyashringa accepted them. But he had no idea that they were unsuitable for a renunciant.

Then she gave him extremely fragrant flower garlands and beautiful shining clothes to wear.

Next, the prostitue sported with a ball, laughing and delighting herself. Then she repeatedly touched Rishyashringa's body—till at last she embraced him tightly. Overcome with intoxication, she looked at him coyly and continued to tempt him. When she noted that his heart had been aroused, she again and again pressed her body firmly against his. Then she abruptly left his side, glanced at him teasingly and said, "I have to go now to make offerings in the sacrificial fire."

Watching her slink away, Rishyashringa became conquered by lust and devoid of reason. When he no longer could see her, he constantly thought of her, feeling sorely vacant. Sighing repeatedly with upraised eyes, he appeared to be in great agony.

***

When Vibhandaka returned, he saw that his son was sitting by himself, brooding, sighing, and sorrowing. "My son," he asked, "why aren't you chopping the logs for firewood? I hope you've made offerings in the sacrificial fire today, and that you've shined the ladles and spoons. I also hope you brought our calf to its mother, whose milk provides the butter we offer into the fire."

Vibhandaka noticed that his son was definitely not in his usual frame of mind. "My son, you look so melancholy and bewildered. Why are you so unhappy today?"

"Well, a religious student came here a little while ago. He was of medium height, had a lively appearance, golden complexion, and big lotuslike eyes. His beauty shone like the sun. He was as graceful as a god, and his eyes were beautiful and black. And his blue-black hair," he began wistfully, "was long, braided, comely, evenly parted, and fragrant, and was tied up with golden threads.

"And what else was he wearing?"

"He sported a lovely glittering ornament around his neck that looked like lightning. And on his hairless chest, he had two beautifully shaped lumps. His waist was rather slender, his navel pleasing, and his abdomen smooth. A golden string shone from beneath his cloth, just like my waist string."

Rishyashringa paused, desiring to be with her.

"Go on," said his father.

"Well, on his feet and wrists he wore beautiful ornaments that jingled, and those on his wrists resembled my rosary here. When he walked, his ornaments jingled and sounded like happy male geese in the water. And the clothes he was wearing were gorgeous, much more beautiful than mine." Again he stopped to reflect on her.

"Is that all?" asked Vibhandaka suspiciously.

"No. His face—it was so lovely to look at, his voice made my heart joyful, and his words were delightful—like a male blackbird's song. As I listened to him, he touched my soul deeply. Father, just as the forest during springtime looks beautiful when a breeze blows over it, he also looked beautiful when the breeze blew."

"And did he do anything?"

"Yes. He repeatedly bounced what looked like a fruit. And each time he hit it, he whirled himself around. Then—he hugged my body, held my matted hair, brought my lips down to his, and, while keeping them there, made a very pleasant sound."

Vibhandaka's suspicions were now confirmed.

"I offered him water," continued Rishyashringa, "to wash his feet with and fruits to eat. But he refused them, saying that such was his religious observance. Then he gave me some sweets to eat, and they were delicious—much tastier than ours! They didn't have any stones or rinds in them. He also gave me a tasty drink, and when I drank it, I not only found it enjoyable but the ground appeared to move under my feet. And these beautiful scented garlands, strung with silken threads, are his. He scattered them here and then returned to his own retreat."

"But how did he make you feel sad?"

"Well, since he left, my heart has been heavy and my body seems to be on fire. I want to go to him as soon as I can, and I want him to walk around here every day. Father! Please let me go to him now!"

"Absolutely not! You must never go to him because—he's a demon! Demons materialize amazingly beautiful bodies. Their strength is unequaled and their beauty, considerable. They always dwell on hindering a sage's practice of austerities. They attempt to charm us by various tricks. Those terrible beings have made saints fall down from their elevated state of consciousness."

"But Father, I want to—"

"Listen to me!"

Although reluctant, Rishyashringa listened.

"A saint, who is master of his soul and who wants to reach the higher planets where the virtuous go, must not associate with such demons. Their deeds are despicable and their joy is in obstructing the ascetic practices of holy men. Consequently, a virtuous person should never even look at them."

"But he was beautiful—like a god. And the drink he gave me, it was—"

"It was unfit to drink! Completely! Because it was intoxicating—the kind that immoral men drink. And these bright, colorful, scented garlands are not meant for ascetics."

Vibhandaka then went in search of the temptress and, after three days of looking, was unable to find her. He thus returned to the ashram. Then one day, after he went away from the hermitage to gather fruits, the same prostitute came to entice Rishyashringa. When the saint saw her, he was delighted and hastened over to her. "Let's go to your ashram before my father returns!"

The prostitute led Rishyashringa to the boat that was disguised as an ashram. By various devices she had him climb aboard and, unknown to him, one of the other courtesans lifted the anchor. The prostitutes continued to distract and please him in different ways as the craft gradually drifted toward King Lomapada's territory. When they arrived there, the king had the boat moored and had Rishyashringa brought to him. Then he provided the young saint with a wonderful new hermitage—namely, the women's quarters of the palace!

The king suddenly noticed that it was raining and that water began to fill the earth. With his heart's desire satisfied, and full of appreciation, he gave his daughter Shanta in marriage to Rishyashringa.

However, he knew that Rishyashringa's father would be angry and would journey to his palace to inquire about his son's absence. Hence Lomapada, to pacify Vibhandaka, ordered that many cows be placed, and fields be ploughed, beside the road that the saint would trod. He also placed courageous cowherds there and ordered, "When the illustrious saint Vibhandaka asks you about his son, I want you to respectfully join your palms and reply, 'These cows and ploughed fields are your son's, and we are his slaves. We are ready to obey him in whatever he asks of us.'"

* * *

After Vibhandaka gathered some fruits and roots from the woods, he returned to his hermitage. Not finding Rishyashringa there, he began to search for him. When he could not find him, he became extremely angry and suspected that the king was responsible. He therefore decided to, by his mystic power, burn the king, the king's capital, and the king's entire territory. He thus proceeded toward the city of Champa.

Along the way, Vibhandaka noticed the cowherds, rich with cows, who had been placed there by the king. Feeling fatigued and hungry, the saint asked them for assistance. They offered their respects to him and enabled him to spend the night there in a manner befitting a king. Noticing this excellent hospitality, he asked, "Whose cowherds are you?"

One of them replied, "Your son's."

"My son's?"

"Yes. And all these cows and fields are his."

Vibhandaka began to understand what had happened. As he continued his journey, he was supremely honored at various spots along the way by the cowherds. Finally, he saw his son, who resembled the king of the gods. He also saw his daughter-in-law, Shanta, who looked like lightning coming out of a cloud. By now, the sage's intense fury had become completely pacified.

Vibhandaka, whose power matched that of the sun god and the fire god, became pleased with the king. He allowed his son to remain there but advised him, "As soon as your wife gives birth to a son and you've done everything the king would like, you must immediately return to the forest."

At the proper time, Rishyashringa followed his father's advice and returned to the forest hermitage where he had once dwelled. But this time he came with his wife. Shanta submissively and affectionately served him, as the star Rohini serves the moon, as Arundhati serves the sage Vashishtha, as Lopamudra serves the sage Agastya, as Damayanti served King Nala, as Shachi serves the chief god Indra, or as Indrasena—Narayana's daughter—served the sage Mudgala.

As the sage Durvasa was talking, a heavenly messenger on a chariot appeared in front of Mudgala.

Chapter Ten

Mudgala Rejects Heaven

The sage Mudgala gave so much charity with an unselfish heart that, although eligible to enter the pleasurable heavenly planets, he rejected them for a more sublime place. We also must learn to be charitable, for this will help us overcome the greed and envy that prevents us from gaining wisdom and virtue.

In Kurukshetra there dwelled a holy sage named Mudgala. He was truthful, free of hatred, and a controller of his senses. He obtained his food by picking up ears of corn and various grains left on the fields by farmers after they had gathered and carried away the rest of them. Though this very austere saint lived like a pigeon, he pleased his guests, performed sacrifices and celebrated other rites. Along with his wife and son, he ate normally for a period of two weeks. But during the following two weeks he gathered some corn and subsisted like a dove. When he celebrated various rites, he ate the food remnants of the deities and the guests.

On favorable lunar days, when Mudgala would perform a sacrifice, the chief god Indra, accompanied by other heavenly beings, would partake of the food offerings. On such days this sage, with a happy heart, also satisfied his guests with food. As he eagerly and sincerely distributed the food, the balance of the corn would miraculously increase. It would increase so plentifully that he would feed hundreds and hundreds of Brahmins.

One day the renowned sage Durvasa arrived there. Without wearing any clothes, he appeared like a crazy person. Having heard about the vows Mudgala had observed, Durvasa decided to test him. He thus deliberately began to speak in an insolent manner, saying, "Brahmin, I've come here to obtain food!"

Mudgala replied, "You are welcome." Then, to the apparently hungry ascetic, he reverently offered water for washing his feet and mouth; then he offered him delicious food for filling his stomach. Ravenously hungry, the excited Durvasa consumed all of it. Then Mudgala gave him more food. After eating it, Durvasa smeared his body with the leftover particles and departed.

During the next season, Durvasa again arrived and consumed all the food Mudgala served him. At that time, without eating any food himself, Mudgala went out and gathered corn. Hunger could not shake his peace of mind, and wrath, deception, humiliation and agitation could not enter his heart.

The sage Durvasa appeared before Mudgala in the same insolent way for six consecutive seasons. And each time he could not detect any disturbance in Mudgala's heart. Rather, he always found the ascetic's heart pure. Consequently, Durvasa was very satisfied with him and said, "On this earth, there is no one as sincere and generous as you. The pangs of hunger drive a person's sense of virtue far away and make him lose all patience. The tongue relishes enjoyable preparations, so it draws people towards them. Food sustains physical life, and the mind is whimsical and difficult to control. Controlling the mind and senses are certainly ascetic disciplines.

"When one has gained something by hard effort, it is difficult to give it up. But you have accomplished this. I feel grateful and satisfied in your presence. You possess self-control, perseverance, fairness, restraint of the senses and faculties, compassion, and virtue. By your actions you have transcended the material world and have thus entered the path of bliss. Yes, even the residents of the heavenly planets are talking about your great deeds of charity. When it's time for you to leave this world, you will ascend to the higher regions even in your present body."

As the sage Durvasa was talking, a heavenly messenger on a chariot appeared in front of Mudgala. The chariot was yoked to swans and cranes, hung with bells, perfumed with celestial fragrance, painted artistically and had the power to go wherever it was ordered. The messenger said to Mudgala, "Your good deeds have brought this chariot here. Please mount it. You have achieved the results of your austerity."

"Messenger, I would first like you to describe the characteristics of the heavenly residents. What are their disciplines and goals? What does happiness consist of in heaven, and what are the disadvantages there? Righteous men of good birth say that one can make friendship with good persons by merely walking with them for seven steps. In the name of that friendship, and without reservation, please tell me the truth and whatever else is useful for me to know. Then, based on what you say, I will decide what to do."

The messenger replied, "Your understanding is rather simple. Though you have attained that spiritual joy which brings great respect, you're still thinking like an unintelligent person. That place called heaven is far above us. It extends very high, is provided with fine roads, and is roamed by celestial vehicles. Certain persons are not permitted there, and they are the atheists, the untruthful, and those who have not performed ascetic disciplines or conducted glorious sacrifices. But those allowed there are the pious, the emotionally restrained, the masters of their faculties, the conquerors of their senses, and those free of hatred and firm in the practice of charity; also allowed there are the heroes and those who, after conducting the most commendable sacrifices, with restrained senses and faculties, bear marks of a battle.

"Heaven contains numerous regions that are beautiful, gleaming and magnificent, and which can fulfill all material desires. They are ruled by heavenly beings, such as the gods, the celestials, the eminent sages, and others. The golden Mount Meru, the king of mountains, exists there, extending over an area of 297,000 miles.

"Also, the god Indra rules over charming gardens there, and deserving persons are allowed to sport in them. No hunger, thirst, fatigue, fear, or anything detestable or unfavorable is found there. The odors are fragrant, the breezes are delightful to the touch, and the sounds are enchanting to the ear and heart. Sorrow, illness, strain, and remorse are not found there. Persons go there as a result of their praiseworthy acts, and those who live there all look beautiful. They do not sweat, smell or urinate, nor does dust soil their clothes. And their glowing, fragrant garlands never wilt. They drive vehicles similar to the one I have come in. They are free of envy, sorrow, languor, ignorance and ill-will, and they live joyfully.

"Far above these planets are others with even higher heavenly qualities. Foremost among them are the lovely and magnificent regions of Lord Brahma. They are very holy and are venerated even by the gods. Shining by their own illumination, they grant every object of desire. Particular beings called Ribhus live there. They do not experience lust, have no worldly riches, and do not deceive others. Nor do they subsist on sacrificial offerings or nectar. Their heavenly bodies cannot be seen by the senses, and they do not seek the happiness of sense pleasure. Nor do they change their forms at the end of a *kalpa*—that is, 4,320,000,000 years, or a day of Lord Brahma. They do not know illness or disintegration, nor temporary joy or happiness, nor sorrow, anger, or displeasure. Mudgala, even the celestials desire such a lofty state, but this freedom can never be achieved by persons controlled by material desires. Those gods number thirty-three. Wise men who have taken awesome vows and have given away gifts based on scriptural injunctions go to this planet. You have easily earned it by the charity you have given and the praiseworthy deeds you have performed. Therefore you can now enjoy that region.

"Those are the pleasures of the heavenly planets. Now listen to some of their drawbacks: A person in the heavenly planets who is enjoying the results his past meritorious deeds cannot earn those type of merits there. He must continue to enjoy the results of his past merits till they are completely exhausted. After that, to acquire new merits, he must return to earth and again take birth as a human being. The prospect of returning to an inferior region—one which will not be as pleasant and bright—fills him with displeasure and sorrow and is difficult to bear. When he is about to fall, his garland begins to fade, fear enters his heart, and he becomes emotionally agitated and stupefied. These are the big disadvantages of going to heaven, and they extend even up to Lord Brahma's planet.

"Once the soul enters a human body, it acquires opulence and pleasure. However, if, during this new lifetime, it does not acquire knowledge and merits, its next birth will be inferior to the present one. The results of whatever deeds one performs in this world are obtained in the next one.

"I have thus described to you, Mudgala, everything you asked to know. Now, with your approval, we shall easily and rapidly leave this planet."

After deliberating well on the messenger's words, Mudgala said, "O heavenly messenger, I offer my respects to you. Please go in peace. I don't want anything to do with materialistic happiness or the heavenly planets. For they have such prominent imperfections. After one enjoys the pleasures of heaven, he then has to suffer tremendous anguish and great sorrow on this planet. Thus, I don't wish to go to heaven. Rather, I will try to attain that perfect region where people never experience sorrow, anguish or disturbance. You have described the big drawbacks related to the heavenly regions. Now I would like you to describe to me a world that is free of defects."

The messenger answered, "Beyond the planet of Lord Brahma exists the supreme world of Lord Vishnu. It is pure, eternal and effulgent, and is called Para Brahman. Persons who are tied to sense objects cannot go there; nor can those who are controlled by arrogance, lust, ignorance, anger and envy. But those who are free from infatuation, egotism, and opposing emotions, who have controlled their senses, and who have practiced meditation and yoga—they can go there."

After hearing this, the sage said goodbye to the heavenly messenger. He was not interested in going to heaven. He was filled with perfect peace. Praise and criticism were the same to him, as were bricks, stone and gold. Determined to attain Para Brahman or Lord Vishnu's realm, he always meditated on Lord Vishnu. By means of spiritual knowledge, he acquired power and perfect understanding. He thus achieved the supreme eternal state of liberation from the material world.

Kacha burst out of his teacher's stomach, killing him instantly.

CHAPTER ELEVEN

DEVAYANI'S WOES

1

While trying to achieve his mystical goal, Kacha bore much trouble and affliction. Nonetheless, he remained resolutely patient and was ultimately successful. In the same way, when striving for wisdom and virtue, we must be considerably patient; otherwise we may thoughtlessly undo our hard-earned gains.

Long ago the gods and the demons often battled each other for lordship over the three worlds—the upper, middle and lower planetary systems. The gods, desiring victory, established Brhaspati as their priest to perform their sacrifices. The demons established the knowledgeable Shukra for the same reason. There was always vain competition between the two priests.

When any of the demons were killed in battle, Shukra, by his mystic knowledge and power, would revive them. They would then resume their fighting with the gods and kill many of them. But Brhaspati, not knowing the science of *Sanjivani*, or revivification, could not revive the gods.

The celestials were thus greatly aggrieved by, anxious about, and fearful of Shukra. Therefore, they went to Brhaspati's oldest son, Kacha, and said, "Please accept our respects. We beg your kindness and would appreciate if you would do us a big favor. We would like you to obtain the mystic secret of revivification from the illustrious Brahmin Shukra. He resides in King Vrishaparvan's court and always gives protection to the demons. You are younger than he and able to honor him reverently. You can also honor his favorite daughter, Devayani. Truly, you alone can please them by reverence; no one else can. If you please Devayani by your behavior, generosity, kindness and general conduct, you will surely be able to obtain that science."

Kacha replied, "All right, I'll try," and immediately departed for Vrishaparvan's capital. Arriving there, he found Shukra and, after offering him respects, said, "I would like to be your disciple. Please accept me. I am Brhaspati's son and the sage Angiras' grandson. My name is Kacha. If you agree to become my guru, I will practice celibacy for a thousand years. O Brahmin, please order me."

"You are welcome, Kacha. I accept your words and will treat you respectfully; by doing so, I will be respecting your father, Brhaspati."

"Thank you. Then I shall begin my vow now."

From then on, the youthful Kacha began to thoughtfully please both his guru and his guru's young marriageable daughter, Devayani. He pleased her by singing, dancing, playing musical instruments, and by eagerly offering her gifts of flowers, fruits and various services. She, too, sang for and served him as he practiced his vow, gradually falling in love with him.

After five hundred years, some of the demons suspected Kacha's intention and became incensed. One day, while Kacha was tending Shukra's cows in a solitary part of the forest, those angry demons sought him out. Hating Kacha's father, desiring to prevent the science of revivification from being conveyed to Kacha, and having no compunction about killing a Brahmin, they murdered Kacha. Then, to leave no trace of evidence, they chopped his body into pieces and fed it to the jackals and wolves.

At twilight, when Devayani saw the cows return to their sheds without Kacha, she became concerned, went to her father, and told him about it. "I fear that he is lost or dead. Father, I can't live without him!"

Shukra replied, "If he is dead, then I shall revive him and bring him here."

By his mystic power, he summoned Kacha to his presence. The parts of Kacha's body, having been devoured by wolves and jackals, suddenly burst out of those animals' bodies. Then they reunited into a single form, and he happily appeared before his teacher.

Devayani asked, "What happened to you?"

"I was carrying sacrificial fuel, kusha grass and logs of wood, and was headed towards our house. I was hot and tired, so I sat down, along with the cows, under the shade of a banyan tree. Then some demons approached and asked who I was. I told them I was the son of Brhaspati. As soon as they heard this, they murdered me, chopped up my body, fed it to the jackals and wolves, and then went home joyfully. I am here only because your father revived me."

On another occasion, Devayani asked Kacha to go to the forest to gather some flowers for her. As he did, the demons again killed him, pounded his body into a paste, and mixed it with the water of the ocean.

When Kacha failed to return at the usual time, Devayani informed her father. Then Shukra, by his mystic science, summoned Kacha before him. When he appeared, he related everything that had happened.

At another time Kacha was again slain by the demons. They burned his body to ashes, mixed the ashes with wine, and gave the wine to Shukra, who drank it. Devayani then said, "Oh Father, I sent Kacha to gather wild flowers. But he hasn't returned. I'm sure he's lost or dead. If so, I can't live without him!"

Shukra said, "My dear daughter, Kacha has gone to the region of death. Though I keep reviving him, he continues to be killed. What can I do? Devayani, do not grieve or cry. A person like you should not mourn for one who is mortal. As a result of my powers, you are worshiped three times a day during the prayer hours by the Brahmins, the gods, and the other celestials—in fact, by the whole universe! Devayani, it is impossible to keep him alive; for no sooner do I restore him than he is again killed."

"Father, why should I not mourn for him? Was he not the grandson of the great sage Angiras and the son of the great sage Brhaspati? Was he not a celibate and an ascetic? And was he not always alert and skilled in everything? Oh Father, if I don't see Kacha, I will starve myself to death and follow him. He is so dear to me!"

Shukra replied angrily, "These demons want to hurt me, for they keep killing my disciple. They are followers of Lord Shiva and want to strip me of my Brahminical character by making me participate in their crime. And such a crime—killing a Brahmin—has a terrible end and would burn even Indra."

Urged by Devayani, Shukra summoned Kacha from the region of death. But Kacha, who was in his guru's stomach and was afraid of coming out for fear of killing him, said, "My lord, please be kind to me. It is I, Kacha, who worship you. Kindly treat me as your own dear son."

"How did you enter my stomach?"

Kacha replied, "I was killed by the demons, burned, reduced to ashes, and mixed into the wine you drank."

Shukra turned to Devayani. "I can bring Kacha back only at the expense of my life. There is no other way he can come out except by tearing open my stomach."

"Father, if you die, I will also die—just as I will if Kacha remains dead."

Shukra said to Kacha, "You are already successful because Devayani respects you so highly. I've decided to teach you the science of revivification, provided you are not Indra disguised as Kacha. It is not right for a Brahmin to be murdered. Therefore, I'll teach you this science now. After you receive it and I bring you back to life, please act kindly."

Right after Shukra taught Kacha the science, Kacha burst out of his teacher's stomach, killing him instantly. However, since Kacha now knew the science, he immediately revived his guru. Then he said to him, "You have poured nectar in the form of this science into my ears; thus I regard you as both my father and my mother. How can I ever forget the great service you have done for me? How can I ever be so ungrateful as to hurt you? Persons who gain true knowledge from their gurus—who are always objects of worship and the most precious of all precious objects on earth—but who injure them, come to be hated on earth and ultimately go to the regions of the damned."

It was then that the learned Shukra realized that Kacha had tricked him into revealing the secret science of revivification—and only because the sage had been under the influence of wine. Had he been in his normal, alert consciousness, he would not have been so careless. Angry with himself, he proclaimed, "From this day on, any Brahmin who does not resist the temptation to drink wine shall be considered to have lost his piety and slain a Brahmin, and will be despised in this world and the other worlds. I set this restriction on the behavior and the dignity of Brahmins everywhere. Hence, let the honest, the Brahmins, the gods, those who respect their superiors, and the three worlds listen!"

Shukra summoned the foolish demons and bellowed, "How foolish you are! You should know that Kacha has satisfied his desires. From now on he will live with me. He has obtained the priceless knowledge of reviving the deceased and has become as powerful as God Himself!"

The demons, very surprised, departed for their homes. Kacha also, after staying with Shukra for a thousand years and then taking his permission, prepared to return to the region of the gods.

When Devayani heard that Kacha was about to leave, she approached him and said, "Kacha, you shine most brightly in behavior, knowledge, austerity and modesty. Do you recall how I acted affectionately towards you while you observed your vow of celibacy?

Now that you have completed the vow, I would like you to turn your affection towards me—and marry me."

"Devayani, I honor and worship you as I do your father—in fact, even more so. But I'm not interested in marriage."

"What?!"

"I—I'm sorry."

"Have you forgotten the love I showed you—when the demons killed you so many times?"

"No, Devayani, I—"

"Then how can you just abandon me now—after I showed you such friendship and devotion? Have I hurt you in any way? I'm truly devoted to you."

"Yes, you are, but it would be sinful for me to marry you."

"Sinful? What are you talking about?"

"Please try to understand. True, you are virtuous and beautiful. But you once resided in your father's body—as a soul within his semen before conception. And I, too, resided in his body—within his stomach mixed with wine. Thus, since we both emerged from his body, we are, in effect, brother and sister!"

"Oh, that's ridiculous!"

"Please, Devayani. We've spent so many happy days together. But now it's time for me to return home."

"Home?"

"Yes. Would you kindly bless me with a safe journey?"

"Kacha, if you refuse to marry me—even after I proposed to you—"

"Devayani—"

"Then by my curse, the knowledge you've gained from my father will not bear fruit."

"I've refused your proposal only because you're my guru's daughter—not because you have any flaw. And besides, my guru hasn't ordered me to marry you."

Devayani glared at him.

"Though your curse may act on me, it won't act on whomever I may convey my knowedge to."

"Kacha! Please don't go."

"I'm sorry, Devayani, but—I have to."

Devayani felt as if her life were leaving her.

"Goodbye, Devayani," Kacha said gently. "And—thank you for everything."

Kacha then quickly traveled to the planet where Indra, the king of the gods, dwelled. When the celestials saw him, they, with Indra at their head, joyfully welcomed him. Next, they worshiped him, and then one of them said, "You have truly benefitted us. What a great accomplishment! You'll be famous forever."

When Kacha taught the gods the science of revivification, they considered their goal—to defeat the demons—as already attained. They gathered together and said to Indra, "The time has come for showing valor. Please, kill your enemies!"

"Yes, I will!"

2

King Yayati made a serious commitment to Devayani's father. But when he deliberately failed to keep it, he experienced tremendous woe. In the course of developing wisdom and virtue, it is important that we try to meet our commitments, as this helps us to develop confidence in ourselves and trust from others.

Accompanied by the celestials, Indra set out on his mission. However, along the way, he saw some beautiful maidens sporting in a garden lake. To have some fun, Indra transformed his body into wind, approached their garments on the bank, and mixed them up.

Shortly after, the maidens came out of the water and went to the heap of clothes. Sharmishtha, the daughter of King Vrishaparvan, mistakenly took Devayani's clothes. When Devayani saw this, she condescendingly remarked, "Since you're my disciple, why have you taken my clothes? Your conduct is improper and no good can come to you!"

But Princess Sharmishtha quipped, "Hmph! Your father occupies a lower seat than my father. He always honors my father with downcast eyes—like one who is hired to chant others' prayers—whether the king is sitting relaxed or lying down."

Devayani began to boil with anger.

Sharmishtha continued, "You're the daughter of one who chants others' praises and accepts others' charity. But I—I'm the daughter of one who is praised—and *gives* charity instead of *accepting* it. Oh beggar-woman, you can beat your breast, use foul speech, swear hatred to me, yield to anger, or weep angry tears in vain. But just remember, if I wish, I can hurt you—but you can't do anything to me! I don't even consider you my equal!"

Sharmishtha threw Devayani into a blind well.

Hearing this, Devayani became enraged and began to pull at Sharmishtha's clothes. However, the latter threw Devayani into a blind well. Believing Shukra's daughter to be dead, Sharmishtha went home angrily.

Later, King Yayati, who had been hunting, arrived there. The two horses yoked to his chariot, as well as the other single horse with him, were fatigued. Besides this, the king was thirsty. So he he looked about, saw a well, approached it and looked inside. To his great surprise, he noted that it was not only dry—covered with creepers and long grass— but that there was an effulgent maiden in it. Her nails resembled burnished copper and her earrings were studded with heavenly jewels.

"Who are you?" he asked. "How did you fall into this well? And— whose daughter are you?"

"I am Shukra's daughter. He brings back to life the demons slain by the gods. He is not aware of what's happened to me. Here is my right hand. Please take it and lift me out of the well. I know you are nobly born, virtuous, famous, and valorous."

As King Yayati caught her hand and lifted her up, he could not help glancing at her beautiful tapering thighs. He then left courteously and returned to his capital.

Saddened, Devayani said to her maid, "Ghurnika, go quickly and tell my father what has happened. I don't wish to enter King Vrishaparvan's city now."

Ghurnika hastened to Shukra's house and, upset over Devayani's ordeal, said, "O great Brahmin, Devayani was assaulted by Sharmishtha, the king's daughter."

Shukra, his heart heavy, hurried out and found her in the forest. Clasping her affectionately, he sadly said, "My daughter, the woe that comes to people is the result of their past misdeeds. You must have committed a wrong in the past for which you have just been punished."

"Punishment or not, please listen to me attentively, Father. Hear what Sharmishtha said to me." Devayani repeated those derogatory words and then added, "She said I must worship her in the hope of gaining her favor."

Shukra replied, "Devayani, you're not the daughter of a hired chanter of praises or of one that seeks charity and accepts gifts. No, you're the daughter of one who praises no one but is praised by everyone! King Vrishaparvan knows this, and so does Indra and King Yayati. Lord Brahma is my power, and he himself said that I am a master of all things on heaven and earth. I can cause rain for the benefit of all beings and nourish the annual plants that feed all living creatures."

In this way, by such pleasant, significant words, Shukra tried to placate his angry, saddened daughter. Then he tried to appeal to her philosophically. "Devayani, try to realize that one who is undisturbed by another's words can conquer everything. The sages say that a true charioteer holds the reins of the horses tightly. Similarly, a true person does not allow his anger to rise but controls it. Further, he shakes off his rising anger by showing forgiveness. A person who controls his anger and disregards the wicked words of others, surely obtains life's four goals, namely, righteousness, wealth, pleasure and salvation.

"If one person performs sacrifices energetically every month for one hundred years, and another person feels no anger towards anything, the latter person is surely superior. Though boys and girls cannot distinguish between what is proper and improper and argue with each other, the wise never emulate them."

"Father, I know the difference in power between anger and forgiveness. But a guru should never forgive a disciple who acts disrespectfully toward him if he wants to benefit the disciple. Consequently, I no longer wish to live in a country where wicked conduct is regarded highly. If a wise person desires good, he should not live among wickedly inclined persons who speak badly about good conduct and noble birth. Rather, he should dwell where good conduct and noble birth are practiced and honored. Sharmishtha's malicious words burn in my heart, just as when wood burns. I can't think of anything more miserable in the three worlds than to worship one's foes who possess good fortune while one possesses none. The wise have said that death would be better for such a person."

Seeing how disturbed his daughter had become, Shukra himself became angry. He approached the king, who was seated, and without considering his words, said, "Vrishaparvan, like the earth, wicked deeds do not bear fruit immediately. They do so gradually and covertly, destroying those who execute them. Such fruits come either to oneself, to one's son, or to one's grandson. Wicked actions must bear their fruit. Like rich foods, they can never be digested. And, because you are responsible for your subjects' committing them, I am leaving you and your relatives."

Surprised, the king said, "But what did my subjects do?"

"They killed the Brahmin Kacha, who was righteous, knowledgeable in religious principles, and diligent in his service while he lived in my house. And just awhile ago your daughter badly maltreated my daughter. For these reasons I can no longer remain with you. And I am not lying.

You take your offenses much too lightly and make no effort to correct them."

"Shukra, please be merciful to me. Piety and truth always dwell in you. If you leave us, we shall have to enter the depths of the ocean. For truly, what else could we do?"

"Whether you enter the depths of the sea or fly away in every direction, I don't care. I can't bear my daughter's sorrow. She's ever precious to me. My life depends on her well being. If you want to please me, then try to please her. I've always sought your well being by my ascetic merits, just as Brhaspati seeks the well being of Indra."

"Shukra, whatever we demon leaders possess—our elephants, cows, horses, even my lowly self—are yours! You are the absolute master of them all."

"If what you just said is true, that I'm the lord of the demons' wealth, then you must go and please Devayani."

Shukra then led King Vrishaparvan to the spot in the forest where Devayani was waiting. But he had him stand aside so he could first talk to her alone. After he related to her the conversation he had just had with the king, she quickly replied, "O Father, if you are indeed the master of the demon king and all his riches, then tell the king to come here and say so in my presence."

Shukra signaled the king to approach them, and when he did, he told him what Devayani wanted.

The king replied, "Devayani, whatever you wish, I am willing to grant, no matter how difficult it may be."

"All right. Then I want your daughter Sharmishtha, with her thousand maids, to become my servant—and to follow me wherever my father gives me away in marriage."

Vrishaparvan summoned a maidservant who had been attending him and explained to her what had transpired. "Go and bring Sharmishtha here quickly to fulfill Devayani's wish."

When the maidservant reached Sharmishtha's apartment, she related everything that had just happened.

Evaluating the situation and all that could be lost if she refused, Sharmishtha replied, "I will gladly do Devayani's bidding. For I don't want to be blamed for either her or her father's leaving the kingdom."

Accompanied by a thousand maids and riding on a palanquin, Sharmishtha arrived where Devayani, Shukra, and the king had been waiting. Sharmishtha approached Devayani and said, "I'm your servant—along with my thousand maids. And yes, I'll follow you wherever your father gives you away in marriage."

"Oh?" replied Devayani with mock surprise. Then, with a note of sarcasm, "But I'm the daughter of one who chants your father's praises and who begs and accepts charity. But you, on the other hand, are the daughter of one who is worshiped. So—how can *you* be *my* servant?"

Catching the meaning, Sharmishtha answered, "It's my duty to make my father and my relatives happy. And if that's what it takes, then that's what I'll do."

Devayani said to her father, "I'm now satisfied and am ready to re-enter the demon capital. And I now know that your science and power of knowledge are not worthless."

Shukra entered the city with a joyful heart, and the demons worshiped him with great respect.

***

After some time, Devayani, along with Sharmishtha and her thousand maids, proceeded to the same forest as before for recreation. When she reached the same spot as she had previously, she began to ramble about freely. Served by all those companions, she felt extremely joyful. In a light-hearted, sporting mood, they began drinking the honey in flowers and eating different types of fruit.

At that moment King Yayati, the son of Nahusha, again appeared in the area. He had been wandering about, searching for deer, and was now fatigued and thirsty. When he saw Devayani, Sharmishtha, and the other maids, he noted that they were adorned with heavenly ornaments and, from the flower honey they had imbibed, were overcome with sensuous languor. Devayani was smiling sweetly, had the fairest complexion of them all, and was incomparable in beauty. She was reclining relaxedly while Sharmishtha was gently massaging her feet.

Yayati went over to them and said, "Young ladies, I'd like to know who you are and who your fathers are. It appears that all these maids are serving both of you."

Devayani replied, "Sir, I'm the daughter of Shukra, the guru of the demon race. And my companion here is my servant. She waits on me wherever we go. Her name is Sharmishtha, and she's the daughter of the demon king Vrishaparvan."

"Oh? But why is this lovely princess your servant?"

"Sir, as everything is the result of fate, this too is. But you—you look and are dressed like a king. And you speak nobly, as the Vedic scriptures sound. What is your name, where do you come from, and whose son are you?"

"My name is Yayati. I'm the son of a king, and a king myself. During my student days, when I was observing the vow of celibacy, I listened to all the Vedic scriptures."

"And what brings you here? Is it to collect lotuses or to fish or to hunt?"

"I've been hunting for deer. But I'm thirsty now, so I'm looking for water. I'm also quite fatigued. However—If you want me to leave, just tell me."

"No, no, not at all. I'd prefer you to stay. In fact, I—I'd like you to become my friend and—and my husband."

"Oh beautiful one, I'm completely unworthy of you. For you're the daughter of the illustrious Brahmin Shukra, and I—I'm merely a warrior king."

"In earlier times members of the priestly caste married members of the warrior caste. You're the son of a sage and thus you yourself are a sage. Therefore, please marry me."

"True, the four orders—namely, the priestly, warrior, merchant and laborer—have sprung from one body. Nonetheless, their duties and purity aren't the same, for the priestly is above them all."

Devayani said, "Before you lifted me out of that well some time ago, my hand had never been touched by any man. Nor has it been touched since. For this reason I accept you as my husband. I'm sure you realize that because you touched me, no other man would want to touch me now. For he'd feel that I belong only to you."

"But the wise say that a Brahmin should be avoided more so than an angry, poisonous snake."

"Why do you say that?"

"Because in one moment, an angry snake can kill only one person, whereas an angry Brahmin, just by his desire, can kill entire cities and kingdoms. Thus, I can't marry you unless your father offers you to me."

"All right, if that's the only way you will accept me."

Devayani sent a maidservant to her father and she told him what had occurred. Shukra hastened to the area where Devayani was waiting. When Yayati saw him, he offered obeisance and then stood up with palms together, awaiting the sage's commands.

Pointing to King Yayati, Devayani said, "Father, here's the son of King Nahusha. When I was stuck in the well, he took hold of my hand

and lifted me out. Please give me in marriage to him. For I don't want to marry anyone else."

"King Yayati," said Shukra, "since my daughter has accepted you as her husband, I give her over to you. Please accept her as your wife."

"Gladly. But first I would like a blessing from you—namely, that when I marry Devayani and produce a child in her, I won't be guilty of the sin of producing a child from both castes."

"I'll absolve you from that sin. Just maintain Devayani virtuously. May you always be happy in her company." He then pointed to Sharmishtha. "This other maid, King Vrishaparvan's daughter—you must always respect. But you must never have sexual intercourse with her. Do you understand?"

"Yes." Then, out of reverence, Yayati walked around Shukra. And shortly after, he and Devayani were married ceremoniously. Later, King Yayati, along with Devayani, Sharmishtha, and the thousand maidens, returned to his capital happily.

* * *

Yayati's capital was very opulent, like the city of Indra. In his palace he entered the inner apartments with Devayani and established her there. Devayani asked him to establish Sharmishtha in a mansion among the Ashoka trees in his garden. He surrounded her with one thousand maids and respected her by making all arrangements for her food and clothes.

Yayati, for many years, sported blissfully with Devayani. After some time, she conceived and later gave birth to an excellent boy. But Sharmishtha, still childless, became anxious and said to herself, "It's time for me to have a child, yet I haven't even chosen a husband. What should I do? How can I satisfy my wish? Devayani has become a mother, but I—I'll simply spend my youth in vain. Of course, I could choose Devayani's husband for my husband. But—should I? Why not? Yes, that's what I will do. I'll try to obtain a son from him. But will that righteous king see me privately?"

Just then, the king happened to wander by lackadaisically. Seeing her, Yayati halted and remained silent. When Sharmishtha beheld him and realized they were alone, she approached him, joined her palms respectfully, and said, "King, you know that I'm both pretty and high-born. And I'm at that time of life when I should have a child. Therefore, I would like you to—produce one in me."

The king smiled helplessly. "I'm sorry, but—when I married Devayani, Shukra ordered me to never have sexual intercourse with you."

"King, it's been said that lying is not sinful when done under five different circumstances: Namely, when one is joking, or seeking a woman for enjoyment, or getting married, or saving a person from death, or losing one's fortune. Therefore, when you promised to have sex with only Devayani, why not consider that you were lying then? What is the harm?"

"Because a king should always be a perfect example to his people. If he lies, he surely meets with destruction. As for myself, even if I was threatened with the greatest loss, I wouldn't lie."

"But one may regard her friend's husband as her own. And one's friend's marriage may also be regarded as her own. My friend has chosen you as her husband. Thus, you are as much my husband as you are hers. So I beg you, please satisfy my desire."

"I've taken a vow to always grant what someone asks me for. So—I will oblige you."

They then spent some time together and, after a while, parted affectionately. As a result of their union, Sharmishtha conceived and later gave birth to a beautiful boy.

When Devayani learned of this, she became jealous and began to think unpleasant things about Sharmishtha. Devayani went to her and asked, "Why have you committed the sin of yielding to lust?"

"I committed no sin. What happened was that I met a great sage, who was highly virtuous and well versed in the Vedas. Since he was capable of granting boons, I asked him to bless me with a son, and he did. Therefore, I committed no sin."

"Oh, if that's how it happened, you're quite right. But—what's the sage's name, his family name, and his ancestry?"

"Devayani, when I looked at him and saw his ascetic and energetic effulgence, I felt it was unnecessary to ask those questions."

"Well, if that's what actually happened, Sharmishtha, then I have no reason to be angry with you."

They talked and laughed, and then Devayani returned to her palace apartment.

After some time, Devayani became the mother of two sons. They were known as Yadu and Turvasu, and were like Lord Indra and Lord Vishnu in splendor. Sharmishtha, by Yayati's help, became the mother of three sons, whose names were Drahyu, Anu and Puru.

One day Devayani and Yayati went into a lonely part of the king's gardens. There they encountered three gorgeous children who were frolicking with perfect confidence. Surprised by their presence, Devayani asked, "Whose children are they? Why, in beauty they look like children of the gods, and in splendor, I think they resemble you." Without even waiting for the king to reply, she asked the children, "Who are your parents?"

The children pointed to the king and revealed that Sharmishtha was their mother. The children then approached the king to clasp his knees, but Yayati would not dare to fondle them in Devayani's company. The boys began to cry and hastened to Sharmishtha, who was standing nearby.

Devayani called Sharmishtha and exclaimed, "You lied to me! How dare you do this when you're my dependent? Don't you fear the sin of illicit sex?"

"Devayani, all that I said about the sage is completely true. I have acted properly, according to the rules of righteousness. Thus, I'm not afraid of you. When you selected the king as your husband, I, too, selected him. According to custom, a friend's husband is also one's husband. Devayani, you are a Brahmin's daughter, so you deserve my worship and respect. But you don't know that I hold this royal sage, Yayati, in even greater respect."

Devayani turned to the king and said, "You have ill-treated me! Therefore, I won't reside here any longer." Her eyes full of tears, she hastened to her father. The king was sorry to see her like this and, very frightened, followed her, trying to placate her anger. But Devayani, her eyes angry red, could not be passified. When she reached her father, she bowed down low, and then stood up. Yayati, right after her, did the same.

"Father, vice has defeated virtue. The low have risen and the high, fallen. Once again I've been wronged by Sharmishtha."

"Wronged? How?"

"My husband has produced three sons in her and, unfortunately, only two in me. And he's famous for his knowledge of the rules of righteousness."

Shukra glared at the king. "Even against my order?"

"Yes," answered Devayani. "He has violated it."

Shukra then said to the king, "Since you have pleasurably engaged in vice while fully knowing the rules of righteousness, I curse you with unconquerable old age!"

Yayati replied, "But sage, I was propositioned by Sharmishtha to give her a child because she had come of age to give birth. I acceded to her request from a sense of virtue and not lust. It is stated in the Vedas that if a woman is of age to have a child and she asks a man to produce one in her, he must oblige her and take responsibility for her and the child. Isn't that so?"

"Yes, but—"

"And if he refuses her request, he loses virtue and is considered to be a killer of the embryo. To avoid that sin, I had sexual relations with Sharmishtha."

"Yes, but you forgot one thing: You are dependent on my grace. Therefore, as my dependent, you should not have yielded till you received my permission. Thus you went against my wishes, took what you had no right to take, and became guilty of the sin of theft."

At that moment King Yayati suddenly lost his youth and became a weak old man. He then pleaded, "Shukra, I haven't had enough youthful pleasures or enough gratification with Devayani. Please be merciful and take away this old age."

"No! Once I decree something, it must occur!"

"But—"

"However, if you wish, you may transfer your old age to someone else."

"To someone— you mean, perhaps to one of my sons?"

"If he agrees."

"Then please decree that whichever of my sons agrees will become the next king."

"So be it. And he will also gain long life, great renown, and many children."

* * *

The aged Yayati returned to his capital. Sometime later, when Yayati's children had become young men, he one day summoned Yadu, his oldest. He asked him to surrender his youth to him for a thousand years in exchange for Yayati's decrepitude. But Yadu replied, "Father, when one is old, there are many difficulties in drinking and eating. Other effects are white hair, wrinkles, moroseness, laziness, deformities, weak limbs, thinness, incapacity to work, and defeat by friends and comrades. For these reasons, I don't want your old age. But perhaps one of your other sons might be interested."

Displeased by Yadu's answer, Yayati exclaimed, "My son, you've sprung from my heart! Yet you won't offer me your youth. All right, if that's the way you feel, then none of your children will ever be kings!"

Yayati then asked his son Turvasu for his youth, but Turvasu also refused. Cursing him, Yayati said, "You wretch! You will become the leader of those whose practices and principles are unclean. Yes, you will be the king of those low caste men who produce children with high caste women, who eat meat, who are wicked, who enjoy with the wives of their superiors, who act like birds and beasts, and who are sinful and non-Aryan!"

Yayati next asked his son Drahyu for his youth, but he also refused, as he wanted to continue enjoying sense pleasures. Yayati exclaimed, "Oh? Well, if that's what you want, then rest assured your most cherished wishes will never be fulfilled! And you'll be king in name only of that area where there are no roads and no places to swim."

Then Yayati asked his son Anu for his youth, but Anu also refused for similar reasons. Yayati exclaimed, "You find so many faults in old age; therefore, old age will overcome you! Your children also, when they become youths, will die! And you will not be able to perform fire sacrifices!"

Finally, Yayati asked his youngest son, Puru, who humbly replied, "Father, I'll take your weakness and old age. You can have my youth and enjoy life's pleasures."

"Thank you, Puru. I'm very pleased with you. Thus the people in your kingdom will have all their desires fulfilled." He then transferred his old age to Puru's body and received Puru's youth. This made him extremely happy.

Yayati again began to indulge in his favorite activities as he fully desired. He did so to the limit of his powers and, according to the seasons, obtained the highest pleasure from them. However, he never acted contrary to the principles of religion. He offered sacrifices to the gods, foodstuffs to the ancestors, and charity to the poor. He gave food and drink to all persons worthy of hospitality, gave protection to the merchants and farmers, gave kindness to the lower caste laborers, and gave punishment to all criminals. Yayati gratified every one of his subjects. Enjoying whatever objects he desired, the king became exceedingly happy. The only time he was sad was when he thought about his youth ending at the expiration of the thousand years.

When the righteous king noted that the one thousand years had elapsed, he called his son Puru and said, "My son, I have fully enjoyed the pleasures of life. However, our desires are never satisfied by yielding to them. Rather, they only increase in intensity as does the sacrificial fire when clarified butter is poured on it. If a person owned everything on earth—rice, barley, silver, gold, gems, animals and women—he still would not be content. Thus, the thirst for worldly enjoyment, which is man's fatal disease, should be renounced. Of course, this is difficult for the sinful and the wicked. But only those who have done this can know real happiness.

"During the last thousand years, day after day, my thirst for material pleasure has increased. But now it's time for me to renounce it and fix my mind on the Supreme Lord. Therefore, I will now retire to the forest and pass my remaining days peacefully—with the innocent deer and without interest in worldly objects. Puru, I'm very pleased with you. May you be prosperous! Here, take back your youth. And also take my kingdom."

As Yayati regained his old age, Puru recovered his youth. The king now desired to install Puru, his youngest son, on the throne. However, the members of the four orders, with the Brahmins at their head, approached him, and one of them said, "King Yayati, why are you giving the throne to Puru? You're passing over your oldest son, Yadu, Devayani's child and Shukra's grandson. The next oldest is Turvasu, then Drahyu, then Anu, and *then* Puru. Why does your youngest son deserve the throne? This is not the proper practice."

Yayati replied, "O members of the four orders, please listen to why my kingdom should not be given to Yadu, my oldest son. It is said by the wise that a son who disobeys his father is no son at all. But the son who obeys his parents, who pursues their good, who is pleasing to them, is truly the best of sons. My sons Yadu, Turvasu, Drahyu, and Anu disobeyed me when I asked for their help. But Puru alone obeyed me and cared about me. Thus, Puru is my friend, and though he is the youngest, he should be my successor. Even Shukra decreed that the son of mine who would obey me would become my successor and bring the entire earth under his command. Therefore, I beg all of you to allow me to install Puru."

One of the persons there replied, "Yes, King, it's true—the son who has good qualities and pursues the good of his parents is worthy of prosperity, even if he be the youngest. Consequently, Puru, who has pursued the good, is worthy of the throne. And since Shukra himself ordered this, we have no further comment."

Yayati installed Puru on the throne. After performing the initiatory ceremonies for retiring to the forest, he left his capital, followed by the Brahmins and the monks.

Yadu's sons became known as the Yadus. Those of Turvasu became known as the Yavanas. The sons of Drahyu were called the Bhojas. The sons of Anu were referred to as the Mlechchas. And those of Puru were called the Pauravas, from whom came the Kauravas and the Pandavas.

The brothers began to clobber each other continuously.

CHAPTER TWELVE

SUNDA'S AND UPASUNDA'S FALL

Two powerful and inseparable brothers, because they lacked the detachment necessary to curb their lustful urges, became bitter enemies. Similarly, unless we learn how to discriminate and detach ourselves from our lower desires, they will darken our future and make wisdom and virtue almost impossible for us to attain.

L ong ago a powerful Daitya (demon) named Nikumbha was born in the mighty demon dynasty of the infamous Hiranyakashipu. He was blessed with tremendous vigor and power, and he produced two sons known as Sunda and Upasunda. They both had wicked hearts and cruel dispositions. Having the same determination, they were always absorbed in accomplishing the same work and aims. In joy or sorrow, they always shared with one another.

Speaking and doing what was pleasing to each other, the brothers never journeyed anywhere unless they were together. They had the same character and traits and appeared to be one person divided into two. Crowned with tremendous energy, the two brothers gradually matured physically.

They both harbored the same goal—to conquer the three worlds. After they were properly initiated, they journeyed to the Vindya Mountains and engaged in severe ascetic practices to acquire merit. They matted their hair, clad themselves in tree bark, and fasted from food and drink. They covered their entire bodies and heads with dirt, subsisted only on air, stood on their toes, and even flung portions of their flesh into the sacrificial fire. With their arms upraised and eyes steadfast, they practiced these austerities for a long period.

Seeing the harshness of their disciplines, the gods became frightened. They thus began to create many obstacles to hinder the brothers' success. Repeatedly, the gods tempted them with opulent goods and gorgeous women. But the brothers did not veer from their vows. The gods again endeavored to hinder them by creating the following illusion:

The sisters, mothers, wives, and other relatives of the demons hastened in panic towards them—their hair, adornments and robes in disarray—as a titan weilding a lance chased and struck them. The women begged the brothers, "Oh please, save us!" But all this came to naught, for the brothers remained fixed in their vows. Then the women and the titans disappeared from sight.

Finally, the grandsire, Lord Brahma himself, always looking after the welfare of everyone, appeared before those remarkable demons. He asked them to request the blessing they wanted.

The brothers, who were sitting, stood up. Each clasped his own palms and said, "O Lord Brahma, if you have been satisfied with our austerities and are favorable to us, then allow us to have knowledge of all armaments and of all powers of illusion. Grant us immense strength and the ability to assume any form we wish. And finally, permit us to also become immortal."

"You shall be granted all that you wish—except immortality. You have undertaken harsh ascetic practices only to attain lordship over the three worlds. Therefore, I cannot give you the blessing of immortality."

The brothers replied, "O Grandfather, then please enable us to be fearless of any moving or unmoving created being in the three worlds— except from each other, ourselves."

"So be it!"

The grandfather made them stop their austerities and then returned to his own realm.

After that, those powerful demons could not be killed by anyone in the universe. When they returned to their own kingdoms, all their friends and relatives, learning about the blessings they had won, became very pleased. Sunda and Upasunda then cut off their matted hair and wore crowns on their heads. Wearing expensive robes and adornments, they appeared extremely attractive. They forced the moon to rise, out of season, over their city every night.

Their friends and relatives indulged themselves in fun with joyful hearts. In every house, all that could be heard every day were the sounds of eating, feeding, giving, laughing, singing and drinking. In various quarters there were tumultuous outbursts of mirth mixed with applause. The people, absorbed in every type of entertainment and game, were hardly aware of the passage of time.

When the celebrations ended, Sunda and Upasunda, yearning for lordship over the three worlds, sought counsel and ordered their troops to be marshalled. After they had secured the approval of their friends, relatives, ministers and elders, and had performed the preparatory rites of departure, they went forth at night when the constellation Magha was in the ascendant. With joyous hearts they left with a huge demon force, which was decked in armor and outfitted with maces, axes, lances and clubs. As they departed, the poets chanted auspicious songs of praise signifying future victories.

These demon brothers, who could travel anywhere at will, soared into the sky and went to the heavenly region. The gods, who were aware of the boons Lord Brahma had granted them and who knew that the brothers were coming, departed from heaven and looked for shelter on Brahma's planet. The two demons soon conquered Lord Indra's heavenly planet, the various Yaksha and Rakshasa tribes, as well as every being who flew in the sky.

After leaving, the brothers conquered the Nagas, or snake people, of the nether region, then the ocean inhabitants, and then all the barbarian tribes. They next wanted to conquer the entire earth; therefore, on the eastern shore of the great ocean, they called together their soldiers and declared, "Brahmins are our enemies! By their sacrificial food and water offerings, they enhance the vigor and strength of the gods. Therefore, all of us, working together, must totally eradicate them from the earth!"

Harboring this malicious resolution, the brothers went forth in all directions. They immediately and violently slayed the Brahmins who were executing those sacrifices, as well as their assistants, and then left for some other spot. Their soldiers entered the sanctuaries of the self-controlled sages and threw their sacrificial fires into the waters. And though the sages angrily cursed them, their curses were frustrated by the blessings that Brahma had bestowed on the brothers. When the sages noted this, they abandoned their rites and vows and fled in all directions. Even the sages who had achieved success in asceticism and whose desires were completely under control—those masters who were fully absorbed in meditation on the Deity—ran away, as snakes do at the approach of Lord Vishnu's carrier, Garuda.

Next, the soldiers demolished the holy ashrams and sacrificial jars and containers, their contents strewn all over the ground. The entire universe became vacant and appeared as though all its creatures had been annihilated during the designated period of general dissolution.

After all the sages had left and concealed themselves, the two demons began to assume, at will, different kinds of bodies. Appearing as crazed elephants, the demons hunted for the sages, who had hidden themselves in caves, and then killed them. Sometimes the demons would appear as lions or tigers, or would become invisible and, upon seeing the sages, would immediately slay them.

Thus, the Brahmins and kings were annhilated, and all study, sacrifices, rites, ceremonies, marriages, festivals, and trade ceased. Agriculture was disregarded and the cows were no longer cared for. Towns and hermitages became deserted. The earth, with bones and skeletons strewn all over it, assumed a horrifying appearance. Indeed, it became dreadful to look at. After the brothers had conquered all the heavenly planets and had eliminated all their rivals, they began living in the city of Kurukshetra.

The residents of the sun, moon, other planets, stars and constellations, beholding Sunda's and Upasunda's malicious acts of universal slaughter, became deeply aggrieved. The celestial sages and yogis, ever peaceful and self-restrained, felt compassion for the universe and went to Lord Brahma's planet for advice.

There, they saw the grandfather seated with the gods, yogis, and sages around him, including Mahadeva, Agni, Vayu, Soma, Surya, Shakra and others. The visiting sages mournfully told Brahma in detail exactly what the two demons had done, how they had done it, and in what order. All the celestials and illustrious sages then pressed the subject before Brahma. After deliberating for a moment, the grandsire concluded in his mind what had to be done to reverse the situation. He therefore summoned Vishwakarma, the celestial architect. When Vishwakarma arrived, Lord Brahma said, "I want you to create a young woman who is able to conquer anyone's heart."

After bowing down with respect to Brahma, Vishwakarma, that celebrated craftsman of the universe, created a celestial damsel with painstaking application. She was almost a mass of gems, and in beauty she was incomparable among women in the three worlds. Even the slightest part of her body could compel persons to gaze at her. Like Shri, the goddess of fortune, she could conquer the hearts of all beings. Since she had been created from every kind of gem in minute amounts, Lord Brahma called her Tilottama. As soon as he awakened her consciousness, the maiden, with joined palms, bowed down to him and said, "O creator of the universe, what do you want me to achieve, and for what reason have I been created?"

Brahma instructed her accordingly.

Offering obeisance to the grandsire, she replied, "It shall be done."

Then she proceeded to circumambulate the eminent members of the assembly. Brahma and Mahadeva were sitting and facing the east, the other gods were facing the north, and the sages were facing in all directions.

As Tilottama circled the assembly, only Indra and Mahadeva managed to retain their mental tranquility. However, as she neared Mahadeva, he became so eager to see her that he instantly materialized another head on the southern side of his body; when she was behind him, he created a head on the western side; and when she reached the northern side, he fashioned a fourth head. Thus, he came to have a thousand large, slightly reddish eyes in front, behind, and on all sides.

As Tilottama circled about, all the sages and the other gods, except Lord Brahma, gazed at her in all directions. Therefore, as the lovely damsel left, all of them felt that her task was virtually accomplished. The grandsire then adjourned the meeting and the celestials and sages departed.

* * *

The two demon brothers, having conquered the three worlds, were now unrivalled. Free of the fatigue of exertion, they considered themselves as persons who had nothing more to do. They had plundered all the wealth of the gods, celestials, demons, titans, and saintly kings, and began to spend their days in great joy. Finding no rivals anywhere, they gave up all striving and, like the celestials, devoted their time to sensual pleasure and fun. They experienced great enjoyment by yielding to such pleasures as lust, perfumes, garlands, food, drink, and other delights in quantity. They did this in houses, woods, gardens, and on hills—wherever they wished.

One day, for the purpose of enjoying themselves, the brothers went to a plateau of the Vindhya mountains. It was perfectly even and stony, and overgrown with flowering trees. Having brought for their enjoyment the most beautiful women, the demons, with joyful hearts, sat on a fine seat. Wanting to please the brothers, those women, accompanied by music, began to dance and sing sweetly many songs of praise to them.

Then Tilottama came strolling along. She was dressed in a red silk gown that revealed all her beauty. Picking wild flowers, she slowly proceeded to the spot where the brothers were. The demons were intoxicated from drink, and upon seeing that exceedingly beautiful woman, they were overwhelmed. Both of them left their seats and hastened to the maiden. Smitten with lust, each of them wanted her for himself. They were drunk with power, wealth, treasure and wine. Crazy from all these and driven by passion, they spoke angrily to each other.

Sunda grabbed Tilottama's right hand and Upasunda, her left. Then Sunda angrily said to his brother, "She's my wife and thus your superior!"

Upasunda replied, "No, she's my wife and thus your sister-in-law!"

For a while, each continued bellowing, "She's mine and not yours!" till both were overcome with rage. Maddened by Tilottama's loveliness, they soon forgot their fondness for each other. Once their reason disappeared, they clutched at their deadly maces and cried out, "I was the first to catch her hand!"

"No, I was!"

"No you weren't. I was!"

"Get away from her!

"No, you get away!"

The brothers then began to clobber each other continuously until finally, their bodies soaked with blood, they dropped to the ground, dead.

Seeing this, the women and the other demons who had accompanied them there became filled with fear and grief. Consequently, they hastened away and took refuge in the subterranean regions.

Lord Brahma, the celestials, and the great sages then arrived where the dead brothers lay. The grandsire congratulated Tilottama. Bestowing a boon on her, he cheerfully said, "Lovely maiden, you shall wander through the highest region of heaven. Your brilliance will be so great that no one shall ever be able to gaze at you for any length of time."

Brahma then reestablished the three worlds under Indra's rule and returned to his own realm.

* * *

Thus we can see that if we are controlled by lust, our power, no matter how prodigious it may be, can easily be lost.

Four fierce-looking Rakshasas suddenly appeared and moved towards the king to kill him.

CHAPTER THIRTEEN

RESPECTING THE BRAHMINS

When the haughty King Sala disrespected a Brahmin by callously appropriating the holy man's horses, the consequences were disastrous for him. Thus, we should be especially respectful to holy persons and their property, for this will help us gain their favor and blessings, which is one of the best means of achieving wisdom and virtue.

King Parikshit ruled over the state of Ayodhya and belonged to the Ikshvaku dynasty. One day the monarch went out hunting alone and, as he rode his horse and pursued a deer, the animal led him far away from where people lived. He became fatigued, hungry, and thirsty from the long ride. Seeing a dark, dense forest, the king entered it. Soon he beheld an enchanting pond, and he and his horse bathed in it. Refreshed by the water, he placed some lotus stalks and fibers before his horse, and reclined at the side of the pond.

He began to hear sweet music and thought, "I don't see any footprints of people here. Who is playing the music and from where is it coming?" Then the king saw a young woman of exquisite beauty gathering flowers and singing. As she approached him, he asked, "Who are you and who is your father?"

She replied, "I'm a maiden."

Overwhelmed by her beauty, he exclaimed, "I'd like to marry you!"

"Oh? Well, first you must promise me something."

"Yes, certainly. But what?"

"That you'll never make me look at water."

"Water? All right. I promise."

King Parikshit married her, delightedly sported with her there, then sat quietly with her.

A while later, the king's troops arrived and, seeing him, gathered around him. Heartened by their company, the king, with his new wife, entered a beautiful conveyance that took them to the capital. There he

161

began to dwell with her in seclusion. Even persons who were close to the king could not speak to him.

Then one day the chief minister asked the women attending to the king's needs, "What do you do here?"

One of them said, "We see a matchlessly beautiful woman. And the king just plays with her. When he married her, he promised he would never show her water."

After that, the chief minister had an artificial forest made, abounding with trees, flowers and fruits. He also had a pond dug in a lonely area and filled it with nectar-sweet water. Then he had the pond overlaid with a net of pearls.

One day the chief minister approached the king in private and said, "I've found a wonderful forest that has no water. You can sport merrily in it."

The king, with his lovely wife, entered that enjoyable forest and played with her. After a while, he became hungry, thirsty, fatigued and exhausted. Seeing a shaded, leafy recess of madhavi creepers, he and his beloved entered it. There, the king saw a clear, shining pond. Forgetting his earlier promise to his wife, he escorted her to it, and they both sat down on its bank. Then he suggested, "Why don't you take a refreshing dip?"

Agreeing, she jumped in, went under the water, but never came up.

When the king tried to find her, he was unsuccessful. Therefore, he ordered his men to bail the pond. After they did, he saw a frog in it sitting at the entrance of a hole. Thinking that some frogs had eaten his wife, the king became furious. He issued a proclamation that all frogs in his country should be killed; and that anyone who wanted to speak with him would have to offer him as tribute some dead frogs.

Because frogs in great numbers were horribly slain, the frogs informed their leader. He in turn materialized a human form and, in the guise of an ascetic, approached the king. He said, "Don't yield to anger. Rather, be merciful. Don't kill innocent frogs. A soul sunk in ignorance loses his prosperity and ascetic merit. Why should you perpetrate such evil? What end can you serve by it?"

Overwhelmed with grief due to the death of his beloved, King Parikshit declared, "No, I will not forgive the frogs. Instead, I will destroy them! Those wicked creatures have devoured my beloved. They deserve to be killed. Therefore, don't interfere!"

Pained, the king of the frogs, replied, "Your Highness, please be merciful. I'm king of the frogs and my name is Ayu. The woman who was your wife is my daughter, and her name is Susobhana. What she has done, without a doubt, is an example of bad behavior. Previously, she also deceived other kings."

"But I want her back! Please give her to me."

The king of frogs then granted his daughter to King Parikshit and said to her, "You must now wait upon and serve the king." Then he angrily added, "You've deceived numerous kings, so for this untruthful conduct, your children will be disrespectful to the Brahmins!"

Because of her companionable qualities, the king was deeply in love with her and felt he had gained rulership over the three worlds. He offered obeisances to the king of frogs and, in a voice choked with joy and tears, said, "Indeed, I've been blessed!" The king of frogs said goodbye to his daughter and returned home.

***

After some time, King Parikshit produced three sons from her. Their names were Shala, Dala, and Vala. Years later, the king installed his oldest, Shala, on the throne and retired to the forest to practice asceticism and achieve Divine realization.

One day Shala went out hunting on his chariot. Seeing a deer, he shot an arrow into it, but the deer raced away. The king turned to his charioteer. "After it—fast!"

"You can't catch it," replied the charioteer. "But if you had Vami horses, you could."

"Vami horses? Tell me what you know about Vami horses—or I'll kill you!"

Afraid of the king, the charioteer became alarmed. But he was also afraid of being cursed by the owner of those horses, the sage Vamadeva. He thus remained silent.

The king raised his sword and exclaimed, "Tell me—or else!"

The charioteer was very frightened and shuddered, "The Vami horses belong to— to the sage Vamadeva. They—they're as fast as the mind."

"Oh? Then drive me to Vamadeva's retreat!"

The charioteer drove him there, and the king said to Vamadeva, "I shot an arrow into a deer, but it escaped. I'd appreciate if you'd give me your two Vami horses so I can catch it."

"All right. But as soon as you do, I'll expect you to return them."

The king took the horses, yoked them to his chariot, obtained leave of the sage, and went looking for the deer. He said to his charioteer, "These are gems of horses. Brahmins don't deserve to have them. Therefore, don't return them to Vamadeva."

Soon the king saw the deer, pursued it, and easily captured it. Later, he returned to his capital and housed the Vami horses in the inner apartments of his palace.

In the meantime the sage mused, "I loaned the prince my fine horses and he's joyfully sporting with them. But he was supposed to return them to me. What a shame. It's because he's still young."

After one month had passed, Vamadeva said to one of his disciples, "Atreya, go to the king and tell him that if he's finished using my horses, he should return them to me."

Atreya did as he was told, but the king replied, "These two horses deserve to belong only to kings. Brahmins should not own such valuable gems. Why does a Brahmin need horses like these? Go and return to your ashram peacefully."

When Atreya returned to the hermitage and related everything to Vamadeva, the sage became angry. He thus personally went to the king and demanded, "Give me back my horses!"

But the king refused.

"I said give me back my Vami horses! They helped you accomplish your purpose, which you couldn't have done otherwise. You're violating an ethical principle and thus exposing yourself to the punishing noose of Varuna or death."

"But four of the best asses or mules can carry you, or even four fast horses. Why not take them? These two Vami horses should belong to warriors. You really have no right to them."

Vamadeva was provoked by these words and exclaimed, "If I have observed all my Brahminical vows, then, at my command, may four ferocious and powerful Rakshasas—with frightening bearing and iron bodies—appear. Then, let them pursue you, cut your body into four parts, and carry you on their sharp lances!"

The king insolently replied, "No, may they, at my command, make you and your disciples lie down before me."

"When I loaned you my Vami horses, you said you would return them. You should thus give them back to safeguard your life."

"But you don't need these horses, since it's not ordained for Brahmins to pursue deer. I will therefore punish you for violating the ordinance."

Vamadeva retorted, "A Brahmin cannot be punished in thought, word or deed. One who realizes this by ascetic discipline attains renown in this world."

At that moment, four fierce-looking Rakshasas suddenly appeared. Carrying lances, they moved towards the king to kill him.

The king shouted, "No, I'll never give you back the Vami horses!"

One moment later, the king lay dead on the ground.

When the Ikshvaku citizens discovered that their king had been killed, they installed Dala on the throne. Vamadeva traveled to and approached the new king, and said, "All the holy scriptures say that persons should make offerings to the Brahmins. If you are afraid of sin, then return my Vami horses to me now!"

This angered the king and he exclaimed to his charioteer, "Quick, bring me a poisoned arrow so that I can pierce Vamadeva with it. Then I'll watch him lie on the ground in pain and be torn apart by the dogs!"

The charioteer handed him the arrow and the king strung it to his bow.

Vamadeva replied, "I know you have a ten year old son named Senajita. Instead, I order you to immediately shoot the arrow at him!"

Helplessly, the king shot the arrow. It traveled to the inner apartments and killed the prince. As soon as the king learned of this, he angrily declared to his comrades, "Members of the Ikshvaku race, I will now benefit all of you by killing this Brahmin!" He turned to his charioteer. "Bring me another poisoned arrow." After he received it, he again turned to his comrades and said, "You lords of the earth, just see my power!"

Vamadeva answered, "You will not be able to aim or even shoot it at me."

As the king tried to aim the arrow, he found himself incapacitated. Amazed, he said to his friends, "I—I can't aim this arrow and kill the Brahmin." Realizing his foolishness, he added, "May Vamadeva, who is blessed with a long life, remain alive!"

Vamadeva then advised him, "Take this poisoned arrow and touch your queen with it. In this way, you can purify yourself of the sin of trying to kill a Brahmin."

After the king followed the sage's instructions, the queen begged, "Vamadeva, please allow me to teach my pathetic husband, from day to day, about what brings true happiness. May I always serve the Brahmins and, by such service, attain the holy regions after death."

Vamadeva replied, "Queen, you have saved this noble dynasty. Therefore, beg from me a blessing. Whatever you ask, I shall grant. And you should rule over your family and the glorious Ikshvaku kingdom."

The princess begged, "I ask that my husband now be freed from his sin and that you may be engaged in thinking of the welfare of his son and relatives."

"Granted!"

King Dala then became very happy and, after bowing down to the sage, returned the Vami horses to him.

***

Thus we can see that arrogance towards holy persons begets self-destruction, whereas humility towards them begets blessings.

"When a husband discovers his wife is habituated to drugs and incantations, he fears her as if she were a snake hidden in his bedroom."

CHAPTER FOURTEEN

DRAUPADI ADVISES SATYABHAMA

Queen Draupadi explained to Queen Satyabhama that by her being extremely diligent in her services to her powerful husbands, she was able to win their hearts completely. Similarly, if we perform our various services diligently, we will attract the grace of the Divine, whose blessings are invaluable for attaining wisdom and virtue.

The Pandava princes and their wife Draupadi had been exiled from their kingdom and were now living in the forest. One day Lord Krishna and His wife Satyabhama chanced to visit them. Draupadi and Satyabhama went into the ashram and, with joyful hearts, laughed blithely and sat down relaxedly. For a long time they had not seen each other. They always spoke pleasantly to one another, and now they began to discuss subjects that arose from stories about the Kuru and Yadu dynasties.

Satyabhama asked, "Draupadi, I know that you're able to rule your husbands, who are as strong and handsome as the chief gods. But why are they so obedient to you and never upset by you? Is it due to your fulfilling vows, performing austerities, reciting incantations, or taking drugs? Or is it due to your gaining scientific knowledge, having a youthful appearance, reciting specific affirmations, executing ceremonies or applying make-up? Please explain what you're doing so I may get Krishna to always obey me also."

"Satyabhama, you're asking me about the practices of evil women. It's improper for you to imagine that I would ever use such means, since you are intelligent and a favorite of Krishna. When a husband discovers his wife is habituated to drugs and incantations, he fears her as if she were a snake hidden in his bedroom. If a man is afraid, can he have tranquillity? And without tranquillity, how can he be happy? A wife can never make her husband obedient by reciting incantations.

"We know that enemies can transmit painful diseases by various means. For example, if an enemy sends a gift laced with poison, the person who tastes or touches it may quickly die. At times women have caused their husbands to develop dropsy, leprosy, weakness, impotence, blindness, and deafness. This is the path of sin, for a wife should never cause even the slightest harm to her husband.

"The eternal virtue for a woman is based on her concern for her husband. The husband is the wife's god, or master, and her shelter; truly, she has no other refuge. Why, then, should she hurt her husband in even the slightest degree? Whether I'm sleeping, eating or ornamenting myself, I never act against the will of my husbands. Always directed by them, I never speak badly about my mother-in-law."

After Draupadi paused for a few seconds, Satyabhama asked, "Is that all?"

"No, there are also other things—such as the way I act towards my exalted husbands. For example, I lay aside my vanity, restrain my desire and anger, and always wait on them and their other wives with devotion. I control my jealousy and, with love in my heart and without feeling humiliated by the work I do, I serve my husbands. I'm afraid to say what is wicked or untrue, or to look or sit or walk improperly, or to glance at them in a way that reveals the feelings of my heart. My husbands are powerful fighters, effulgent like the sun or fire, attractive as the moon, endowed with terrible might and valor, and able to kill their enemies by merely glancing at them.

"My heart is not disposed to any other male, be he human, celestial, Gandharva, young, ornamented, wealthy, or handsome. I never bathe, eat, or sleep till my husbands and our servants have. Whenever my husbands return from the field, woods or town, I immediately get up and offer them my respects by providing them with water and a seat. I always maintain the house, household articles, and food to be eaten in a neat, clean way. I store the rice carefully and serve the food at the right time. I never speak in a wrathful and annoying way, and never imitate sinful women. Nor do I ever laugh except at a joke, and I don't remain long at the house gate. I never spend much time when answering nature's calls or when in the pleasure garden beside the house. I always abstain from laughing loudly, from yielding to intense passion, and from anything that might be unpleasant.

"I'm always busy serving my husbands, and I never desire to be away from them. When my husbands leave home to visit some relative, in their absence I don't wear any kind of flowers or scented paste, and I practice austerities. Whatever my husbands don't drink, eat, or enjoy, I also don't. I always seek the good of my husbands and always wear ornaments and follow instructions. Day and night, without the slightest idleness, I always discharge those obligations of which my mother-in-law informed me, namely, those regarding relatives, charity, worshiping the gods, offerings to the ill, boiling food to offer to the ancestors and respectable guests on favorable days, and service to those who merit our concern. With humility and under accepted regulations, I attend to my modest, truthful, ever virtuous husbands, as if they were poisonous snakes that could easily be agitated.

"My dear Satyabhama, as a result of my diligence, enthusiasm and humility to superiors, my husbands have become obedient to me. Every day I personally wait on their honorable and truthful mother, Kunti, with food, drink, and clothes. I never show partiality to myself over her in respect to food and dress, and I never criticize her adversely, for she is the earth's equal in forgiveness.

"In the past, eight thousand Brahmins dined daily on golden plates in Yudhishthira's palace. And Yudhishthira entertained eighty thousand household Brahmins, assigning thirty serving girls to each. In addition to these, pure food was carried on golden plates to ten thousand celibate swamis. I used to properly worship with food, drink and clothes all those Brahmins who recited the Vedas. Yudhishthira had a hundred thousand nicely clothed serving girls who wore bracelets, golden necklaces, expensive garlands, sandal paste, gold, and jewels—and all were adept in singing and dancing. Satyabhama, I knew the names and features of every one of those girls, as well as what they did, what they had done, and what they did not do.

"Further, Yudhishthira also had one-hundred-thousand maidservants who fed guests on golden plates. While Yudhishthira dwelled in Indraprastha, one-hundred-thousand horses and one-hundred-thousand-elephants followed him. When he reigned over the earth, those were his assets. However, I was the one who regulated the amount of them and who drew up the rules to be followed regarding them; I was also the one who had to hear all the grievances about them. Yes, I was aware of what everyone did or didn't do, whether they were palace maidservants, other classes of servants, or even cowherds and shepherds of the royal household.

"Between my husbands and me, I alone knew the king's income and expenses and what his entire wealth consisted of. Moreover, my husbands gave me the responsibility of feeding all those whom they were expected to care for. Day and night, sacrificing my comfort, I bore this heavy burden—which could not be borne by evil-hearted persons—and remained lovingly devoted to my husbands. As my spouses were employed in the pursuit of righteousness, I, alone, supervised their treasury, which was always filled, like the vessel of Varuna. I served my husbands day and night, bearing hunger and thirst; thus, my days and nights were the same to me. I was the first to wake up and the last to retire.

"Everything I've just mentioned, Satyabhama, has always been my charm for making my husbands submissive to me, and I've always known this art. But I've never employed the wiles of evil women, nor do I ever desire to employ them."

Satyabhama bowed her head to Draupadi and said, "Princess, kindly forgive me for imputing such to you. But we were talking lightly, and I did not first consider what I said."

"No offense taken. But let me tell you how to attract your husband's heart in an undeceitful way. By doing such, my friend, you'll be able to draw your husband away from other women. Understand that in all the worlds, including that of the gods, for a wife there is no god equal to her husband. When he's satisfied with you, he'll grant your every wish; but when he's wrathful, you may lose what you've gained.

"The wife obtains children and different objects of pleasure from her husband. You can obtain from your husband delightful beds, seats, robes, garlands, perfumes, fame, and the Divine world itself. But one cannot achieve happiness here by easy means. Rather, the woman who is chaste obtains happiness from bearing trials. Therefore, always worship your husband Krishna with friendship, and delight in suffering physically for Him.

"Offer your husband beautiful seats, lovely garlands, different fragrances, and quick service, that he may feel you truly love him and thus become devoted to you. When you hear your husband's voice at the door, get up from your chair and stand ready to greet him. As soon as he enters the room, show your respect by immediately offering him a seat and a foot bath. Even if he orders a serving girl to do something, you get up and do it yourself. Allow Krishna to know this mood of your mind and to know that you worship Him with your whole heart.

"If your husband says something to you, even if it doesn't deserve to be kept secret, don't babble about it to your co-wives; for if they talk about it to Krishna, He might become annoyed with you.

"By every means at your disposal, you should feed those who are dear and devoted to your husband, and always strive for His happiness. Stay away from those who are inimical and opposed to your husband, as well as from those who want to hurt Him or are habituated to dishonesty. In front of men, give up all playfulness and casualness, and hide your impulses by keeping silence. And you should not remain or speak in private even with your sons or your co-wives' sons.

"Further, you should associate with only those women who are nobly born and pure, and avoid those who are grouchy, addicted to intoxicating drinks, gluttonous, larcenous, sinful, and whimsical. By acting virtuously, you'll be respectable and attain good fortune; such conduct is capable of negating animosity and also leads one to the higher spiritual world. Therefore, adorn yourself in expensive garlands and ornaments, anoint yourself with ointments and superb fragrances, and revere your husband."

***

Although Princess Draupadi's standard of a wife's duty may be exceedingly high for today's woman, it nonetheless should serve as a helpful ideal to aspire for in the pursuit of wisdom and virtue.

Shakuni grabbed the dice and threw them. When he saw what appeared, he said, "I win!"

CHAPTER FIFTEEN

THE DEADLY DICE GAME

Although King Yudhishthira was generally self-controlled, he once yielded to a weakness that ultimately resulted in a colossal tragedy. Unless we develop self-control, we may be irresistibly tempted to engage in self-destructive activities, which can significantly harm whatever wisdom and virtue we have acquired.

After King Yudhishthira performed a great sacrifice at his capital city, Indraprastha, he was recognized by all the invited monarchs of the world as the emperor. In tribute, the kings lavished upon him numerous gifts of great value. His cousin, the envious Prince Duryodhana, was amazed by the magnificent assembly hall there and began thinking about it. With his uncle Shakuni, he studied the entire building and saw in it many heavenly designs—designs which he had never before seen in his own city, Hastinapura.

One day the prince circled the hall and encountered a crystal surface. However, mistaking it for a pool of water, he drew up his pants. But as soon as he realized his mistake, he felt like a fool. Then, mistaking a lake with crystal petals in it for land, he fell into the water with his clothes on.

Seeing this, the mighty Pandavas—Bhima, Arjuna, Nakula, and Sahadeva—along with many servants, laughed loudly. Then the servants quickly brought Duryodhana some dry, attractive clothing.

Unaccustomed to tolerating insults, Duryodhana could not bear his cousins' laughter. However, he hid his feelings and did not even glance at them.

When the Pandavas again saw Duryodhana lift up his pants to cross a section of dry land which he mistook for water, they again laughed loudly.

Later, Duryodhana mistook a crystal door to be open when it was actually closed. As he tried to pass through it, he accidentally banged

173

his head, causing his brain to reel. Next, the prince mistook a crystal door to be closed that was actually open. As he stretched out his hand to open it, he lurched forward and fell over. Then he came upon another door that was actually open but which he thought was closed. Therefore, he walked away from it.

After awhile the prince said goodbye to the Pandavas and set out to return to Hastinapura. He could not forget the vast wealth the Pandavas had collected in the Rajasuya sacrifice or the many miscalculations he had made in his wanderings through their assembly hall. These made him burn with envy and vengeance.

Duryodhana recalled how happy the Pandavas were; how all the visiting kings had paid their respects to them; how everyone—young and old—had served them well; and how the Pandavas had become so prosperous and resplendent. These memories made Duryodhana grow pale.

During the journey, Duryodhana was so obsessed with these recollections that he didn't speak a word to Shakuni—even though his uncle spoke to him frequently. After a while, noticing that his nephew had become absent-minded, Shakuni said, "Duryodhana, why are you acting like this?"

"Why? Because Yudhishthira—with his brother Arjuna's help—is now the ruler of the world! And because he performed a Rajasuya sacrifice that was as glorious as those performed by Lord Indra, king of the gods. Thus, I'm filled with envy, and my heart burns day and night.

"I feel as dried as an empty pond in the summer. Therefore, I will throw myself into a fire or poison myself or drown myself. I can't go on living. What man in the world is so strong that he can bear to see his enemies enjoy prosperity and himself suffer poverty? Seeing their command over the world and their immense wealth, along with that wonderful sacrifice, who would not burn up?

"By myself, I can't amass such royal opulence. Nor do I have any allies who could help me. Because of this, I am bent on killing myself. I consider fate to be supreme and all endeavors useless.

"In the past, I tried to destroy Yudhishthira. But he repulsed all my efforts and has grown wealthy—the way a lotus grows in the water. Just see, day by day, Dhritarashtra's sons are waning while Pandu's are waxing. For all these reasons, I'm very sad and filled with envy. Please speak to my father about this."

"Duryodhana," said Shakuni, "you shouldn't be envious of Yudhishthira. Pandu's sons are enjoying the good fortune they earned.

You devised countless plans to kill them—even made some attempts— but couldn't succeed. Those tigerlike men evaded all your intrigues.

"For their wife, they've obtained Draupadi, and for their allies, they've gained King Drupada, his sons, and the glorious Krishna—all capable of conquering the world. The Pandavas have grown as a result of their own exertions. Why should this make you sad? When Arjuna satisfied Agni, the fire god, Agni rewarded him with the bow Gandiva, two inexhaustible quivers, and many heavenly weapons. With that extraordinary bow and by the power of his own arms, he brought all the kings of the world under his control. And when Arjuna saved the demon Maya from a big fire, Maya, as a reward, built him that marvelous assembly hall. Why does that make you sad?

"You said you have no allies. But that's false. Your many brothers obey you. Drona, his son, Karna, Kripa, King Saumadatti, my brothers, and I—we're all your allies. Unite with us and you'll defeat the whole world."

Duryodhana said, "With you and those great fighters, I will conquer the Pandavas. If I can defeat them, then the whole world, all the kings, and that opulent assembly hall will be mine."

Shakuni replied, "Even the demigods can't conquer in battle Arjuna, Krishna, Bhima, Yudhishthira, Nakula, Sahadeva, and Drupada and his sons. They're all powerful fighters who wield the largest bows, are expert in weaponry, and enjoy combat. But I know a means to defeat Yudhishthira. Listen to me and then use it."

"If there is no danger to our friends and other famous men, tell me how."

"Yudhishthira likes to play dice, but he doesn't play very well. If he's asked to play, he's unable to resist. I'm an expert at dice. No one on earth or in the three worlds is equal to me. Just ask him to play. And I'll win his kingdom and his wealth for you. But Duryodhana, first tell your father about this. If he orders me, I will do it."

"Uncle Shakuni, it will be better if you tell my father. I will not be able to."

Shakuni and Duryodhana entered Dhritarashtra's chamber and found him seated on his throne. Shakuni said, "Duryodhana has become pale, thin, dejected, and anxious. Why don't you ask him why?"

Dhritarashtra inquired, "Duryodhana, why are you so depressed? If it's all right for me to hear, then tell me. Why should you be sad? My vast wealth is at your command. Your brothers and your relatives never do anything that's disturbing to you. You wear the best clothes and eat the best food prepared with meat. You have the best horse. You have expensive beds, beautiful women, excellently furnished palaces, and delightful pleasures. All of them await your command—just as they do for the gods. Therefore, why are you so sad, as if you were poor?"

"Since I've seen Yudhishthira's wealth, none of my pleasures bring me any satisfaction. Rather, his wealth makes me pale and I realize how poor I am. Though his wealth isn't before me, yet I see it. That's why I've become dejected and thin, I've got a burning heart, and I've lost my peace of mind."

Shakuni said, "Prince, I'm an expert at dice and the best in the world. In this game, I have special power. Before I throw the dice, I know exactly what numbers will come up. I know when and when not to bet. Yudhishthira enjoys playing dice, though he has little ability. If he's challenged, he will certainly accept, and I'll beat him at every throw. I guarantee I'll win all his wealth, and you, Duryodhana, will enjoy it."

Dhritarashtra said, "I always follow the advice of my chief counselor, Vidura. He has great wisdom. After I consult him, I'll let you know my decision."

"But he'll advise you against this, said Duryodhana. "And if you follow that advice, I'll surely commit suicide. When I am dead, you can be happy with Vidura and the entire earth."

Dhritarashtra went with Duryodhana in private and said, "My son, give up the idea of playing dice. Vidura doesn't speak favorably of it. What he says is highly beneficial for us. Dice games create conflicts and conflicts destroy a kingdom. You've received position and properties. You've been schooled and are smart in all fields of learning. You have been raised with love in your father's house. And you've gotten the very best of food and clothing. Why do you still sorrow?"

"Why? Father, my prosperity doesn't please me. For when I see Yudhishthira's prosperity, I'm greatly aggrieved." Then he spoke about his embarrassing miscalculations at the assembly hall and the laughter these evoked from the Pandavas. "If I could, I would have instantly killed them and Draupadi right there. Their insults make me burn."

Duryodhana described the expensive articles the kings gave Yudhishthira at the sacrifice: Skins, woolen blankets, fur, cat hair inlaid with golden threads, horses, elephants, donkeys, Brahmans, clarified butter, serving girls, swords, scimitars, hatchets, battle-axes, arrows, gold, silver, ivory, clothes, chariots, and many other things.

"When I saw all those things, I wanted to die. Even with the help of discrimination, I can't enjoy peace. That's why I've become depressed, pale, and thin."

"Don't be envious," advised Dhritarashtra. "An envious man is always miserable and suffers the pangs of death. Yudhishthira is undeceptive, has as much wealth as you, has the same friends as you, but is not envious of you. Then why should you be envious of him?

"If you desire the prestige of performing a sacrifice, our priests can arrange the great one called *Sapatantu*. Then all the kings will respectfully and cheerfully bring you much wealth, jewels and adornments. My child, to desire another's property is very base. On the other hand, to be satisfied with one's own activities produces happiness.

Duryodhana replied, "You know everything, yet you confuse me. As one boat is fastened to another, you and I are tied together. Don't you know what your own interests are? Or do you harbor hateful feelings towards me? All your sons and allies will be destroyed as long as they have you as their king. You should not confuse us, since we are ready to pursue our own interests. Kings should always focus with vigilance on their interests. The only criterion that should guide us is the attainment of success.

"Discontent is the root of wealth, therefore I wish to be discontented. Just as a snake swallows frogs and other creatures, the earth swallows up a king who is tranquil. I desire the Pandavas' wealth. Presently, I'm not sure of my ability to acquire it. But I'm resolved to settle my doubts. I'll either acquire their wealth or die in battle for it. In such a state of mind, why should I care about life?"

Shakuni said, "Duryodhana, by playing dice a skillful man may defeat an unskillful one."

Duryodhana said to Dhritarashtra, "Uncle Shakuni is very skillful at dice. He's ready to capture Yudhishthira's wealth by playing with him."

"Once I talk to Vidura," said Dhritarashtra, " I'll know what to do."

"Vidura always favors Pandu's sons," said Duryodhana. "He'll surely influence you against this idea."

Dhritarashtra replied, "You consider the dice game a great blessing, even though it's really filled with intrigue and will be followed by the horrible consequences of a war."

"Ancient men invented the game of dice," retorted Duryodhana. "There is no killing in it and no fighting with weapons. Therefore, accept Shakuni's offer and quickly order the construction of an assembly hall. By gambling, the door of heavenly happiness will open for us. Indeed, those who gamble with such help deserve such gain. The Pandavas will then become our equals instead of being our superiors. Therefore, let us gamble."

Dhritarashtra replied, "Your words don't appeal to me. But do what you like. You'll have to repent for such action. Words filled with wickedness can never bring future prosperity. Even the wise Vidura, always on the path of truth and wisdom, foresaw this. Destined by fate, the great war is inevitable."

Dhritarashtra was weak-minded. He considered fate as all-powerful and unpreventable. Deprived of his reason and following his son's advice, he loudly ordered his men, "Carefully and immediately erect the most beautiful assembly hall. It'll be called the Crystal-Arched Palace, will have a thousand columns, and will be adorned with gold and lapis lazuli. It'll have one hundred gates and will be two miles in length and in breadth."

Thousands of workers, skilled and intelligent, soon constructed the palace. They told the king it was completed, beautiful and enjoyable, bedecked with every kind of jewel and covered with many-hued carpets inlaid with gold. Then King Dhritarashtra called for Vidura and said, "Go to Indraprastha and bring Prince Yudhishthira and his brothers here as soon as possible. I would like them to see my gorgeous, jeweled assembly hall, and then engage in a cordial game of dice."

"King, I don't approve of this order. Please withdraw it. I fear it'll bring about the end of our dynasty. When Pandu's sons and your sons lose their unity, conflict will definitely ensue among them—all over a game of dice."

"If fate be friendly, this conflict will certainly not sadden me. The entire cosmos moves at the will of its Maker under the dominating authority of fate. It is not free. Therefore, Vidura, go to King Yudhishthira and quickly bring that invincible warrior here."

Against his own will, Vidura boarded his chariot and set out for the Pandavas' palace. His horses were spirited, fast and strong, and took him to King Yudhishthira's city quickly. There he entered the opulent palace and approached his nephew.

Yudhishthira was devoted to truth and had no enemies. He respectfully greeted his uncle and inquired about Dhritarashtra and his sons. Then he remarked, "Vidura, your mind seems to be morose. Have you come here in happiness and peace? I hope Dhritarashtra's sons are obedient to their aged father and that the citizens are also submissive to his rule."

"The king and his sons are well and happy. Surrounded by his kinsmen, he rules like Indra, the king of heaven. His sons are obedient and he has no anguish. But he's inclined towards his own glorification. He ordered me to ask you about your peace and prosperity, and to ask you and your brothers to come to Hastinapura; and, when you arrive, after you see the king's newly built palace, to ask you if it's equal to yours; and also, to invite you to a friendly game of dice. The Kurus have already arrived. There you'll see the gamblers and cheats King Dhritarashtra has invited. This is why I've come here. May you approve of the king's order."

"Uncle Vidura, if we compete at dice, we may argue. Knowing this, what man would agree to gamble? What do you think is proper for us? We'll follow your advice."

"I know that gambling is a cause of suffering, so I tried to discourage the king. Despite this, he dispatched me to you. Knowing all this, do what you think is useful."

"Besides Dhritarashtra's sons," asked Yudhishthira, "which cheating gamblers are there, ready to play? Who will we have to stake our wealth against?"

"Shakuni, the king of Gandhara—he's an expert at dice; also Vivingati, the king of Chitrasena, and Satyavrata, Purumitra, and Jaya."

"It appears that the most dreadful, deceitful gamblers are there. I don't want to gamble, and I don't intend to—unless Shakuni challenges me."

King Yudhishthira then ordered that preparations be made at once for his trip.

* * *

The next day the king set out for the Kuru capital with Vidura, his brothers, mother, relatives, priests, attendants, household women, and his queen, Draupadi. Blazing with royal splendor, he did not deliberate on Dhritarashtra's summons.

Having arrived in Hastinapura, Yudhishthira, with his brothers, went to the king's palace. He approached and embraced the king, as well as other Kuru personages.

Accompanied by his brothers, Yudhishthira entered King Dhritarashtra's apartment. He saw his aunt, the venerable and dutiful Queen Gandhari, surrounded by her daughters-in-law. He greeted her and she blessed him. The king, as a gesture of affection, smelled the heads of the five Pandavas. And all the Kurus, seeing them, became very happy.

The next morning the Pandavas were awakened by poets playing sweet music. After they finished their morning religious duties, they entered the assembly building and were greeted by the gambling-match spectators. The Pandavas, led by Yudhishthira, approached all the kings. They worshiped those who were deserving, greeted others respectfully according to age, and sat down on clean, costly seats.

Shakuni said to Yudhishthira, "Everyone is here and has been waiting for you. Let the dice be thrown and the rules of the game be established."

Yudhishthira replied, "Dishonest gambling is sinful. There's no warrior power or morality in it. Thus, don't try to defeat us dishonestly."

Shakuni answered, "Yudhishthira, it is from the motive to win—a not very honest motive—that one noble person approaches another to prove his family superiority. Also, it is from the motive to defeat—a not very honest motive—that one pundit approaches another to prove his knowledge superiority. But such motives are scarcely considered truly dishonest. Similarly, a skilled dice player approaches a less skilled one with a motive to defeat him. Now if you think I'm driven by dishonest motives, and if you're afraid to play with me, then don't play."

"Once I'm invited, I never refuse. This is my fixed vow. Who am I supposed to play with? Is there anyone here who can bet as much as I? If so, then let the game begin."

Duryodhana replied, "I'll supply jewels, gems and all kinds of wealth. And my uncle Shakuni will play for me."

"One person gambling for another seems to be against the rules. Don't you agree?"

"Yudhisthira, he's my nephew, the same family. What's the difference?"

"Well, if you insist on this arrangement, then let's play."

When the game began, all the kings there, led by Dhritarashtra, sat down. Bhishma, Drona, Kripa, and Vidura, their hearts despondent, sat behind them. Other kings sat separately and in pairs on high, beautifully made, gorgeously colored seats. The assembly looked magnificent—like a band of angels in heaven.

Yudhishthira said, "I stake these valuable pearls. They are covered with pure gold and were obtained by churning the ocean a long time ago. What will you stake?"

Duryodhana replied, "I possess much jewelry and great wealth. But I'm not proud of them. See if you can win them."

Shakuni then grabbed the dice and threw them. When he saw what appeared, he said, "I win!"

"You won my stake unfairly," said Yudhishthira. "But don't be so proud. I have many lovely jars and each one is filled with gold, silver, and other minerals. I now stake them."

Again the dice were cast. And Shakuni said to Yudhishthira, "See, I win."

Yudhishthira said, "I now stake my chariot—sacred, triumphant, and royal—that's drawn by eight white, noble horses."

The dice were thrown and Shakuni said, "Look, I have won."

Yudhishthira continued to lose. He lost thousands of servant women and men, elephants, chariots with horses and warriors, special horses, and jewels.

During the gambling, Vidura said to Dhritarashtra, "Listen to me. My words may be repugnant to you, as medicine is to one who's ill and about to die. When Duryodhana was born, he cried jarringly, like a jackal. It was well known then he had been predestined to cause the end of our Bharata dynasty. You should know that he will cause everyone's death. He's creating animosity with the Pandavas and does not see the fall awaiting him."

Dhritarashtra remained impassive.

"You should order Arjuna to kill Duryodhana," continued Vidura. "Then the Kurus can pass their days in happiness. Understand that for the sake of a family, one of its members may be sacrificed; for the sake of a village, a family may be sacrificed; for the sake of a province, a village may be sacrificed; and for the sake of one's own soul, the whole earth may be sacrificed. Therefore, don't harm the Pandavas because of your desire for gain. Otherwise, you will have to repent later."

Dhritarashtra remained unresponsive.

"You're ecstatic that Duryodhana is winning. But this success will cause war and lead to many men's death. You still approve of this conflict with Yudhishthira. You yourself are a mine of wealth. You can earn by other means as much wealth as you want to earn by gambling. By winning the Pandava's great fortune, what do you hope to gain? Better to win the Pandavas themselves, for they can be more useful to you than whatever wealth they have. Therefore, send Shakuni back home. Don't fight with Pandu's sons!"

Hearing this, Duryodhana exclaimed, "Vidura, you're always glorifying the renown of our foes and disdaining the sons of Dhritarashtra. We know who you really like. You wish success on your favorites and defeat on your unfavorites. Not knowing we had a snake

Dushasana grabbed Draupadi's cloth and tried to strip her naked.

on our laps, we nurtured you. The wise have declared that there is no sin worse than hurting one's master. Don't you fear this sin? If so, then don't insult us! We shouldn't give shelter to one who befriends our enemies. Therefore, Vidura, go wherever you like. You're like an unchaste wife who, though well-treated, leaves her husband."

Vidura snapped back, "You're an evil-hearted man, and you can never be brought to the path of virtue. You're like an unchaste wife in the house of a noble person. Without a doubt, good advice doesn't appeal to you. Well, if you want to hear pleasant words, then talk to idiots and fools. But it's rare to find a person who speaks or listens to fitting but unpleasant words. A king's true ally is one who says what may be unpleasant but necessary. You should drink the medicine of humility: though it's bitter, pungent and revolting, it will help you regain your sobriety. I always wish your father and brothers prosperity and renown."

Shakuni turned to Yudhishthira and said, "You have lost much of the Pandavas' wealth. If you still have anything left, tell us what it is."

Yudhishthira said he still had an untold amount of wealth and defied him to stake an equal amount. Shakuni did. Then, using unfair means, he won again.

Yudhishthira staked his cows, horses, calves, goats, sheep, land, and country, and lost them all. Next, he staked and lost each of his brothers—Nakula, Sahadeva, Arjuna, and Bhima.

Shakuni asked, "Do you have anything else to stake?"

"I myself am unwon. If you beat me, I'll do what you order."

Shakuni won again. He said, "King, you still have one stake left—your wife Draupadi. Stake her and win yourself back."

"My wife? Yes, I—I stake her."

But the elders in the assembly blurted out, "No! No!"

Most everyone there was upset, and many of the kings expressed their grief. Bhishma, Drona and Kripa—all great teachers—were sweating profusely. Vidura held his head between his hands, looked downwards, sighed deeply, and appeared as if he had lost his reason.

But Dhritarashtra's heart was happy and, unable to conceal his feelings, he asked, "Did Shakuni win?"

Karna, Dushshasana, and others laughed loudly while some in the assembly wept openly.

The dice were again cast—and Shakuni won!

Duryodhana then proudly said to Vidura, "Bring Draupadi here. Make her sweep the chambers and then stay in the women servants' quarters."

Vidura exclaimed, "You wretch! Don't you know that by speaking so harshly you're binding yourself with ropes? That you're dangling from the edge of a mountain cliff? That you're a deer provoking the fury of many tigers? That angry poisonous snakes are on your head? Don't further provoke the Pandavas or you'll go to Yama, the lord of death. In my opinion, Draupadi cannot become your slave. For she was staked by Yudhishthira *after* he had lost himself. Not being his own master, he had no right to stake her. "

Drunk with pride, Duryodhana bellowed, "To hell with you, Vidura!" He looked at the doorkeeper and ordered, "Bring Draupadi here. You need not be afraid of the Pandavas."

The doorkeeper went hastily, entered the quarters of the Pandavas, and approached their queen. He said to Draupadi, "Yudhishthira became drunk from the dice game and Duryodhana has won you. I have come to take you to Dhritarashtra's palace and engage you in some menial work."

"What are you saying?" asked Draupadi. "What prince would stake his wife? The prince could not find anything else to stake?"

"It was only after he had nothing left that he staked you. The King first staked his brothers, then himself, then you."

"Go ask my husband whom he lost first—himself or me. After you find out, come back here."

The doorkeeper returned to the assembly and said to Yudhishthira, "Draupadi wants to know whose master you were when you lost her. She asked who you lost first—yourself or herself?"

But Yudhishthira just sat there like a crazed person bereft of reason, giving no answer, good or bad.

Duryodhana then ordered, "Draupadi should come here and ask her question. And everyone here should listen to the exchange between her and Yudhishthira."

The doorkeeper, now distressed, returned to the palace and said, "Princess, you have been called to the assembly."

Draupadi replied, "It's been said that morality is the highest duty in the world. When nurtured, it blesses us. It should not leave the Kauravas. Return to the assembly and repeat my words. I'm prepared to do whatever the elders, versed in morality, tell me."

The messenger returned to the assembly and reiterated Draupadi's words. But all the elders sat looking downward, silent, understanding the desire and determination of Dhrtarashtra's son.

Joyful Duryodhana said to the doorkeeper, "Bring her here! The Pandavas must answer her question in front of her."

Afraid of Draupadi's anger, the doorkeeper asked the assemblymen, "What should I say to her?"

Duryodhana turned to his brother Dushasana and said, "This dumb doorkeeper is afraid of Bhima. So go and bring her here by force. Our enemies are now our dependents. What can they do to you?"

Dushasana, his eyes blood-red, got up and hastened to Draupadi's quarters. He entered her room and condescendingly said, "Come, come, Draupadi. We've won you. Now accept us Kurus as your lords."

Draupadi, in terrible distress, stood up, rubbed her pale countenance with her hands, and ran to the area where the women of Dhritarashtra's household were.

Dushasana roared loudly and chased after her. Then he grabbed her long, dark-blue wavy hair and dragged her out of the palace and into the assembly hall. She trembled like a banana tree in a hurricane and cried out, "You dog! It's improper for you to bring me here. I'm having my period. And I'm wearing only one piece of cloth."

When Dushasana disregarded her plea, she began to pray to Lord Krishna.

Dushasana blurted out, "Period or no period, one piece of cloth or naked, you've been won and made our slave! And you will live with our women servants!"

Draupadi said angrily, though faintly, "There are persons in this assembly who are expert in all fields of knowledge. They're dedicated to the performance of sacrifices and other ceremonies. Some of them are my superiors. Thus, I shouldn't remain before them in this condition. You pig! Stop dragging me!"

"Shut up, slave!"

"My husbands will never excuse you even if you have the gods as your friends. Yet—no one here chastises you. So all of them must be in agreement with you. How horrible! Has the virtue of the Bharata dynasty vanished? If not, then the Kurus in this assembly would never remain silent in this matter. I guess Drona, Bhishma, Vidura, and Dhritarashtra have lost their power. Otherwise, why are these topmost leaders remaining silent during this terrible crime?"

Draupadi glanced at her angry husbands. They were not so pained by the theft of their kingdom, their wealth and their most precious jewels as they were by Draupadi's modest yet angry glance.

Dushasana, noticing Draupadi glancing at her helpless husbands, dragged her even more forcefully and, laughing loudly, shouted, "Slave! Slave!"

When Karna heard this, he became exceedingly happy and approved of it by chuckling loudly. Shakuni also applauded Dushasana. But everyone else in the assembly—except these three and Duryodhana—was filled with sorrow.

Bhishma said to Draupadi, "Morality is truly subtle. On the one hand, one who has no wealth can't stake others' wealth; on the other hand, wives are always under the command and direction of their husbands. Hence, I can't judge this issue."

Dushasana spoke many unpleasant, rough words to Draupadi, who was sobbing pitifully and glancing momentarily at her husbands.

Bhima, seeing his wife in that undeserved condition—dragged during the time of her period and her upper garments loosened—could endure no more. His blazing eyes focused on Yudhishthira, and he angrily exploded. "Gamblers keep whores in their houses, yet out of kindness don't stake them. Our enemies have won our gems, animals, wealth, coats of mail, weapons, kingdom, ourselves, and yourself. None of this has made me angry, since you're our master. But your staking Draupadi—that I consider terrible. She's an innocent woman and doesn't deserve such treatment. She obtained us as her husbands, but it's because of you that she's being persecuted by the base, mean, cruel, and ignoble Kauravas. That's why I'm angry with you and will burn your hands. Sahadeva, bring me some fire!"

Arjuna interceded, "Bhima! Before this, you never spoke such words. Without a doubt, your high morality has been ruined by these savage enemies. You should not satisfy our enemies' desires. Better, exercise the highest morality. Yudhishthira is our virtuous older brother. He was summoned by the enemy and asked to play. Respecting the custom that a warrior never refuses a challenge, he played."

Bhima replied, "If I had not known that our brother was respecting that challenge, I would have forced his hands together and burned them in a big fire!"

Dhritarashtra's son Vikarna cried out to the assembly, "Kings, answer the question Draupadi asked. If we don't answer her, we'll all go to hell immediately. Why don't the oldest Kurus—Bhishma, Dhritarashtra, and Vidura—say anything? And our teachers Drona and Kripa are here. Why don't you great souls answer her question? Why don't all the other kings here answer her?"

But all the kings remained silent.

Vikarna again and again appealed to the kings, then rubbed his hands and sighed deeply. Finally, he said, "Kauravas, whether or not you answer the question, I will state what I consider fair and moral. It's been said that hunting, drinking, gambling, and fornicating are the four vices of kings. King Yudhishthira was intensely engaged in gambling. After the king bet and lost himself, Shakuni urged him to stake Draupadi. And he did.

"Considering all this, I believe that Draupadi has not been won."

A loud uproar arose from the assembly. The members applauded Vikarna and denounced Shakuni.

But Karna angrily challenged, "Vikarna, the elders here have remained silent. And why? Because they believe Draupadi has been won properly. But only you, because you are young and speak as if you're mature, are angry. You are ignorant of morality. How can you say Draupadi has not been won when the oldest Pandava wagered all his belongings—and Draupadi was included in those belongings? When Shakuni mentioned Draupadi, the Pandavas approved of her as a wager. How then can you consider her as not won?

"Maybe you think that because she was brought here wearing a single piece of cloth, this is immoral. Well, here's what I think: For a woman, the gods have prescribed only one husband. But Draupadi has many. Thus, she's definitely an unchaste woman. To bring her here wearing one piece of cloth—even to strip her completely—isn't an act that should surprise one. Shakuni won whatever wealth she and the Pandavas had. Dushasana, this Vikarna is only a boy. Take off the Pandavas' robes and also Draupadi's cloth."

The Pandavas removed their upper garments and threw them down.

Then Dushasana grabbed Draupadi's cloth and tried to strip her naked. As he began, Draupadi prayed aloud, "O Lord Krishna, don't you see that the Kauravas are dishonoring me? O Lord, save me from sinking in this Kaurava ocean. I'm very pained." She covered her face, cried loudly, and thought only of Krishna, Lord of the whole universe.

When the Lord heard her cries for protection, He was deeply touched. Appearing invisibly there, He asserted His mystic power. As Dushasana pulled off Draupadi's cloth, another one miraculously appeared over her body. As he continued pulling, more and more cloths of various colors appeared over her body—until hundreds and hundreds of cloths were soon lying on the floor. Baffled, Dushasana could not expose Draupadi's body!

There arose an uproar in the assembly. The kings, seeing this miracle, applauded Draupadi and chastised Dushasana.

Bhima squeezed his hands, his lips trembling in fury, and made a frightening vow: "O kings, hear me! I promise that in battle I will tear open the chest of this evil-minded scoundrel, Dushasana, and drink his blood. If I don't accomplish this, then may I not attain the higher realm of my ancestors!"

These words made everyone's hair stand on end. All congratulated Bhima and condemned Dushasana, who, exhausted and humiliated, sat down.

Seeing the Pandavas in that chagrined state, the kings exclaimed, "Hell on Dushasana!" Others said, "The Pandavas haven't answered the question Draupadi asked them."

Then Vidura waved his hands and silenced all. "Everyone here should reflect on what the answer is to Draupadi's question."

No one spoke at that moment, but then Karna said to Dushasana, "Take this serving-woman away to the inner apartments."

As Dushasana tried to pull the helpless, modest Draupadi out of the assembly, she shook and sobbed pitifully to her husbands. Then she offered her respects to all the venerable elders and said to them, "I want to know—am I or am I not a servant? I'll gladly accept your answer. This low wretch is hurting me badly and I can't take it any longer. Do you or don't you consider me won?"

Bhishma replied, "I've already said that morality is subtle. But it seems to me that Yudhishthira is an expert in this matter. He should say whether or not you've been won."

Though Draupadi was sobbing pitifully and kept appealing to the kings, they, in fear of Duryodhana, remained silent. Seeing this, Duryodhana smiled faintly and said, "Draupadi, your question depends on your husbands. They should answer it. Let Bhima, Arjuna, Nakula, and Sahadeva say, for your sake, that Yudhishthira is not their master. That will make Yudhishthira look like a liar. Then you'll no longer be our slave. Yes, let the virtuous Yudhishthira himself state whether or not he's your husband. And depending on what he says, accept either the Pandavas or us immediately. Indeed, all the Kaurava leaders here are feeling your misery. But they cannot answer your question."

Duryodhana's words made most of the Kauravas very happy. The kings looked at the Pandavas and were curious to hear what they would say.

Bhima said, "Had Yudhishthira, our eldest brother, not been our master, we never would have excused the Kurus for all this. He's the lord of our devotional and ascetic merits and the master of even our lives. If he thinks he's been won, then we also have been won. If this weren't true, then who in the world, after touching Draupadi's hair, would escape with his life? I haven't done anything terrible because I've been repeatedly urged by Arjuna to respect our older brother and remain silent. But if Yudhishthira were to order me, I would kill Dhritarashtra's wicked sons, as a lion slays many small animals."

Karna said to Draupadi, "You are now a slave! Your husbands are also slaves. They can't continue to be your masters. Therefore, select another husband—one who won't gamble you away into slavery."

Duryodhana said to Yudhishthira, "Your brothers are under your command. Answer Draupadi's question: Has she or hasn't she been won?" Then, to encourage Karna and offend Bhima, Duryodhana exposed his large thigh to Draupadi.

Bhima's reddened eyes opened, and he vowed, "If I do not break your thigh in a fight, then may I not attain the region of my ancestors!" Sparks of fire radiated from angry Bhima's sense organs.

Vidura said, "This terrible, threatening crisis has been sent by fate. O Kauravas, listen to this high principle: If Yudhishthira had wagered Draupadi before he himself had been won, he would certainly have been considered her lord. But if a person wagers something when he's incapable of having any wealth and he's beaten, the winner's gain is like the wealth of a dream."

Duryodhana replied, "I will abide by Bhima's, Arjuna's, or the twins' words. But they must state that Yudhishthira isn't their lord. Then I will free Draupadi from her bondage."

Arjuna said, "King Yudhishthira was definitely our lord before he started playing. But then he lost himself. Thus, all the Kauravas should judge whether, after that, he could be anyone's master."

Suddenly, from a distance, a jackal howled loudly. An ass brayed. Fearsome birds shrieked from all sides. Bhishma, Drona, and Gautama shouted out, "Amen! Amen!" Then Vidura and Gandhari disclosed the significance to King Dhritarashtra of that scary portent.

The king said, "O Duryodhana, you wretch! As soon as you insulted the Pandavas' wife Draupadi, death conquered you." But Dhritarashtra desired to save his relatives and friends from death, therefore he comforted Draupadi. He said, "Princess, ask for any blessing from me. You're chaste and virtuous, and first among my daughters-in-law."

Draupadi replied, "I ask that you free Yudhishthira from slavery. Thoughtless children must never call his son the son of a slave."

"So be it. Ask for another blessing. You deserve more than one."

"May Bhima, Arjuna, and the twins—with their chariots and bows—regain their freedom."

"So be it. Now ask for a third blessing. For two aren't enough to adequately honor you."

"I don't deserve a third blessing. So I won't ask for it. Once my husbands are freed, they'll achieve prosperity by their good deeds."

Karna sarcastically said, "We've never heard of anything like this—where a beautiful wife saves her husbands."

Bhima, angered, asked Yudhishthira, "Should I kill all these enemies now or should I do it outside this palace? Then again, why do I need your order? I can kill them right now, and then you can rule the world, unrivaled."

Like a lion amidst a herd of weaker animals, Bhima glanced angrily and repeatedly about. Though Arjuna tried to pacify him, Bhima's anger was so intense that smoke, sparks, and fire shot out of his ears and other senses. He was so frightening to behold that his furrowed brow made him look like death personified at the time of the cosmic dissolution.

Then Yudhishthira embraced and forbade Bhima, "Don't be like this. Be still and tranquil."

When Bhima was pacified, Yudhishthira approached his uncle Dhritarashtra with palms folded and said, "You are our master. Tell us what we should do. We wish to always remain submissive to you."

"Yudhishthira, you are blessed. Leave here in serenity and security, and rule your own realm with your wealth. Follow the counsels of peace. See only the merits and not the faults of your enemies. Forgive their bad deeds and remember their good ones. And don't remember Duryodhana's harsh words. I let this dice game occur to see all our friends from your city and to examine the strength and weakness of my children. Those who have you for their ruler and Vidura for their counselor can never have any grief. For you are virtuous, Arjuna is patient, Bhima is powerful, and the twins are respectful. Thus, return to Indraprastha. May there be brotherly love between you and your cousins, and may your heart always be fixed on virtue."

The Pandavas, with their wife Draupadi, soon mounted their chariots and, with happy hearts, proceeded towards their exquisite city.

***

When Dushasana learned that his father had ordered the Pandavas to return to their capital, he went at once to Duryodhana, who was with his advisors, and said, "After all our trouble, the old man has given back all our winnings to our enemies!"

The vain Duryodhana, Karna, and Shakuni then conspired to try to recover the Pandavas' wealth. They hastily approached King Dhritarashtra in private. Duryodhana artfully said, "Father, the Pandavas are now outfitted with weapons and seated on their chariots. They're as angry as poisonous snakes and will surely kill us. Arjuna is holding his bow, breathing hard, and glancing angrily about. Bhima is whirling his heavy club. Nakula is holding his sword and shield. And Sahadeva and Yudhishthira have indicated clearly what their intentions are. Their chariots are full of various weapons. And they're whipping their horses to hasten to their capital to mobilize their troops. They can't forgive us for their injuries or Draupadi's.

"Father, listen to our plan: We want to again gamble with Yudhishthira. The wager will be that the losers will wear deer skins, live in the forest for twelve years, and live unrecognized in some inhabited country for one more year. But if the losers are recognized during the last year, they'll have to live in the forest another twelve years. If unrecognized, their kingdom will be returned.

"After Shakuni defeats the Pandavas and they're exiled, we'll become strongly rooted in the kingdom. We'll make alliances, mobilize an unconquerable army, and if the Pandavas re-surface, we'll defeat them. Father, please approve of this plan."

Dhritarashtra replied, "Then bring back the Pandavas—even if they have gone far away—for another match."

When the plan was discovered by the leaders—Drona, Somadatta, Vahlika, Gautama, Vidura, Ashwathaman, Bhurisravas, Bhishma, and Vikarna—they opposed it. "Do not play," they said. "Let there be peace."

But Dhritarashtra was biased towards his sons. He disregarded the advice of all his sage friends and relatives and called back the Pandavas.

When Dhritarashtra's virtuous wife Gandhari learned of his decision, she said, "When our son Duryodhana was born, Vidura remarked, 'He cried repeatedly and harshly like a jackal. Without a doubt, he will prove to be the death of our dynasty. So it will be useful to kill him.' My lord, please don't accept the advice of evil young men. Don't be the cause of the destruction of this dynasty. Abandon Duryodhana. Because of fatherly affection for him, you haven't been able to. But now you must; otherwise our dynasty will die. Let your mind be guided by the advice of peace and goodness. Wealth accumulated through evil deeds is soon lost; but wealth won by virtuous deeds takes root and descends to succeeding generations."

The king replied, "If our dynasty is to be destroyed, then let it happen freely. I can't stop it. It shall be as my sons wish. The Pandavas will return here and my sons will gamble with Yudhishthira."

The royal messenger reached the Pandavas and relayed King Dhritarashtra's message—that Yudhishthira should return for another game of dice.

Yudhishthira replied, "Beings reap good and bad fruits according to Providence. Whether or not I play, those fruits are unavoidable. It is a challenge for me to play and an order from the aged king. Therefore I can't refuse, even though I know it will hurt me."

The Pandavas returned to the Hastinapura assembly house. Even while knowing of Shakuni's trickery, Yudhishthira agreed to play with him. Shakuni then spelled out the wager.

When the members of the assembly heard it, they raised their arms and shouted, "Curses on Duryodhana's friends. They should tell him of his terrible danger. And his father's duty is to tell him clearly."

Hearing these remarks, Yudhishthira ignored them.

Then Shakuni seized the dice and threw them. "Just see," he said, "I win!"

The defeated Pandavas prepared for their exile to the forest. They discarded their royal outfits and dressed themselves in deerskins.

When Dushasana saw them, he exclaimed, "King Duryodhana's absolute rulership has now begun. And you Pandavas have been defeated and distressed, plunged into eternal hell. You once laughed at Duryodhana and boasted that you had no equals in the world. But now you'll have to regard yourselves as no more than empty husks of rice. And what will be your joy, Draupadi? Better to choose a new husband from among us Kauravas. Why should you serve the Pandavas any longer?"

"You evil-minded wretch!" shouted Bhima. "You speak only what the sinful speak. As you pierce our hearts with word-arrows, I will one day pierce your heart in battle and remind you of this insult. And I will send all your followers, along with your descendants and relatives, to the house of death."

Dushasana danced mockingly around the Pandavas and shamelessly said to Bhima, "O cow! O cow!"

Then the joyful Duryodhana mimicked the leonine walk of Bhima.

Bhima replied, "You fool! Don't think by this you've gained any power over me. Soon I will kill you with all your followers and remind you of this."

As the Pandavas were leaving the Kaurava court, Bhima said, "If we ever fight with the Kauravas, I will kill Duryodhana, Arjuna will slay Karna, and Sahadeva will annihilate Shakuni."

Arjuna confirmed that in battle, with his arrows, he would slay Karna, his followers, and his allies if, fourteen years hence, Duryodhana did not respectfully return their kingdom. Sahadeva then vowed to kill in battle Shakuni and his followers. And Nakula promised to kill all Duryodhana's brothers who, during the dice game, made harsh and derogatory remarks to Draupadi.

The Pandavas said goodbye to all their relatives and friends.

Vidura said to them, "One who is defeated by evil means has no reason to be distressed by such a defeat. You're all very powerful, incomparable and inseparable—the envy of everyone. Resolve to achieve victory, give in charity, and control your emotions. You may depart with our blessings. We hope to see you return unharmed and crowned with success."

Bowing low to the elders Bhishma and Drona, Yudhishthira said, "So be it."

* * *

As the Pandavas left Hastinapura, some astonishing phenomena occurred: lightning flashes lit up the sky, but without clouds; the earth began to shake; a solar eclipse took place even though Rahu—which covers the sun—was not in the proper conjunction; meteors began to fall, keeping the city on their right; jackals, vultures, ravens, beasts, and birds began shrieking and crying loudly from the temples, sacred trees, walls and roofs. All these augured destruction for the Bharatas as a result of Dhritarashtra's evil advice.

While King Dhritarashtra and Vidura were conversing in the assembly, a great saint suddenly appeared there and said, "As a result of Duryodhana's offense, in fourteen years, Bhima and Arjuna will destroy the Kauravas." The saint then rose into the sky and vanished.

And of course, his prophesy came true.

"O Lord, we pray that you protect the universe, the gods, and Indra from this overwhelming dread."

CHAPTER SIXTEEN

AGASTYA DEFEATS
THE DEMONS

1

By pleasing his wife, who demanded from him something unusual, Agastya was able to fulfill an extremely important desire of his. Similarly, if we wish to acquire virtue and wisdom, we should try to please others by expertly using our knowledge and abilities. This helps us develop harmony and pleasure in our social relationships.

In the city of Manimati there lived a Daitya (or demon) named Ilwala, and he had a younger brother called Vatapi. One day Ilwala asked the illustrious Brahmin Agastya to grant him a son equal in prowess to the god Indra. But Agastya refused. This so infuriated the demon that he became a killer of Brahmins and executed his animosity in the following way:

Vatapi, by his mystic power, would transform himself into a ram. Ilwala would cook his flesh and feed it to a Brahmin. While the food was digesting, Ilwala would shout to his brother, "Vatapi, come out!" Hearing his brother's call, Vatapi would instantly re-assume his true form and, laughing loudly, burst out of the Brahmin's stomach, frequently killing him.

At about this time the famous sage Agastya saw his departed forefathers in hell hanging upside down in a pit. "Why are you suffering like this?" he asked.

"Because you've not produced children." they replied. "If you can produce a fine son, we can be freed from this hell. And you, too, will achieve the fortunate condition of those who beget children."

"Ancestors, I shall fulfill your wish. Do not worry."

195

Agastya began to consider how to perpetuate his family line. He concluded that there was no woman worthy of him with whom he would like to have children. Therefore the sage decided to create such a woman. He fashioned in seed form a female who would have a beautiful body and a noble soul. Then he arranged for it to take birth in the line of the king of Vidharba, who had been practicing asceticism for the purpose of having children.

When the girl was born, the king informed the Brahmins, and they in turn blessed her and gave her the name Lopamudra. The child, exceedingly beautiful, began to grow rapidly like the brilliant flame of a fire. Upon attaining puberty, a hundred ornamented virgins and a hundred maids served her obediently. Shining among them, she possessed excellent conduct and manners. Despite this, due to fear of her father, no man dared to ask her to marry him. Lopamudra was devoted to truth and, by way of her behavior, she satisfied her father and relatives. Realizing she was now of a marriageable age, the king considered whom he should give his daughter to.

When Agastya felt that Lopamudra was ready to assume the responsibilities of household life, he approached the king of Vidharba and said, "Please give your daughter to me in marriage."

Because the sage lived a harsh, austere life and the king wanted his daughter to live in ease and comfort, the monarch fainted. He was averse to offer his daughter, but when he considered the sage's mystic powers, he was afraid to refuse. For if he did, the ascetic might curse and destroy him. He explained the situation to his daughter and asked what she wished. But she remained silent.

In due time, Lopamudra, seeing her father and mother grievous, went to them and said, "Please do not sorrow because of me. Father, save yourself and give me to Agastya." Hearing this, the king arranged to offer his daughter to the sage with proper ceremony.

Shortly after, Agastya asked his new wife, "Do you think you can discard your expensive robes and adornments?"

Lopamudra immediately cast them away and clad herself in rags, barks and deerskin; then she became her spouse's partner in vows and deeds. They proceeded to Gangadwara, and Agastya began to undergo the harshest of austerities. Lopamudra was very satisfied, and out of profound respect for Agastya, began to serve him. And he, too, began to show deep love for her.

Then one day, after Lopamudra had just bathed and was in her fertile period, she blazed with ascetic brilliance. Very pleased with her for her services, purity, self-control, grace, and beauty, Agastya called her for sexual intercourse. However, his wife joined her palms respectfully and bashfully said, "The husband undoubtedly marries to have children. However, I would appreciate if you would reciprocate my love for you in a specific way. I would like you to have union with me on an opulent bed—like the one I used to sleep on in my father's palace. I would like you to be adorned in flower garlands and other ornaments. And I, also, would like to be wearing costly ornaments. But if I have to wear these red ascetic rags during that time, I could not unite with you."

"But I don't have the kind of wealth your father has."

"No, but you have the wealth of asceticism, and by that power you can bring here in a moment whatever exists in the world."

"Yes, that's true. But that would be a waste of my spiritual power. Therefore, ask me to do something that would not reduce my spiritual power."

"Agastya, my fertile period will not last long. And I don't want to unite with you unless you fulfill my wish. I also don't wish to reduce your spiritual power in any way. But somehow or other you should do as I'd like—without hurting your ascetic merit."

"My dear wife, if in your heart you have definitely decided on this, then I will go searching for wealth. Meanwhile, you remain here and do as you like."

Agastya then went to visit the opulent King Srutarvan to beg for wealth. Hearing of the Brahmin's arrival in his kingdom, the monarch went out with his ministers and welcomed the sage with honor. After immediately offering him refreshments, he joined his palms and humbly asked Agastya the purpose of his visit.

"King, I've come here to obtain wealth. Please give me a part of yours, to the extent that you're able and without hurting anyone."

The king informed the sage that his income equaled his expenses, but the sage could take whatever amount of wealth he desired. Since the king could not afford to donate any wealth, Agastya declined, realizing that if he took any, it would result in harm or deprivation to the king's subjects.

The sage, along with King Srutarvan, then paid a visit to King Vardhnaswa, who welcomed him with great respects. When the sage disclosed his reason for coming, the king informed him that his income equaled his expenses, but that the saint was free to take whatever he liked. Not wanting to inconvenience any of the subjects, Agastya again declined to take anything.

Consequently, he, along with Kings Srutarvan and Vardhnaswa, paid a visit to the extremely wealthy King Trasadasyu. Again, Agastya encountered the same result he had with the two previous kings—income equaled expenses. After the Rishi refused to take any wealth, one of the kings suggested, "There's a demon named Ilwala who has a tremendous amount of wealth. Let's go to him today and ask for some." Approving this idea, Agastya and the kings left for the demon's residence.

As soon as Ilwala heard that the kings and the Brahmin had arrived in his territory, he and his ministers went out to meet and properly honor them. Then the demon prepared a scrumptious feast for them, which included, of course, ram's meat. But before eating it, the kings learned that the meat was none other than Ilwala's transformed brother Vatapi. This knowledge both disgusted and depressed the kings, nearly driving them out of their senses. But Agastya said to them, "Don't despair, for I will eat up the great demon."

The sage sat down on a fine seat, and Ilwala, with a smile, began to serve the food. Agastya ate up every morsel of it. When the dinner was over, Ilwala, in his usual manner, called his brother to come out. But the only thing that came out of the sage's stomach was a horrendous belch that was as loud as thunder. Surprised, Ilwala repeatedly called, "Oh Vatapi, come out!"

Agastya burst into laughter and said, "How can he come out? I've already digested the demon."

When Ilwala heard this, he became morose and hopeless. Joining his palms respectfully, he asked, "Why have you come here, and what can I do for you?" Agastya smilingly replied, "We know that you have great power and wealth. These kings are not too wealthy. Yet I have a great need for wealth. Give us what you can without hurting anyone."

"How much wealth do you want?"

"Give each of these kings ten thousand cows and an equal amount of gold coins. And give me twice as much, as well as a golden vehicle and two horses that run as fast as thought. "

The demon regretfully gave away profuse wealth and his chariot, to which were yoked two horses.

Those horses drew the kings, Agastya, and all that wealth in but a moment to the sage's ashram. Obtaining Agastya's leave, the saintly kings left for their individual cities. Soon after, when Lopamudra saw that Agastya had fulfilled all her desires, she said, "Now produce in me a child who will have tremendous power."

"Lopamudra, I've been pleased by your behavior. Please listen to my proposal regarding children. Would you like to have a thousand sons? Or a hundred—each one equal to ten? Or ten—each equal to a hundred? Or only one—who can defeat a thousand?"

"Just one. For one good knowledgeable son is preferable to many bad ones."

"So be it."

After Lopamudra conceived, Agastya left for the forest. The fetus, growing for seven years, finally emerged from Lopamudra's womb. He was to be known as the resplendent and very knowledgeable Dridhasyu. He was endowed with great strength and, even as a child, would carry bundles of sacrificial fuel into Agastya's ashram. Later, he also became known as Idhmavaha [the bearer of the sacrificial wood]. When the sage saw his son with such qualities, he became very happy.

2

When we are beset with overwhelming problems, we should, as did the gods in this story, humbly pray to the Supreme Lord for guidance and strength to overcome them. By praying regularly and humbly, we develop an inner life wherein virtue and wisdom quite naturally grow and flourish.

In the the golden age, also known as the Age of Enlightenment, there existed certain Danava or demon tribes that were violent and unconquerable. Known as Kalakeyas, they were empowered with frightening valor. Under Vritra's leadership, they outfitted themselves with various weapons and chased the gods, headed by Indra, in all directions. The gods then decided to destroy Vritra; thus, they went to the abode of Lord Brahma to seek his advice.

When Brahma saw the celestials standing before him with their palms joined reverently, he said, "Gods, I know why you've come and what you want. So I will tell you how you may kill Vritra. There's a great saint named Dadhicha. Go and ask him to donate his bones to you. After he gives up his body, you should use his bones to create a terrible, high-powered weapon. It should be called Vajra. It will have six sides, make a terrifying roar, and be able to destroy even the most mighty enemies. With it, Indra will destroy Vritra. I have nothing more to say except that you should do this quickly."

After taking leave of Lord Brahma, the gods, with Lord Vishnu at their head, went to Dadhicha's forest retreat. It was filled with flowering trees, humming bees, melodious birds, wandering buffalo, boar and deer, sportive elephants, and roaring lions and tigers. Lying on the bank of the Saraswati River, the sanctuary truly resembled heaven. When they saw Dadhicha himself, he looked like the glowing sun, his beauty shining like Lord Brahma's. The gods bowed down at his feet and entreated him for the blessing they desired.

Well pleased with them, Dadhicha said, "I will help you. Yes, I will give up my body and you can use its bones accordingly." By an act of will, he irretrievably withdrew himself from his body and left this world.

The gods then took the sage's bones to the celestial architect Twashtri and explained to him what they wanted. Pleased to serve them, Twashtri took the bones and carefully and attentively fashioned from them the mighty Vajra weapon. He happily said to Indra, "With this best of weapons, burn those terrible demons to ashes. Then, with your followers, joyfully rule the entire kingdom of heaven." Twashtri handed the Vajra to Indra, who gladly and respectfully accepted it.

At that time, Vritra had conquered and occupied heaven and earth. Indra, backed by mighty celestials, then confronted the demon. Vritra was guarded on all sides by the Kalakeyas, who had huge bodies and carried upraised weapons that looked like mountain peaks. Though the fight between the gods and the demons ended soon, it was extremely appalling. Swords and scimitars clashed loudly, and severed heads flew into the air and dropped to the earth. The Kalakeyas, wearing golden armor, attacked the gods with iron-mounted bludgeons and looked like moving mountains on fire.

The gods, unable to bear the shock, broke ranks and fled in fear. Seeing this, as well as Vritra growing in courage, Indra grew deeply despondent. He became afraid of the Kalakeyas and hastened to Lord Vishnu for shelter. The Lord, noting Indra's weakened condition, imparted to him a portion of His own potency. When the gods observed this, they too gave Indra a portion of their potency. The pure Brahmarishis did the same. Blessed, Indra became more powerful than before.

When Vritra learned that Indra had been invested with such potency, he roared terribly several times and shook the earth, sky, directions, heaven, and mountains. Hearing this, Indra was deeply disturbed and frightened, so he hurled his Vajra weapon at him. Struck hard, the demon, wearing gold and garlands, fell down like a huge mountain.

Nonetheless, not knowing whether or not the Vajra had killed Vritra, Indra fearfully raced from the battlefield to a lake for shelter. But the gods and the great sages knew it had killed Vritra, and gladly began to sing praises to Indra. The gods mobilized their forces and began to kill the demons, who were depressed by their leader's death.

Alarmed by the turn of events, the demons retreated and, by their mystic powers, hid in the depths of the sea. There, among the fishes and crocodiles, they began to boldly plot the destruction of the three worlds. Each demon suggested different courses of action according to his own understanding. In time, however, they decided to destroy all persons who had higher knowledge and ascetic virtue, for they knew that the worlds were upheld by asceticism. They declared, "We must quickly destroy asceticism. Let us kill all persons who have ascetic virtues, are knowledgeable about duties and righteousness, and are God-realized. For once we annihilate them, the universe itself will become annihilated." From that time on, they made the ocean their fortress from which they launched their attacks.

The Kalakeyas proceeded to systematically destroy the universe. Under the cover of night, they entered various retreats—such as those of sages Vasishtha, Chyavana and Bharadwaja, where holy men were subsisting on only fruits and roots or air and water—and wreaked havoc. The demons slayed the ascetics horrendously, leaving many of the bodies without flesh, blood, marrow, entrails and limbs. Before night ended, the Kalakeyas returned to the sea, and in the morning all that could be seen, scattered along the ground, were heaps of bones, broken sacrificial jars, smashed libation ladles, and extinguished sacred fires. Everyone in the universe became terrified by the Kalakeyas, and the world, bereft of Vedic learning, sacrificial festivals, and religious ceremonies—became bleak.

Many who survived the killings fled fearfully in every direction, some to caverns and some to mountain streams and springs; others merely died out of fear of death; and still others, brave archers, eagerly tried to find and confront the culprits, but were unable.

As a result of such universal destruction, the gods became disturbed. With Indra among them, they gathered together apprehensively and discussed the matter. Consequently, they went to the divine, birthless Narayana—the undefeated Lord of Vaikuntha (the eternal spiritual world)—and sought His protection.

After bowing to Him, they humbly said, "O Lord, You are the creator, preserver and destroyer of us and the world, with its moving and non-moving beings. O lotus-eyed one, You, in earlier days, for the benefit of all beings, assumed the form of a boar and lifted the sunken earth from the sea; You assumed the half-man, half-lion form to save Your devotee Prahlada from his mighty demon father, Hiranyakashipu; You assumed the form of the dwarf Vamana to dethrone the unconquerable demon Bali as sovereign of the three worlds, exile him, and re-establish Indra as sovereign; You killed the demon Jambha, a powerful archer who always hindered the performance of sacrifices. These achievements, and countless others, are all Yours. O Lord, we are afraid, so we have come to You for shelter. That is why we are telling You about our present difficulties. We pray that You protect the universe, the gods, and Indra from this overwhelming dread.

"Through Your favor, all created beings multiply. They pacify the inhabitants of heaven by making offerings to them and to the departed ancestors. Protected by You and free from affliction, people live depending on each other and thus multiply. Now the people are beset by this danger, and we do not know who, at night, is slaying the Brahmins. If the Brahmins are annihilated, the earth itself will be annihilated; and if the earth ceases to exist, heaven also will cease. O mighty-armed Lord of the universe, we beg that, for Your pleasure, You act in such a protective way that all the worlds may not cease to exist."

Lord Vishnu replied, "Gods, I know why human beings are being destroyed. I will tell you about it, so listen to Me with your minds free from sorrow. There is a very savage army called the Kalakeyas. At one time, under Vritra's leadership, they were ravaging the entire universe. When they learned that Indra slayed their chief, to keep their lives they entered into the ocean. They remained hidden there during the day, but at night they emerged and, with the intention of exterminating humanity, killed the holy men. Because they have taken refuge in the sea, they can't be destroyed. And who, except Agastya, is able to dry up the sea? Unless the sea is dried up, these demons cannot be attacked."

The gods took Brahma's permission and went to Agastya's ashram. The son of Varuna, the ocean god, looked magnificent and was attended by saints, just as Lord Brahma is attended by the gods. He looked like an incarnation of many spiritual deeds. The gods approached and glorified him. One of them said, "O Agastya, once, when we gods were tyrannized by Nahusha, we took shelter of you. Though he was a thorn in the world, he was toppled from his heavenly throne. At another time, when the Vindhya Mountains, in order to block the sun's rays, suddenly began to grow, you ordered the mountain god to stop and he obeyed. You rescued the world from darkness and death and provided it with the highest security. Therefore, whenever we are overcome by insecurity, we take shelter of you. And that's why we are here now—to ask you for a blessing."

"What boon would you like?"

"O saint, we'd like you to swallow up the large ocean. Then we'll be able to kill our enemies, known as the Kalakeyas, along with their followers."

"All right, I'll do what you wish and whatever will make people happy."

Agastya, accompanied by the gods and sages, and followed by humans, snakes, and various celestials—all eager to behold the awesome event—proceeded to the sea. There, they saw the waves heaving in the breeze and heard the surf pounding on the shore, as flocks of various birds skittered and flew about. Agastya said, "I will now drink up this ocean. But as soon as I do, you should be ready to do what you have to."

Agastya, seething with anger, began to drink.

The gods, along with Indra, were deeply amazed; thus, they glorified him with praises. One said, "You are the protector of the gods and the guardian of humanity. By your blessing, the universe and its gods may possibly be saved from destruction."

As the celestials played musical instruments and showered blessings on Agastya, he finished drinking up the ocean. This made the gods very happy, for the demons were now exposed. Thus, the strong, fast gods, roaring loudly, attacked the demons with their divine weapons, and a furious battle ensued. Some of the saints glared at some of the demons and, by their mystic power, burned them to cinders. Though the demons fought hard, the gods, after awhile, finally slaughtered them.

Then the gods again praised the mighty Agastya. "O powerful one, by your kindness the ruthless Kalakeyas have been killed and humanity has received a great blessing. Therefore, we now would like you to re-fill the ocean with the water you've drunk."

"But that will not be possible because I've digested it. You'll have to think of some other means."

Not expecting this reply, the gods were filled with wonder and distress. They therefore, after paying obeisance and saying goodbye to the potent saint, left with Lord Vishnu. They then went to Lord Brahma's place and, respectfully joining their palms, discussed with him what had happened in order to learn how to re-fill the ocean.

Lord Brahma replied, "Gods, go wherever you wish now, for it will be a long time before the ocean resumes its natural state. The ancestors of King Bhagiratha will cause the circumstances by which it will happen."

The gods departed and went their ways, looking forward to the day that the ocean would be replenished.

***

Thus, by humbly praying to God for help and guidance, we not only can overcome our serious problems, but also acquire wisdom and virtue in the process.

The Ganges suddenly burst out of the sky and fell forcefully onto Lord Shiva's head.

CHAPTER SEVENTEEN

BHAGIRATHA AND THE GANGES

To achieve extremely difficult goals, it is sometimes necessary to observe severe austerity, as did King Bhagiratha, who saved his tormented ancestors from a hellish condition. Such austerity builds inner strength and determination, which are indispensable for acquiring virtue and wisdom.

King Sagara belonged to the Ikshvaku dynasty and was endowed with beauty and power. As a result of his military ability, he became king of the earth. Nonetheless, though he had two beautiful and youthful wives, neither of them had borne him a son. With the desire to obtain one and accompanied by his wives, King Sagara went to Mount Kailash to practice harsh austerities. There, he engaged in yoga or contemplation. And after some time, Lord Shiva, who carried a trident and generously offered blessings, appeared before him. As soon as King Sagara saw him, he, along with his queens, fell at his feet and prayed to have a son.

Lord Shiva was well pleased with the monarch and said, "You have offered your prayer at an astrological moment that will provide the following: One of your wives will give birth to sixty thousand militant and very proud sons, and all of them will die together. But your other wife will bear you a single courageous son who will perpetuate your family line." Lord Shiva then vanished from sight.

This news made the king very happy; therefore, with his wives, he returned to his palace. It was not long before his spouses gave birth. One of them, the princess of Vidarbha, brought fourth something that looked like a gourd; the other, the princess of Shivi, brought forth a boy as handsome as a god. King Sagara decided to throw away the gourd, but at that moment a disembodied voice, both grave and serious, called to him from the sky:

"O King, don't act so hastily! Don't desert your sons. Instead, remove the seeds from the gourd. Then preserve them in steaming vessels partly filled with clarified butter. You will then obtain sixty thousand sons. This is what Lord Shiva stated. Therefore, don't let your mind be diverted from this course."

Because these words came from above, Sagara had faith in them and followed the instructions. He took the seeds, placed each in a vessel filled with clarified butter, and provided a nurse to care for them. After some time, sixty thousand extremely powerful sons were born. They were terrible and ruthless, and could rise from the ground and fly in the air. Despising everyone and chasing even the gods, celestials, and humans, they were bold and attached to fighting.

All the harassed people, along with the gods, went to Lord Brahma for shelter. But Brahma explained to them why they really had no need to worry. Therefore, they all departed.

Sometime later, King Sagara began to perform a horse sacrifice. He released the special horse and, as it roamed all over the world, his sons carefully watched and protected it. But when the horse reached the waterless sea, which was terrible to behold, it suddenly disappeared from the spot it was standing on. Completely perplexed, Sagara's sons believed it had been stolen. They thus returned to their father and explained exactly what had happened.

Sagara replied, "Go and search for the horse in all directions."

Sagara's sons began looking everywhere, but they were unsuccessful. Therefore, they returned to their father and, joining their palms respectfully, reported, "Father, we've searched every hill, wooded path, ocean, forest, island, river, cave—the whole world—but can't find either the horse or the thief."

These words enraged the king. "All of you—leave immediately! Search for the horse again. And unless you find it, don't return!"

Sagara's sons again scoured the entire earth. As they looked along the ocean floor, they noticed a cleft in it. Curious, they began excavating it in all directions with spades and pickaxes. They encountered demons and snakes that blocked their way. Thus they killed hundreds and thousands of them—cutting off heads and trunks, tearing flesh, and breaking joints and bones. Throughout, their victims cried out excruciatingly.

After digging for a long time, the brothers still did not find the horse. Incensed, they began digging in the north-eastern region of the ocean floor till they at last reached the lower world.

There they finally beheld the horse roaming about. They also saw the resplendent Divine incarnation Kapila sitting nearby. Though delighted to find the horse, they were angered to see Lord Kapila, for they thought he had surely stolen it. Totally disrespecting the sage by ignoring him, they hastened toward the horse to re-claim it. When Lord Kapila saw this, he gazed at the dull-headed brothers angrily, and the brothers immediately burned to ashes.

Later, the sage Narada happened to see those ashes and, by his mystic power, knew whose they were. He thus went to King Sagara and disclosed the fate of his sons. Hearing the terrible news, the king was morose for almost an hour. Then he recalled what Lord Shiva had predicted.

Sagara's other son, Asamanjas, had been born to his other wife, the princess of Shivi. Demoniac in nature, this son would seize weak children by the throat and, as they screamed in terror, fling them into the river. Filled with fear and sorrow, the people obtained a meeting with the king. They stood with joined palms, and one of them respectfully petitioned, "When we are attacked by a hostile, deadly force, it is your duty to protect us. Your son Asamanjas is such a force; therefore, we request you to free us from him."

This unpleasant news made the righteous king sorrowful. Then he declared to his ministers, "From this day on, banish my son Asamanjas from the city! And if you wish to please me, do it soon!" The ministers hurriedly fulfilled the king's order.

Sagara said to his grandson Amshuman, "I'm grief-stricken from having banished your father, from the death of my other sons, from my not recovering the sacrificial horse, and from having halted my sacrificial ceremony. Therefore, my grandson, I'm asking you to bring back the horse and deliver me from the hell I will suffer."

Without delay, Amshuman left the city and went to the spot where his uncles had been killed. Seeing the illustrious Lord Kapila and the lost horse, Amshuman bowed his head to the ground. Then he humbly disclosed to the sage the purpose of his visit. Pleased with Sagara's grandson, the Lord asked him to request a blessing.

Amshuman first prayed for the release of the horse so that his father's sacrificial ceremony could be completed. Next, he prayed for the purification of his deceased uncles.

"I will grant those requests. May you have good fortune! You are forbearing, truthful, and pious. Through you, the king will satisfy all his desires." The Lord also revealed other events that would occur in the future. Finally he said, "You may now take the horse so that your grandfather may finish the sacrifice!"

When Amshuman returned to his grandfather, he respectfully fell at his feet. In response, Sagara lifted him up and lovingly smelled his head. Amshuman told him all that had happened and would happen, and the king, very pleased, praised and glorified him.

After King Sagara finished the sacrificial ceremonies, all the gods appeared and saluted him. Then, after a long period of rule, Sagara installed his grandson on the throne, retired from active life, and left this world for the higher regions. The virtuous Amshuman, following in his grandfather's footsteps, governed the earth far and wide.

Years later, Amshuman begot a virtuous son named Dilipa. When Dilipa learned of the terrible fate of his sixty thousand great-grandfathers, he became very sad. He therefore thought of a way to redeem them. He knew that if the holy Ganges River—which emanated from the feet of Lord Vishnu—could be made to descend from the heavenly realm and then be directed to the spot where the ashes of his great-grandfathers lay strewn, their souls would become purified and released from their present suffering condition. Dilipa thus took extraordinary pains to bring down the Ganges but was unsuccessful.

Dilipa had a handsome, pious son named Bhagiratha, who was truthful and free of hostility. When Dilipa felt he had ruled long enough, he installed Bhagiratha on the throne and retired to the forest to undertake asceticism. After a sufficient period of practice, he ascended to the heavenly world.

Bhagiratha was a powerful ruler, a joy to behold, and a soul of all souls. When he learned how his great-great-grandfathers had died and had been unable to attain to the heavenly kingdom, he became sad. Therefore, to redeem them, he transferred his royal duties to his chief minister and went to the side of the snowy Himalayan Mountains to engage in austerities. He did this to burn away all the ill effects of his past sins, and thereby obtain the blessings of Goddess Ganga.

The spot where Bhagiratha did penance was beautiful, with its mineral-laden peaks, rivers, groves, rocky spurs, and its lions and tigers hidden in caves and pits. The colorful, singing birds and the lotus flowers in the water ponds were also admirable. The place was frequented by various celestial beings. In some areas, the mountain looked golden; in others, silvery; and in still others, sable.

For one thousand years of the gods, or 360,000 earth years, he lived only on water, fruits and roots. Then the presiding goddess of the Ganges—Ganga herself—materialized and asked, "What would you like from me? What can I give you?"

Bhagiratha replied, "O giver of boons, O glorious river, while my great-great-grandfathers were looking for their father's sacrificial horse, Lord Kapila sent them to the god of death. Hence, they can't reach the heavenly realm. Unless you sprinkle your holy water over their ashes, there is no hope of them ascending. Thus, I beg you to descend and flow to their ashes so that their souls may be released."

Ganga, very satisfied with the king, replied, "I'm certainly ready to fulfill your prayer. However, if I, as a river, fall from the sky, I'll land with such a tremendous impact that it'll be difficult for the earth to sustain me. There is no one in the three worlds who can buffer the impact except the blue-throated Lord Shiva. Therefore, try to obtain his blessing by undergoing more austerities."

King Bhagiratha went to Mount Kailash and practiced more severe austerities. After a certain amount of time, Lord Shiva agreed to bear on his head the impact of the Ganges' descent from heaven. Then he asked Bhagiratha to pray devoutly to Goddess Ganga to fall from the sky. When Bhagiratha did, the gods, saints, and celestials assembled there and watched expectantly.

Then the Ganges suddenly burst out of the sky and fell forcefully onto Lord Shiva's head. She raged with whirlpools, teemed with fishes and sharks, and billowed with foam. When she reached the earth's surface, she said to Bhagiratha, "King, show me the way you want me to flow."

Bhagiratha led her toward the sea. As she flowed, she separated herself into three streams and moved in a crooked, tortuous manner. Finally, she reached the vast ocean hole [created by the sage Agastya] and began filling it quickly. Then she flowed down through the cleft in the ocean floor and at last reached the spot where the ashes of King Bhagiratha's great-great-grandfathers lay scattered. The king next performed a water rite in each of their names and freed them. He further adopted Ganga as his daughter, and for this reason she is also called Bhagirathi.

In this way the ocean was refilled and King Bhagiratha's heartfelt wish was fulfilled.

Krishna took the particle of rice and vegetable stuck to the pot's rim and ate it.

CHAPTER EIGHTEEN

KRISHNA SAVES THE PANDAVAS

It was Queen Draupadi's great faith in Lord Krishna that caused Him to miraculously appear before her and save her and her husbands from being cursed by Yogi Durvasa. By developing such faith in the Supreme Lord, we can easily obtain His valuable grace and thereby increase our wisdom and virtue manyfold.

Prince Duryodhana learned that the five Pandava princes and their wife Draupadi were dwelling as happily in the forest as they previously had in the city. But he, along with his sly friend Karna, his brother Dushashana, and others, yearned to make them unhappy by causing them harm. As they were concocting various evil schemes, the righteous and famous yogi Durvasa arrived at Kurukshetra with his ten thousand disciples.

After seeing the quick-tempered ascetic arrive, Duryodhana and his brothers welcomed him with exceeding humility, submissiveness and kindness. Duryodhana personally waited on the sage as a servant and provided him with a very respectful reception. He knew that the famous ascetic hurled curses at the slightest offense or provocation.

While the sage stayed there for a few days, Duryodhana served him painstakingly both day and night. Sometimes the sage would exclaim, "I'm hungry. Bring me some food quickly!" At other times, when he would go out to take a bath and come back at a late hour, he would say, "I have no appetite, so I won't eat anything today!" Then he would vanish from sight. Sometimes he would suddenly appear and demand, "Feed us fast!" At other times he would wake up at midnight and order Duryodhana to give him food; upon receiving it, he would angrily criticize it and refuse to eat it.

After testing Duryodhana in this way for a while and seeing that he was neither incensed nor irritated, the peppery sage became amiably disposed towards him and said, "I have the power to give you three blessings. You may ask for whatever is closest to your heart. May you have good fortune. As I'm pleased with you, you may obtain from me anything that is not antagonistic to religion or morals."

When Duryodhana heard these words, he felt exhilarated with new life. This was because he, Karna, and Dushashana had beforehand agreed on the blessing he would ask for if the sage were happy with his services. Remembering what had been decided earlier, the evil-minded Duryodhana said, "King Yudishthira is the oldest and the best of our generation. That religious man is presently dwelling in the forest with his brothers. I'd like you to be his guest, just as you and your disciples have been mine for awhile. If you wish to do me a favor, then I'd like you to visit him right after his fine, lovely wife Draupadi has served food to the Brahmans, her husbands and herself, and has laid down to rest."

"Is that all?"

"Yes, that's all."

Durvasa then departed with his followers.

Duryodhana felt that he had accomplished all his purposes. For he knew that Draupadi could not provide food for Durvasa's ten thousand disciples after she had taken her meal. Though the pot she cooked in was given to her by the sun god and mystically produced unlimited quantities of food, it did so only before Draupadi took her meal. But once she ate, the pot would become empty—and stay empty till her next meal. Duryodhana felt certain that when this happened, Durvasa would curse the Pandavas for the offense of not providing him and his disciples with food.

Holding Karna's hand, Duryodhana displayed intense pleasure. Karna also, in the company of the prince's brothers, joyfully said to Duryodhana, "By a bit of unusual good luck, you've done well and shall fulfill your wishes. Your enemies will be plunged into a treacherous ocean that will be hard to cross. Pandu's sons will now be exposed to Durvasa's anger. Due to their own shortcomings, they have fallen into a chasm of darkness."

***

One day while the Pandavas were sitting about relaxing and Draupadi was lying down after having eaten, Yogi Durvasa, with his ten thousand disciples, arrived in that forest area. When the celebrated and honorable King Yudhishthira noted this, he and his brothers proceeded to greet them. He folded his palms, pointed to a fitting and comfortable seat, and offered the holy men proper and respectful greetings. Then he said, "Please feel free to go to the stream now, take your bath, and return quickly."

Not knowing how Yudhishthira would adequately feast him and his disciples, the pure sage, along with his followers, proceeded to the river and began bathing.

Princess Draupadi, who was devoted to her husbands, began to worry about how she would provide a feast for the holy men. For at that time, because she had already eaten her meal and the mystical pot would thus produce no more food, she was unable to. Thus, full of anxiety, Draupadi prayed to Lord Krishna, the killer of the demoniac King Kamsa, "O Krishna, son of Devaki; O Vasudeva, Lord of the universe; Your power is indefatigable and You dissipate the obstacles of persons who bow down to You. You are the Supersoul, the creator and the destroyer of the universe. O Lord, You are inexhaustible and the deliverer of the distressed. You are the preserver of the universe and of all manifested souls. You are the highest of the high, the source of mental perceptions, knowledge and morality. O highest and unlimited Being, O provider of all blessings, please be the shelter of the helpless.

"O first Person, You are incapable of being imagined by the soul or the mental faculties. You are the sovereign of all and the ruler of Lord Brahma. I seek Your protection. O Lord, You are always kind toward those who take shelter of You. Hold me with Your kindness! Your dark complexion resembles the blue lotus, Your reddish eyes resemble the petals of the lily, You wear yellow garments and a shiny Kaustubha jewel on Your chest; You are the beginning and the end of creation, and the mighty shelter of all. You are the greatest light and the essence of the cosmos. Your face is pointed in every direction. They call You the highest source and the resting place of all opulences. O Lord of the gods, when You protect someone, he is not afraid of evil. As You once protected me from Dushashana, who tried to strip off my garment before an assembly of men, please free me now from this plight."

Lord Krishna—the glorious Supreme Lord, the master of the world, whose movements are mysterious, who is always good-hearted to His dependents—was residing in His capital, Dwarka, and was in bed with His chief queen, Rukmini. However, realizing Draupadi's difficulties, Krishna instantly transported Himself to the forest where the Pandavas were staying.

Seeing Krishna, Draupadi joyfully bowed down to Him and told Him about the unexpected visit of the holy men as well as all other things.

After hearing Draupadi's problem, Krishna said to her, "I'm very hungry; please give Me some food immediately. Then you may attend to your work."

Hearing this, Draupadi became bewildered and replied, "The pot that the sun god gave me stays full only until I finish my meal; and since I've finished it, there's nothing left."

The lotus-eyed and lovable Krishna said, "Draupadi, this is not the time for joking. I'm suffering from hunger. Go and get the pot quickly and show it to Me."

Draupadi went to the fire, returned with the pot, and gave it to Krishna. He gazed into it intently and noticed that there was a particle of rice and vegetable stuck to its rim. He took the morsel between His fingers and ate it. "May Lord Hari," He said, "the Supersoul of the universe, who receives all sacrifices, be pleased and fully satisfied with this."

Krishna, who had long arms and who relieved suffering, said to Bhima, "Go quickly and invite the holy men here for dinner!"

Bhima immediately proceeded toward the stream where the ascetics were bathing.

Meanwhile, the holy men were in the river rubbing their bodies and looking as though their stomachs were filled. As they came out of the water, they gaped at one another curiously. Turning to Durvasa, one said, "Master, our stomachs feel full, right up to the throat. King Yudhishthira has uselessly prepared a meal for us. What's the best thing for us to do now?"

The sage answered, "If we refuse to accept the meal, we'll commit a terrible offense against that royal saint. The Pandavas might glare at us angrily and kill us. I know that Yudhishthira has tremendous ascetic power. The Pandavas are highly elevated, pious, knowledgeable, protective, steadfast in ascetic disciplines and religious practices, devoted to Lord Krishna, and ever mindful of the principles of good behavior. If inflamed, they can destroy us with their anger as fire consumes a bale of cotton. Therefore, my disciples, I advise you not to return to them but to run away quickly!"

Becoming greatly fearful of the Pandavas, the holy men scattered in all directions.

***

When Bhima reached the river, he did not see them there. He therefore searched all the bathing spots. As he did, he learned from the resident holy men that Durvasa's disciples had run away. Bhima then returned to his camp and told Yudhishthira what had occurred.

Nevertheless, the Pandavas, still expecting the holy men to return, waited for them for some time. Yudishthira suspiciously said, "Those ascetics may come back late at night and deceive us. How can we escape from this problem?"

When Krishna saw them thinking in this way and sighing deeply and frequently, He suddenly appeared before them and said, "While I was aware of your danger from that hot-tempered sage, Draupadi prayed to Me to come here, so I came quickly. But now you have no reason to fear Durvasa. He's scared of your ascetic powers; thus, he's gone away. Righteous men like you never have to worry. Allow Me to return home now. May you always have good fortune."

When the Pandavas and Draupadi heard Lord Krishna's words, their minds became relaxed, cured of the fever of anxiety. Yudhishthira said, "Krishna, by Your help, we've become freed from this unsolvable difficulty, just as persons drowning in the vast ocean reach the shore safely by means of a boat. You may now leave in peace, and may You always have good fortune."

Lord Krishna returned to His capital.

The Pandavas, roving from forest to forest, spent their days joyfully with Draupadi. Thus, the scheme of the evil Duryodhana and his brothers was baffled by Draupadi's devotion and Lord Krishna's mercy.

Lord Brahma, satisfied with Dhundhu's efforts, offered him a boon.

CHAPTER NINETEEN

KING KUVALASHVA'S GLORY

King Kuvalashva had the courage to face the most powerful and destructive demon on earth, Dhundhu, and he defeated him. Similarly, by facing our trials and tests with do-or-die courage, we not only can achieve our goals but can simultaneously grow steadily in wisdom and virtue.

The Brahmin Utanka was highly exalted and had tremendous spiritual potency. He had just learned that the saintly King Vrihadaswa—who was foremost in wielding weapons—was about to renounce his kingdom and retire to the forest to practice spiritual austerities. Utanka approached him and started to persuade him to renounce his ascetic plan.

He said, "King, it's your duty to protect your subjects, and you should perform that duty. By your grace, allow us to be free from all worry and let the earth be free from all peril. You shouldn't give up your kingdom and withdraw to the forest. When you protect the people, you earn great spiritual merit. This type of merit cannot be obtained by living in the woods. Therefore, don't pursue this course. In ancient days, the merit gained by saintly kings from protecting their subjects was incomparable. So please stay here and protect your people.

"I presently can't perform my devotional practices serenely. Near my retreat there's a sea of sand known as Ujjalaka. It's a level area, has no water, and stretches for many miles in length and breadth. A demon leader named Dhundhu lives there, and he's the son of Madhu and Kaitabha. He's ferocious, terrifying and powerful, and lives underground. Before you retreat to the forest, you should kill him. He's now lying still and performing rigorous austerity to conquer the gods and the three worlds. In the past, he acquired from Lord Brahma a blessing that made him indestructible to the gods and demons. If you kill him, that'll be wonderful. You'll surely attain everlasting and immortal renown.

"At the end of every year, when that terrible demon starts to breathe, he causes the earth—with its mountains, forests and woods—to tremble. He also blows up clouds of sand and covers the sun. The earth shakes continually for seven days, and sparks and flames mingled with smoke spread all around. Therefore, I can't be at peace in my ashram. Please kill him. When he's dead the three worlds will be peaceful and happy.

"I fully believe you're capable of destroying him. If you try, Lord Vishnu will add His own power to yours. Long ago the Lord offered a boon, namely, that the king who would kill this demon would be permeated by His, the Lord's, own unconquerable power. But if a warrior with only a small amount of power challenged Dhundhu, he would be defeated, even if he tried for a hundred years."

That undefeated king joined his palms respectfully. "Brahmin, your visit here won't prove fruitless. My son's name is Kuvalashva and he's endowed with firmness and energy. Assisted by his courageous sons, whose powerful arms resemble iron maces, he'll fulfill your wish. But since I've now renounced my weapons, please allow me to retire."

"Certainly," said the sage.

Vrihadaswa said to his son, "Please do what the sage asks." And with that, he retired to the woods.

***

But who was this powerful demon, Dhundhu? And how did he become so potent?

Many millions of years ago, when the world became one huge tract of water and animate and inanimate beings were killed, the whole creation came to an end. At that time, Lord Vishnu, the Supreme Lord, the eternal source and immortal creator of the universe, was lying in yogic sleep on the broad hood of His mighty serpent-couch, Sesha. As the Lord rested, a beautiful, glowing lotus, bright as the sun, arose from His navel. From that lotus, Lord Brahma, the four-headed creator of the world and revealer of the Vedic scriptures, was born. And there, atop the lotus, he sat.

Lord Vishnu was stunningly beautiful. He radiated tremendous light, like a thousand suns concentrated in one mass. He was dressed in a yellow silk dhoti and purple shawl, and He wore a golden crown and a kaustubha jewel around His neck.

After some time, two powerful demons named Madhu and Kaitabha began to terrify and alarm Lord Brahma, making him tremble. Then the stalk of the lotus also trembled, causing Lord Vishnu to awaken from His slumber. When Lord Vishnu beheld those demons, He said to them, "Greetings, mighty ones. I'm pleased with you; thus I'll grant you wonderful blessings."

Those proud and powerful demons laughingly replied, "Rather, You ask us for a boon and we'll give it to You. Ask for whatever comes into Your mind."

"Surely, I'll accept a blessing from you. For there is something I wish. Allow me to kill you! I wish to do this for the benefit of the world."

Madhu and Kaitabha answered, "We've never spoken an untruth—not even in fun, what to speak of other times. We've always been fixed in truth and piety. There's no one comparable to us in strength, body, good-looks, virtue, asceticism, charity, conduct, goodness, and self-restraint. But now we're in a dangerous position. However, do as You wish. No one can conquer over time. Nonetheless, O Lord, there is one boon we'd like: To be killed at a place that's completely uncovered, and to become Your sons. Please don't break Your promise."

"Yes, I'll do everything you wish."

Lord Vishnu then considered where He would slay them. But He couldn't find any place on land or in the sky that was completely uncovered. However, seeing that his thighs were totally uncovered, He placed the brothers on them. Then, with His sharp-edged disc, He chopped off their heads.

The famous Dhundhu, exceedingly powerful and skillful, was the son of Madhu and Kaitabha. He practiced severe austerity, standing erect on one leg and reducing his body to a heap of veins and arteries. Lord Brahma, satisfied with Dhundhu's efforts, offered him a boon. The demon replied, "May the gods, demons, Rakshasas, Nagas, and Gandharvas be incapable of killing me."

"As you wish. Now be on your way."

The demon reverently placed Brahma's feet on his head and then went away.

Remembering the death of his father by Lord Vishnu, the demon began to conquer and harass all the celestials. Finally, Dhundhu arrived at Ujjalaka, the sea of sand, and with his utmost strength, upset Utanka's ashram.

Dhundhu, with the aim of destroying the three worlds, now lay in his underground cave practicing harsh austerities. Meanwhile, King Kuvalashva, with his 21,000 powerful sons and troops, along with Utanka, proceeded towards that place. At the request of the sage, Lord Vishnu, desiring to benefit the three worlds, filled the king with His own energy.

The gods began to rain flowers upon the king and beat their kettledrums. Cool breezes blew, and Indra, the chief god, gently showered water on the dusty roads. Soon the airplanes of the gods, celestials, and great sages hovered high above mighty Dhundhu's dwelling, for they were curious to watch the fight.

King Kuvalashva, assisted by his sons, soon attacked the sea of sand and commanded that it be excavated. With the job completed after seven days, they could then see the powerful Dhundhu. His huge body was shining like the sun and was covering the western part of the desert.

The king's sons assaulted him with keen arrows, maces, heavy and short clubs, axes, clubs with iron spikes, and sharp swords. This angered the demon and made him stand up. Enraged, he swallowed the weapons flung at him. He exhaled fiery flames resembling the *samvarta* fire, which appears when the world is about to be destroyed. With those flames, and in a moment, he burned to death all the king's sons, just as Lord Kapila had burned the sons of King Sagara.

The king, who had tremendous power now, approached the demon fiercely. Then, from his body, a shower of water burst forth that soon extinguished the demon's flames. Next, he killed the demon with the famous weapon known as Brahma, and by this means, he became like a second leader of the three worlds.

Thereafter, King Kuvalashva became known as Dhundhumara, or the slayer of Dhundhu, and came to be regarded as indomitable in battle. The gods and the great sages who had come to witness the fight were so pleased that they said to him, "Please ask us for a benediction."

Filled with great happiness, the king joined his palms and said, "Kindly let me always donate wealth to superior Brahmins. Let me be undefeatable to all my enemies. Let me have friendship with Lord Vishnu. Let me have no hostility towards any being. Let my heart always pursue virtue. And let me dwell in the higher region eternally."

When the gods, sages and Utanka heard this, they were very satisfied and said, "May it be so." The gods and sages blessed him with many other words and then departed for their respective planets.

Although, during the battle, all the king's accompanying sons were slain, Kuvalashva still had three sons. They were known as Drdashva, Kapilashva and Chandrashva. And it is from them that the celebrated line of monarchs of the Ikshvaku dynasty originated.

***

It is said that anyone who listens to this holy story related to Lord Vishnu becomes pious and obtains children (if desired). By listening to it on particular full moons, one becomes blessed with long life, excellent fortune, and freedom from anxiety and disease.

As the priest got ready to feed the boy into the fire, the king's wives could not tolerate the agony of seeing this.

CHAPTER TWENTY

KING SOMAKA'S SACRIFICE

King Somaka learned that we sometimes have to sacrifice something very dear, which may cause us much pain, in order to achieve something even better. To grow in virtue and wisdom, we must be ready to gladly make whatever sacrifices are required, for this helps us to overcome our selfish nature.

There once lived a pious king named Somaka. He had one hundred wives, and they were all satisfactorily matched to him. However, hard as he tried, he was unable to produce a son from any of them. This situation continued till he was very old. Nonetheless, he persisted in trying. Then one day it happened: One of his wives bore him a son, and they called him Jantu.

After this, all the king's wives would surround the child and offer him playthings for his amusement and delight. One day, while this was going on, an ant stung the boy on his hip. As the sting was quite painful, the boy cried out loudly. After understanding why he was crying, the wives became disturbed and also began crying loudly.

Although the king was sitting among his ministers, his family priest beside him, he clearly heard the piercing cries. So he asked an usher to go and determine what the cause was. When the usher returned, he explained exactly what had happened.

Somaka rose with his ministers and hurried towards the women's quarters. Seeing his distraught son, the king comforted him. When Jantu was fully satisfied, the king and his ministers returned to where they had been sitting.

The king exclaimed to his priest, "How horrible to have only one son! I would rather have no son! Human beings are constantly subject to disease and difficulties, and therefore I'm always in anxiety over losing this one son. But if I had many sons, then I wouldn't worry so much about one. I married a hundred women with one purpose: To have many sons. And just see what has happened. Can there be any sorrow greater than mine? Now I'm old and so are my wives, and our only child is as dear to us as our very breath. But is there some ceremony I could perform by which I could obtain one hundred sons?"

"Yes, there is. Would you like me to explain it to you?"

"Please."

"Well, you'll have to offer your present son—into a sacrificial fire."

"What?!"

"Yes—your son."

"But—why?"

"In order to offer his fat to the gods."

The king shook his head in anguish.

"And when all your wives smell that smoke, they'll soon give birth to a hundred brave, strong sons."

"One hundred? Are you sure?

"Yes. And Jantu will be re-born from the same mother he has now."

"But how can we be sure of that?"

"Because he'll have a gold mark on his back."

The king carefully considered the priest's prescription. Realizing it would be good not only for himself but also for the entire kingdom—since many princes would be born from the sacrifice—he anxiously assented.

The priest officiated at the sacrifice in which Jantu was to be offered. As he got ready to feed the boy into the fire, the king's wives could not tolerate the agony of seeing this. Because their hearts were heavy with pity, they forcibly grabbed Jantu's right hand and pulled him away. Weeping painfully, they shouted, "We're ruined!"

But the priest grabbed the hand back and wrenched him away from the women. As the women screamed in anguish, like female ospreys, the priest slaughtered Jantu and duly offered his fat into the blazing fire. As the wives smelled the odor of the burning fat, they fainted and fell to the ground.

Very soon, all those wives became pregnant, and after ten months, each of them gave birth to a son. Jantu was born to his former mother and was the oldest. Strangely, all the king's wives loved Jantu even more than their own sons. As predicted, he had a gold mark on his back, and of all the sons, he had the most spiritual merit.

After some time, the family priest and King Somaka left this world. Somaka saw that the priest was being broiled in a horrible region of hell. He asked him, "Why are you being broiled here?"

"Because I officiated at your sacrifice."

The king turned to the god of death and said, "O Yama, please free my priest. It wasn't his fault. I'm the one who made the request, so I'm the one who should suffer."

But Yama replied, "You can't enjoy or suffer for someone else's deeds." Then he showed him a document. "Here are the results of your deeds."

When King Somaka saw where he was headed, he answered, "No, I don't wish to go to the higher regions without this Brahmin. I want to stay with him—in the realm of the gods or in the depths of hell."

"Then you'll have to suffer here for as long as he does."

"I don't care."

"But after that, you'll go to the higher regions."

When the king and the priest had paid for the sin, they both were released. Because the king was so fond of the priest, he then shared with him all the blessings he had won as a result of his good deeds. Thus they both soared upwards.

* * *

The more we sympathize with and share the sorrows of others, the more we grow in virtue and wisdom. These two qualities can bring us the inner peace, abounding joy, and true happiness we desire.

GLOSSARY

A

Agastya: A sage with great mystic powers. He gave Lord Rama the bow of Lord Vishnu and entertained Him and Sita during their exile in the forest.

Agni: The god of fire.

Airavata: An elephant produced when the gods and demons churned the Milk Ocean. Airavata was appropriated by the god Indra.

Akritavrana: A sage who is a close companion of Parashurama.

Amba: The eldest daughter of the king of Kashi.

Ambalika: The youngest daughter of the king of Kashi.

Ambika: The middle daughter of the king of Kashi.

Amrita: The nectar of immortality produced by the churning of the ocean by the gods and demons; also, the food of the gods.

Amshuman: The name of a king belonging to the solar dynasty who descended from King Asamanjas.

Anga: The country of Bengal proper; its capital was Champa.

Angiras: A great sage who was a mind-born son of Lord Brahma and one of the ten progenitors of mankind.

Anila: One of the eight Vasus, or heavenly beings, who is responsible for creating wind.

Anu: The son of King Yayati by his wife Sharmishtha, a Daitya princess.

Apsara: Wives of the heavenly Gandharvas, or angels.

Arghya: A ceremonious offering, in a conchshell, of water and other auspicious items, such as milk, kusha grass, rice, durva grass, sandalwood, flowers, etc.

Arjuna: The name of the third Pandu prince, who descended from the god Indra. He was a brave warrior, and the famous *Bhagavad-gita* was spoken to him by Lord Krishna.

Arka: An ancient king. Also a synonym for the sun god.

Arundhati: The wife of the sage Vasishtha, the family priest of the house of Ikshvaku.

Aruni: A devoted disciple of his guru Ayodha-Dhaumya.

Ashram: The dwelling of sages and ascetics.

Ashtaka: A king of the Puru dynasty descended from Ajamidha.

Ashvamedha: A horse sacrifice performed by ancient kings to gain sway over kingdoms.

Ashwapati: Lord of the horses. Also a name of many kings.

Ashwatthama: He was the son of Drona and Kripi, and was one of the generals of the Kauravas.

Ashwins: The twin gods—young and handsome—who are the physicans of heaven. They restored the youth of the sage Chyavana.

Asita: A great sage and disciple of Vyasa.

Asumanjas: A king who descended in the solar dynasty from King Sagara.

Asuras: Demons (atheists) who are the enemies of the gods.

Atreya: A disciple of Vamadeva. This sage acquired the power to go from one planet to another.

Atri: A sage and author of many Vedic hymns, and a son of Lord Brahma.

Ayodha-Daumya: A great sage whose disciples were Aruni, Upamanyu, and Veda.

Ayodhya: A city in North India that enjoyed great importance and reputation for many years as the capital of the kings of the solar dynasty.

Ayus: The king of the frogs.

B

Bali: A good and virtuous Daitya king. He was the son of Virochana and grandson of saintly Prahlad.

Bel: A tree whose leaves are enjoyed by Lord Shiva.

Bhagiratha: King Amsuman's son who brought the Ganges River down into this world.

Bharadwaja: A great sage who is the son of Brihaspati and father of Drona, the military preceptor of the Pandavas.

Bharata: A son of King Dushmanta and Shakuntala, he was a partial incarnation of Lord Mahavishnu and very powerful.

Bhima: The king of Vidharbha and Damayanti's father. A different Bhima is the second of the five Pandava brothers, known for his stupendous might. His mother was Kunti and his actual father, Vayu, was the wind god.

Bhishma: The son of King Shantanu and Goddess Ganga. He took a difficult vow to abstain from sexuality for his entire life so that his father could marry Satyavati.

Bhrigu: A Vedic sage and a son of Lord Brahma.

Bhurishrava: A prince of the Balhikas and an ally of the Kauravas.

Brahma: The creator of this universe and of all its creatures. He is born on a lotus sprung from the navel of Lord Vishnu.

Brahmin: One whose social position is to perform priestly and educational work.

Brahmarishi: Great sages or rishis of the Brahman caste.

Brhaspati: A son of the rishi Angiras. He is a great sage and preceptor of the gods, and father of the sage Bharadwaja.

C

Chakravarti: A universal emperor who is born with the mark of Lord Vishnu's discus visible in his hand.

Champa: The capital city of the country of Anga, which was surrounded with numerous champaka trees.

Chedi: The name of a country, the modern Chandail and Boglehand.

Chitrangada: The eldest son of King Shantanu, and brother of Bhishma. He was killed in early life in conflict with a Gandharva of the same name.

Chitraratha: The king of the Gandharvas.

Chitrasena: One of the hundred sons of Dhritarashtra.

Chyavana: A sage who is the son of the rishi Bhrigu.

D

Dadhicha: A famous sage who donated his bones to the gods who used them to create a thunderbolt weapon to defeat the demons.

Daitya: Descendents from Diti by Kashyapa. They are a race of demons and giants who warred against the gods and interfered with sacrifices.

Daksha: A son of Lord Brahma who had many daughters whom he gave in marriage to Kashyapa, Chandra, Dharma, and Lord Shiva.

Dakshina: The payment a student gives his guru on finishing his studies as a mark of his gratitude.

Dala: The son of King Pariksit and Queen Sushobhana of the Ikshvaku dynasty.

Damayanti: A daughter of King Bhima of Vidarbha.

Danava: Descendants from Danu by the sage Kashyapa. Often referred to as demons, they warred against the gods.

Darshana: To see or to be seen by the Deity or a holy person.

Dasharatha: A king of Ayodhya and father of Lord Rama.

Dattatreya: An incarnation of Lord Krishna or Vishnu, he is the son of the sage Atri and his wife Anasuya. He gave Kartavirya Arjuna one thousand arms.

Devaki: The mother of Lord Krishna and wife of Vasudeva.

Devavrata: Another name of Bhishma.

Devayani: The daughter of Shukra, priest of the Daityas, and wife of King Yayati. She bore him two sons, Yadu and Turvasu.

Dhara: Wife of a Vasu, or god, named Drona.

Dharma: A word meaning justice; also the name of the judge or god of the dead.

Dharmaraja: The judge of the dead; also, a title of Yudhishthira, an actual son of Yama, judge of the dead.

Dhoti: An Indian garment worn by men. It consists of a large piece of cloth folded to form pants.

Dhritarashtra: The eldest son of Vichitravirya (but actually Vyasa) and brother of Pandu. His mother was Ambika. He was born blind and so could not become the real King of Hastinapura.

Dhundhu: A demon who harassed the sage Utanka in his devotions, but who was killed by King Kuvalashva.

Dhundhumara: A name of King Kuvalashva, the killer of Dhundhu.

Dilipa: The son of King Amshuman and father of Bhagiratha from the Ikshvaku or solar dynasty.

Drahyu: A son of King Yayati born from Sharmishtha.

Draupadi: The wife of the Pandavas and daughter of King Drupada, King of Panchala.

Drdashva: A famous king of the Ikshvaku dynasty and a son of Kuvalashva.

Dridhasyu: A son born to the sage Agastya by his wife Lopamudra who became a great scholar and ascetic.

Drona: A Brahman generated in a bucket by his sage father Bharadraj. He married Kripi and fathered Ashwatthama. He also taught the military arts to both the Pandava and Kaurava princes.

Drupada: The king of the Panchalas and Shikhandi's father.

Durva grass: A bent grass (*panicum dactylon*) contained in the religious offering of arghya.

Durvasa: A sage, the son of Atri and Anasuya, known for his irascible temper, curses, and blessings.

Duryodhana: The first son of King Dhritarashtra and leader of the Kauravas. He is known for his evil connivings in his attempts to illegally wrest the throne from the Pandavas.

Dushmanta: A valiant king of the Lunar race, descended from Puru. He was the husband of Shakuntala, by whom he had a great son, Bharata.

Dushshala: A daughter of King Dhritarashtra.

Dushasana: The evil son of King Dhritarashtra who tried to strip Princess Draupadi naked in an assembly but who was baffled by Lord Krishna's miracle of increasing the length of her sari.

Dwapara: The third age of the world in which righteousness is diminished by half.

Dwarka: Lord Krishna's capital, situated in the sea to the west of Gujarat. It is said to have been submerged by the ocean seven days after He left this world.

Dyu: One of the eight Vasus, gods who stole the cow Nandini from the sage Vasishtha. He was reincarnated on earth as the great warrior Bhishma.

Dyumatsena: The king of Shalva and father of Satyavan, Savitri's husband, whose life she saved.

G

Gadhi: A king of the Kushika race and father of the sage Visvamitra.

Gandhara: A country and city on the west bank of the Indus River near Attock. It was famous for its breed of horses.

Gandhari: The daughter of King Subala, Gandhara's king, and wife of King Dhritarashtra.

Gandharva: Heavenly beings who prepare soma juice for the gods, are skilled in medicine, and are excellent singers and musicians.

Gandiva: The bow of Arjuna received by him from Agni, the fire god.

Ganga: The sacred River Ganges. It flows from the toe of Lord Vishnu and was brought down by the austerities of King Bhagiratha. Also, the goddess in charge of this river.

Gangadwara: The place where the Ganges River falls from the Himalaya Mountains and where the sage Agastya performed penance with his wife Lopamudra. Also known as Haridwara.

Gautama: A name of the sage Saradwat, a son of Gotoma, and the husband of Ahalya.

Gritachi: A heavenly nymph who sings and dances.

Guhyaka: A Yaksha or member of Kuvera's court.

Gurnika: A companion of Devayani.

Guru: One who teaches a student, through various processes, how to realize his relationship with God.

H

Haihaya: A prince of the Lunar race and great grandson of King Yadu.

Hari: Another name of Lord Krishna or Vishnu.

Hastinapura: The capital city of the Kauravas that is presently near New Delhi.

Himalaya: The famous mountain range in northern India. Often referred to as the Himalayas.

Hiranyakashipu: A king of the Daitya (demon) race known for his severe austerities. Lord Vishnu killed him to protect His devotee Prahlada.

Hiranyavarman: The king of Darsana, whose daughter married Shikhandi.

Homa: A sacrifice in which an oblation is made to the gods by pouring butter into the fire to the accompaniment of prayers and invocations.

Hotravahana: A saintly king who was Amba's grandfather.

I

Idmavaha: A son of the sage Agastya and his wife Lopamudra. Also known as Tridasyu.

Ikshumati: A river that flows near Kurukshetra.

Ikshvaku: The son of Manu Vaivasvat, who was the son of the sun god, Vivasvan.

Ilwala: A demon subdued by the sage Agastya.

Indra: The king of heaven and the god of rain.

Indraprastha: The capital city of the Pandu princes. This name is presently used for a part of the city of Delhi.

Indrasena: The son of King Nala and Queen Damayanti.

Indrasenah: The daughter of King Nala and Queen Damayanti. Also, a wife of the sage Mudgala.

J

Jamadagni: A Brahmin and descendent of the sage Bhrigu, he was the son of Richika and Satyavati, and the father of five sons, one of whom was God's incarnation—Parashurama.

Jambha: The name of several demons.

Jantu: A king of the Puru dynasty, he was the son of King Somaka and the father of King Vrshatanu.

Japa: The practice of uttering a mantra or prayer repeatedly for personal purification.

Jarita: A certain female bird of the species called Sarngakas. She gave the sage Mandapala four sons.

Jaritari: A son of the mother bird Jarita.

Jaya: A word that means victory or triumph.

Jayadratha: A prince of the Lunar dynasty, son of Brihanmanas. He was king of Sindhu and married Dhritarashtra's daughter.

Jitavati: A daughter of King Ushinara. The most beautiful woman in the world, she was a friend of the wife of the Vasu Dyu.

Jivala: A charioteer of King Rituparna.

K

Kacha: A son of Brihaspati who obtained from the sage Shukra the secret of reviving a dead person.

Kailash: A mountain in the Himalayas, north of the Manasa lake, where Lord Shiva abides.

Kaitabha: A demon who, when about to kill Lord Brahma, was killed by Lord Vishnu.

Kalakeyas: Sons of the sage Kashyapa by his wife Kalaka who were powerful, ferocious, and cruel.

Kali: The fourth age, personified by the spirit of evil, during which only one quarter of righteousness remains.

Kalpa: A day and a night of Lord Brahma, each part lasting 4,320,000,000 years.

Kampilya: King Drupada's city in the country of the Panchalas.

Kamsa: He was the son of King Ugrasena, king of Mathura, and an incarnation of the asura Kalanemi. He was killed by his nephew Lord Krishna because of his evil activities.

Kanwa: A sage who found the abandoned Shakuntala in the woods and raised her as his daughter.

Kanyakuvja: An ancient city on the Kali-nadi, an affluent of the Ganges, and lying a little to the west of the latter. Once the capital of a powerful dynasty.

Kapila: An incarnation of God and founder of the Sankhya philosophy.

Kapilashva: The son of King Kuvalashva. He was destroyed by the sage Dhandhu.

Karkotaka: A Naga who helped King Nala during his period of exile.

Karna: He was a son of Queen Kunti by Surya, the sun god, before her marriage to Pandu. Ignorant of being the half-brother of the Pandavas, he was their determined enemy and Duryodhana's friend.

Kartivirya: He was the son of Kritavirya, king of the Haihayas. He had a thousand arms, and was killed by Parashurama for an offense against his family.

Kashi: The city of Varanasi or Benares, a sacred pilgrimage spot.

Kashyapa: He was a great sage who was the son of Marichi, Lord Brahma's son.

Kaumadaki: The name of Lord Krishna's club or mace, which He received from the god Agni when He assisted him in burning down the Khandava forest.

Kaustubha: A celebrated jewel obtained at the churning of the ocean by the gods and demons, and worn by Lord Vishnu on his chest.

Keshini: A maidservant of Queen Damayanti.

Khandava: A forest and country on the banks of the Yamuna River. In it the Pandavas built the city of Indraprastha and made it their capital. The forest was once consumed by the god Agni.

Kripa: He is the son of the sage Sharadwat, and the adopted son of King Shantanu. He was one of the Pandavas' teachers of the military art.

Krishna: A manifestation of God who lived in Vrndavana as a cowherd, in Mathura as a prince, and in Dwarka as a king. He spoke the *Bhagavad-gita*—the song of God.

Kundina: The capital of Vidarbha.

Kunti: The mother of three of the Pandavas.

Kuru: A prince of the Lunar race and son of Samvarna by Tapati. He ruled in the N.W. of India over the country about Delhi.

Kurukshetra: A plain near Delhi where the great battle between the Kauravas and the Pandavas was fought. It lies S.E. of Thanesar near Panipat.

Kurus: A people dwelling about Kurukshetra who are connected with King Kuru of the Lunar race. He was the ancestor of both Pandu and Dhritarashtra, but the name Kaurava is generally applied to the latter.

Kusha: A great effulgent sage of ancient India in the line of the sage Vishvamitra.

Kusha grass: A sacred grass used for religious ceremonies. It has long stalks and pointed leaves, like rushes.

Kuvalashva: A king of the Solar race who, with his sons, attacked and

killed the great demon Dhundhu, who had disrupted the devotions of
the sage Uttanka.

Kuvera: The god of wealth and treasurer of the gods.

L

Lakshmi: The goddess of fortune.

Lomapada: A king of the country of Anga.

Lopamudra: The wife of the sage Agastya.

M

Mada: Created by the sage Chyavana, this fearsome monster persuaded
the god Indra to share the Soma drink with the Ashwins.

Madhavi: A name of Goddess Lakshmi.

Madhu: A demon slain by Lord Krishna.

Magha: An important, sacred month—February. One who bathes at
Prayag during this month will be freed from all sins.

Mahabhisha: A king of the Iksvaku dynasty, also known as Shantanu.

Mahadeva: Another name of Lord Shiva.

Mahendra: One of the seven mountain ranges of India.

Malava: The country of Malwa.

Malini: A name of the city of Champa.

Mandara: A great mountain used by the gods and demons to churn
the ocean.

Manibhava: The god of travel.

Manimati: A city in which the demon Ilwala lived.

Manu: This name belongs to fourteen progenitors of mankind and rulers
of the earth, each of whom rules for a period of 306,720,000 years or
71 sets of the four yuga cycles.

Mantra: A sacred or mystical hymn devised to produce a mystical
effect or influence matter.

Marut: The god of the wind.

Maruts: The forty-nine Vayus who assist Indra.

Matali: The charioteer of Indra, the chief god.

Maya: Illusion personified as a female form of heavenly origin, created for the purpose of beguiling an individual who wants to enjoy sense pleasure.

Menaka: A heavenly nymph sent to seduce the sage Vishvamitra from his austerities, and who later became the mother of Shakuntala.

Meru: A sacred mountain said to be the abode of the gods.

Mlechchas: Descendents of Anu, King Yayati's son. A degraded people who eat meat without restriction.

Mudgala: A great sage known for his unflappable mentality and high spiritual aspirations.

N

Naga: A creature that has the head and arms of a human being and the neck and trunk of a serpent.

Nahusha: A famous king of the Lunar dynasty, and father of King Yayati.

Nakula: The fourth of the Pandava princes and one of the twin sons of Madri, the second wife of Pandu.

Nala: A virtuous king of Nishada.

Namuchi: A demon slain by Indra with the foam of water.

Nandini: The cow of plenty belonging to the sage Vasishtha, said to have been born of Surabhi.

Narada: A great devotee sage born from Lord Brahma.

Narayana: Another name of Lord Vishnu.

Nikumbha: A demon who was killed by Lord Krishna.

Nirukta: An etymology or glossary devoted to explaining difficult Vedic words.

Nishadha: The country of Nala, probably the Bhil country.

P

Palanquin: A conveyance on which a person sits and which is carried by four men, each man carrying a pole on his shoulder.

Panchala: The name of a country sometimes identified with the Punjab and near Hastinapura.

Pandavas: The descendents of King Pandu.

Pandu: The father of the Pandu princes or the Pandavas.

Parashurama: An incarnation of Lord Krishna or Vishnu. He was the fifth son of the sage Jamadagni and Renuka.

Parikshit: The son of Abhimanyu by his wife Uttara; grandson of Arjuna and father of Janamejaya. He succeeded Yudhishthira on the throne, and the *Shrimad Bhagavatam* was narrated to him by Shukdeva Goswami just before Parikshit was killed by the curse of a snake bite.

Parjanya: The god of clouds and rain. Also called Indra.

Parnada: The Brahman who, for Damayanti, discovered where Nala was hiding.

Parvata: A sage who was the nephew of the sage Narada.

Paurava: A descendent of Puru of the Lunar race.

Paushya: A king whose wife gave her earrings as a gift to the sage Uttanka.

Pipal or *Pippala*: A fig tree.

Pishacha: A fiend, evil spirit, vilest of malevolent beings.

Prabhasa: A place of pilgrimage on the coast of Gujarat near Dwarka.

Prahlada: A great devotee whom Lord Vishnu (in His Narasingha incarnation) protected from death by his demon father Hiranyakashipu. Prahlada was an enlightened king.

Prasenajit: The father of Renuka, wife of the sage Jamadagni.

Praswapa: A mystical weapon that induces sleep in one's opponent.

Pratardhana: Son of Divodasa, king of Kashi, and a mighty warrior.

Pratipa: A king of the Lunar dynasty and a father of King Shantanu.

Pratusha: A son born to Dharmadeva of his wife Prabhata. He is one of the Vasus—the god of light.

Pundit: A learned person versed in the scriptures.

Puru: The sixth king of the Lunar race, youngest son of Yayati and Sharmishtha. His descendents were called Pauravas, and from this race came the Kauravas and Pandavas.

Purumitra: One of the eleven valiant sons of Dhritarashtra.

Purvachitti: A celebrated celestial maiden and dancer.

Pushkara: An evil brother of King Nala.

R

Rahu: A planet responsible for creating eclipses.

Rajasuya: A royal sacrifice performed at the installation of a king. It implied that he who instituted it was a king over all kings, and his tributary kings were expected to attend the rite.

Rakshasa: Generally a demon or a fiend who disturbs sacrifices, harasses devout persons, devours human beings, and vexes and afflicts people in many ways.

Rantideva: A pious and benevolent king of the Lunar race, sixth in descent from Bharata. He was very rich, religious, and charitable.

Renuka: The daughter of King Prasenajit, wife of the sage Jamadagni and mother of God's incarnation Parashurama.

Ribhus: A son of Sudhanva, a descendent of the sage Angiras. Spiritually advanced beings who live in the region of Lord Brahma.

Richika: A sage descended from Bhrigu and husband of Satyavati, son of Urva and father of Jamadagni.

Rig: The original Veda, or holy book, from which the Yajur and Sama Vedas are derived. It consists of many hymns addressed to the personifications of the powers of nature.

Rishi: A great sage or self-realized being.

Rishyashringa: A hermit son of the sage Vibhandaka who descended from the sage Kashyapa. He performed a sacrifice for King Dasharatha that effected Lord Rama's birth.

Rituparna: A king of Ayodhya of the Ikshvaku dynasty.

Rohini: Daughter of Daksha and fourth of the lunar asterisms, the favorite wife of the moon.

Rukmini: The daughter of Bhishmaka, king of Vidarbha, and the first wife and chief queen of Lord Krishna.

Rumanvan: The eldest of the five sons born to the sage Jamadagni by his wife Renuka.

S

Sagara: A king of Ayodhya of the Solar race and son of King Bahu.

Sahadeva: The fifth Pandava brother. His mother was Madri and his actual father was one of the twin Ashwins (physicians of heaven).

Sahajanya: A heavenly nymph accomplished in dancing.

Sama: The third Veda or holy scriptures of the Vedic religion. Its verses or hymns were often chanted at sacred sacrifices.

Samanta-panchaka: A holy pilgrimage place founded by the incarnation of God Parashurama. He made five rivers here, through which warrior's blood flowed.

Samhitas: A collection of hymns addressed to various nature gods. These songs are in the form of mantras.

Samvarta: A son of the sage Angiras and a younger brother to the sage Brhaspati.

Samvodhana: A weapon that awakens one from sleep.

Sanjivani: A secret method of reviving the dead that the sage Shukra knew and, when he was inebriated, disclosed to Kacha.

Saraswati: A sacred river that falls from the Himalayas and is lost in the sands of the desert, but in ancient times flowed on to the sea. Also the name of Lord Brahma's wife.

Sarvabauma: A king of the Bharata dynasty. He was the son of Viduratha and the father of Jayatsena.

Sarvadamana: Bharata, the heroic son of Shakuntala.

Satyabhama: One of Lord Krishna's wives, daughter of King Satrajit.

Satyavan: The virtuous husband of Savitri, who saved him from death.

Satyavati: The mother of Vyasa and the wife of King Shantanu. She bore two sons, Citrangada and Vicitravirya.

Satyavrata: A king of the Solar race descended from Ikshvaku. He is also known as Trishanku and was raised to heaven by the sage Vishvamitra.

Saumadatti: Bhurishravas, the son of Somadatta.

Savitri: The daughter of King Ashwapati and Queen Malati, and the wife of the pious Satyavan, whose life she saved.

Senajit: A king who was the son of King Vishvajit. He wrote a treatise on the duties of a king.

Shachi: The wife of Indra, king of the gods.

Shaivya: A king of ancient India, and close friend of the sages Narada and Parvata. Another Shaivya was the grandson of King Ushinara, King Shivi's father.

Shakra: A name of Indra, chief of the gods.

Shakuni: Queen Gandhari's brother and uncle of the Kaurava princes. He was a skillful gambler and a cheat.

Shakuntala: The abandoned daughter of Menaka and Vishvamitra. She was adopted and raised by the sage Kanwa in a forest retreat.

Shala: Son of King Parikshit of the Ikshvaku dynasty. He refused to return two horses he had borrowed from the sage Vamadeva.

Shalihotra: An expert in the science of horses.

Shalwa(s): The name of a country in the west of India, or Rajasthan; also the name of its king.

Shalya: The king of Madras and brother of Madri, second wife of Pandu. He fought for the Kauravas in the battle of Kurukshetra.

Shanta: King Lomapada's daughter, who was married to Rishyashringa.

Shantanu: A great king of the Lunar race, son of Pratipa, father of Bhishma.

Sharmishtha: The daughter of King Vrshaparvan, king of the Asuras. She became a maidservant of Damayanti as a consequence of offending her.

Sharyati: A king in the Ikshvaku line. His daughter Sukanya married the aged sage Chyavana.

Shiva: The god who destroys this world at the designated time.

Shivi: He was the king of Ushinara, and also the son of Ushinara. He was known for his charity and devotion.

Shraddha: Faith in God and the scriptures.

Shri: Another name of the Goddess Lakshmi.

Shrutasena: The younger brother of the serpent Takshaka.

Shukracharya: He was the son of Bhrigu and priest of Bali and the Daityas. His daughter Devayani married King Yayati of the Lunar race.

Shwetaki: A king who was greatly occupied with performing sacrifices.

Sindhu: The country along the Indus River.

Soma: The juice extracted from the Soma creeper. It is believed that the gods fondly accept Soma in sacrifices.

Somadatta: A king of the Kuru dynasty and the son of King Balhika.

Somaka: A son of Sahadeva, he was the king of Panchala and is known for sacrificing his son to obtain one hundred sons.

Stuna: A Yaksha who had mystic powers and lived in a forest mansion.

Sudaman: He was a king of Dasharna.

Sukanya: The wife of the recluse Chyavana. She was responsible for his regaining his youth from the Ashwins.

Sunda: A demon for whose destruction the heavenly nymph Tilottama was sent down from heaven to create friction between him and his brother Upasunda.

Surabhi: The cow of plenty produced by the churning of the ocean and who granted every desire.

Surya: The sun god.

Sushena: A son of the sage Jamadagni.

Sushobhana: A Manduka princess who became King Parikshit's wife and bore him three sons.

Suvala: The king of Gandhara and father of Gandhari, Dhritarashtra's wife.

Swami: A monastic who has taken vows of sense control and renunciation for the purpose of God realization.

Swayamvara: A ceremony in which an unmarried woman selects her husband among eligible invited suitors.

T

Takshaka: A serpent and son of Kadru, chief of snakes.

Tilottama: An apsara, heavenly nymph. Exquisitely beautiful, she brought about the destruction of the two demons Sunda and Upasunda.

Turvasu: The son of King Yayati by Devayani.

Twashtri: The chief architect of the gods; also known as Vishwakarma.

U

Uddalaka: Another name of Aruni, disciple of Ayodha-dhaumya.

Ujjalaka: A desert near the ashram of the sage Uttanka. The demon Dhundhu lived in this desert.

Upamanyu: A dutiful disciple of the teacher Ayodha-daumya.

Uparichara: A Vasu or demigod who became the king of Chedi by Indra's command. His daughter Satyavati gave birth to the sage Vyasa.

Upasunda: A Daitya (demon), son of Nisunda and the brother of Sunda.

Urvashi: A celestial nymph.

Ushinara: Another name of King Shivi. Also, a country.

Utanka: An ideal disciple of Veda, who was the disciple of Ayodha-daumya.

V

Vahuka: A disguised form of King Nala given by the Naga Karkotaka.

Vaikuntha: The spiritual world where Lord Vishnu and His devotees reside.

Vaishravana: The god of wealth.

Vajra: The thunderbolt of Indra, said to have been made from the bones of the sage Dadhicha.

Vamadeva: An ancient hermit whose horses were borrowed by King Shala, who refused to return them and was then killed by some titans.

Vamana: An incarnation of Lord Krishna (or Vishnu) in the form of a dwarf. He appeared in the Treta yuga from the sage Kashyapa and his wife Aditi.

Vami: A fast horse.

Varshneya: King Nala's charioteer who later became King Rituparna's charioteer.

Varuna: The god of the oceans.

Vasishtha: A celebrated Vedic sage to whom many hymns are attributed. He was a mind-born son of Lord Brahma.

Vasudeva: Another name of Lord Krishna or Vishnu.

Vasumanas: A king of the dynasty of Ikshvaku descended from Haryashva and Madhavi.

Vasus: The gods of water, the pole-star, moon, earth, wind, fire, dawn, and light.

Vatapi: A demon consumed by the sage Agastya.

Vayu: The god of wind.

Vedas: The holy books containing Divine knowledge that is the foundation of the Vedic religion.

Vibhandaka: The son of the great sage Kashyapa. He was a forest ascetic who fathered the sage Rishyashringa.

Vichitravirya: Name of a king of Hastinapura whose mother was Satyavati and father was Shantanu.

Vidarbha: A country, probably Bihar, whose capital was Kundipura.

Vidura: A son of the sage Vyasa and a maidservant. He was a counselor to his brother King Dhritarashtra of Hastinapura.

Vikarna: A son of King Dhritarashtra.

Vindhya: The mountains that stretch across India and divide Hindustan from the Dakhin or south.

Virasana: A yogic posture in which one kneels, sitting on one's heels and placing one's hands on one's knees.

Viravahu: He was a king of the country of Chedi.

Vishnu: A name of God, who maintains and restores the universe. He resides in both Vaikuntha (the transcendental world) and in every atom of creation (in the material world).

Vishvamitra: A royal hermit of immense attainments. His father was King Gadhi of Kanyakubja.

Vishwachi: A celestial nymph who sings and serves the god Kuvera.

Vishwakarma: The architect of the gods.

Vishwavasu: A brother of the incarnation of God Parashurama.

Vrihadgarbha: The son of emperor Shivi.

Vrishaparva: He was born from the sage Kashyapa and his wife Danu, and he had a daughter named Sharmishtha.

Vritra: The demon of drought and uncongenial weather. He was killed by the god Indra.

Y

Yadu: A son of King Yayati of the Lunar race, and founder of the line of the Yadavas in which Lord Krishna was born.

Yajur: The second Veda containing hymns and chants. It was taught by Vyasa to Vaishampayana.

Yaksha: A class of supernatural beings who serve Kuvera, the god of wealth. Sometimes they appear as imps of evil.

Yama: The god governing death and righteousness.

Yamuna: A sacred river in India that rises in a mountain called Kalinda.

Yayati: The fifth king of the Lunar race, and son of King Nahusha. He had two wives, Devayani and Sharmishtha.

Yogi: A person fixed on a spiritual course of uniting or linking his soul with the Supreme soul.

Yudhishthira: The eldest of the five Pandava princes and the son of Dharma, or the god of righteousness (although he is referred to as Pandu's son).

MAHABHARATA

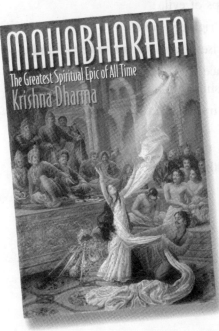

The Greatest Spiritual Epic of All Time

This most cherished of all Indian classics recounts the story of five heroic brothers, the Pandavas. Robbed of their kingdom and exiled by their envious cousins, they encounter many hardships, culminating in an apocalyptic war. As we accompany them on their extraordinary adventures and spiritual journey, we meet sages, warrior kings, virtuous heroines, and a host of celestial beings. Among them is Krishna, a divine incarnation and, as you will discover, the pivotal character of the book. It is due to Krishna's presence that the work is revered as a sacred text. It contains the *Bhagavad-gita*, a masterpiece of spiritual wisdom, embraced by millions and one of the world's most significant treatises on karma, reincarnation, and yoga.

"Dharma successfully captures the mood and majesty of a rich and ancient epic. A well-wrought saga that will be appreciated by Western readers... Highly recommended."
—*The Midwest Book Review*

"Rarely, if ever, has an ancient epic received such modern blockbuster treatment... The narrative moves effortlessly, often as racily as a thriller, without compromising the elevated style and diction. The visual imagery is every bit as impressive as anything achieved in the cinematic editions."
—Mahesh Nair, *India Today*

Hardbound, 6 x 9 inches, 940 pages, 16 color plates, 18 b&w drawings, $39.95

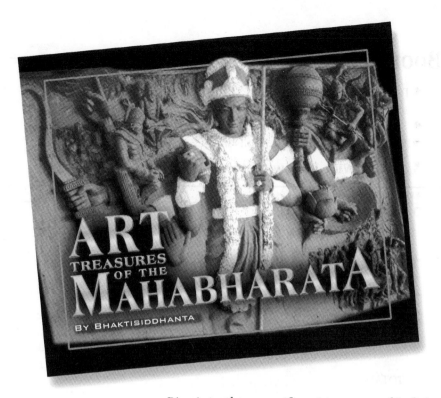

BOOK ORDER FORM

◆ Telephone orders: Call 1-888-TORCHLT (1-888-867-2458)
   (Please have your credit card ready.)
◆ Fax orders: 559-337-2354
◆ Postal Orders: Torchlight Publishing, P O Box 52, Badger, CA 93603, USA

🌏 **World Wide Web: www.torchlight.com**

PLEASE SEND THE FOLLOWING:	QUANTITY	AMOUNT
☐ *Bhagavad-gita As It Is*		
Deluxe (1,068 pages)—$24.95	x_____	= $_____
Standard (924 pages)—$12.95	x_____	= $_____
☐ *Art Treasures* of the Mahabharata—$24.95	x_____	= $_____
☐ *Mystical Stories* from the Mahabharata—$17.95	x_____	= $_____
☐ *Ramayana*—$27.95	x_____	= $_____
☐ *Mahabharata*—$39.95	x_____	= $_____
Shipping/handling (see below)		$_____
Sales tax 7.25% (California only)		$_____
TOTAL		$_____

(I understand that I may return any book for a full refund—no questions asked.)

PLEASE SEND ME YOUR CATALOG AND INFO ON OTHER BOOKS BY TORCHLIGHT PUBLISHING.

Company _____

Name _____

Address _____

City _____ State _____ Zip _____

PAYMENT:

☐ Check/money order enclosed ☐ VISA ☐ MasterCard ☐ American Express

Card number _____

Name on card _____ Exp. date _____

Signature _____

SHIPPING AND HANDLING:

USA: $4.00 for the first book and $3.00 for each additional book. Air mail per book (USA only)—$7.00.

Canada: $6.00 for the first book and $3.50 for each additional book. (NOTE: Surface shipping may take 3 to 4 weeks in North America.)

Foreign countries: $8.00 for the first book and $5.00 for each additional book. Please allow 6 to 8 weeks for delivery.